Transnational Hispaniola

TRANSNATIONAL HISPANIOLA

New Directions in Haitian and Dominican Studies

Edited by
April J. Mayes and Kiran C. Jayaram

University of Florida Press
Gainesville

Publication of this paperback edition made possible by a Sustaining the Humanities through the American Rescue Plan grant from the National Endowment for the Humanities.

First cloth printing, 2018
First paperback printing, 2022

27 26 25 24 23 22   6 5 4 3 2 1

Library of Congress Cataloging-in-Publication Data
Names: Mayes, April J., editor. | Jayaram, Kiran, editor.
Title: Transnational Hispaniola : new directions in Haitian and Dominican
    studies / edited by April J. Mayes and Kiran C. Jayaram.
Description: Gainesville : University of Florida Press, 2018. | Includes
    bibliographical references and index.
Identifiers: LCCN 2017041397 | ISBN 9781683400387 (cloth)|
ISBN 9781683402688 (pbk.)
Subjects: LCSH: Hispaniola—Social conditions—History. | Haiti—Social
    conditions—History. | Dominican Republic—Social conditions—History.
Classification: LCC F1916 .T73 2017 | DDC 972.93—dc23
LC record available at https://lccn.loc.gov/2017041397

University of Florida Press
2046 NE Waldo Road
Suite 2100
Gainesville, FL 32609
http://upress.ufl.edu

UF PRESS

UNIVERSITY
OF FLORIDA

CONTENTS

FIGURES

Transnational Hispaniola

An Introduction

APRIL J. MAYES AND KIRAN C. JAYARAM

In January 1905, Dr. Francisco Henríquez y Carvajal, a Dominican politician in exile in Cuba, sent a letter to Dr. Anténor Firmin, the former Minister of Finance, Commerce, and Foreign Affairs of Haiti, who was living his own exile in St. Thomas, then a Danish colony. Henríquez y Carvajal informed Firmin that he and a "group of Antilleans resident in Cuba . . . who labor to realize [Eugenio María de] Hostos's and [José] Martí's ideal," planned to publish a biography about the "illustrious Antilleans who, to varying degrees, contributed to the morale and intellectual elevation of our people" (Firmin 1910, 9).[1]

Antillanistas believed that Cubans, Dominicans, Jamaicans, Haitians, and Puerto Ricans constituted a natural brotherhood based on their common colonial histories, their shared resistance to slavery, their transcolonial struggles for political independence, and their shared vulnerability to the growing power of the United States.[2] By 1905, though, Firmin and Henríquez y Carvajal were the only remaining actors in that activist generation. Henríquez y Carvajal encouraged Firmin to participate in the project: "Permit me to call upon your consistent support that you have given to your home country, the first of the Antilles and the second of the Americas to proclaim the rights of man in this continent" (Firmin 1910, 122).

Like Henríquez y Carvajal, Anténor Firmin (1850–1911) had worked professionally in France and had been repeatedly forced into exile as a result of political conflict. Perhaps these commonalities and his adherence to *antillanismo* prompted Firmin's enthusiastic response: "It is in this spirit [of Caribbean unity], that I join with your cause and give you all my heart and all my love" (Firmin 1910, 130). Firmin, who had studied and published works on anthropology, spent his intellectual energy refuting the scientific consensus of the day that the personal, social, and cultural attributes of African-descended people made them subordinate to whites.[3] In addition to this important work, Anténor Firmin helped organize the first Pan-African Congress, which was held in London in 1900, thus serving as one of the founders of pan-Africanism, a global, intellectual, artistic, and political movement aimed at mobilizing African-descended people in a common struggle against racism and colonialism (Fleuhr-Lobban 2000, 460). Firmin's support for Antillean unity was thus part of a broader liberationist project in which a Caribbean federation played an important role.

What Is Transnational Hispaniola?

This brief nostalgic exchange between Dominican and Haitian statesmen is one example of the kinds of political engagements and intellectual collaborations that motivate the intellectual project of transnational Hispaniola, an endeavor that unites scholars, artists, and activists who work toward social, cultural, and political change across Hispaniola and among its diasporas/*diásporas*/*dyaspora*. We believe that scholarship and creative expression are crucial elements of overcoming the legacies of authoritarianism and dictatorship in the Dominican Republic and Haiti. Transnational Hispaniola scholars and artists understand their creative and intellectual work as connecting with and supporting social movements that resist political exclusion, racism, anti-Haitian xenophobia, gender inequality, and discrimination based on sexuality across the island and within its diasporas (Mayes et al. 2013, 26–32).

We opened our introduction with this exchange of letters between Henríquez y Carvajal and Firmin to emphasize a few salient points about how we conceive transnational Hispaniola as engaged scholarship. First, this initiative is a recuperative project that encourages analysis of moments of collaboration and convergences of interests among Haitians and Dominicans. An important element of the concept of transnational Hispaniola is that Dominicans and Haitians have long cooperated with each other in political, social, and economic projects that challenge oppression. We consider it our job to find and share those stories. It is also our responsibility to understand and teach about moments of violent conflict and oppression between the two countries. While conflict is one of many ways to frame Dominican-Haitian relations, it is also the most simplistic, reductive, and overused. The conflict narrative is often accompanied by equally pessimistic adjectives—broken, divided, and pathological—that renders it questionable as a guiding principle for change.

Second, we understand that while focusing on moments of cooperation and reconnecting them to larger global processes is just one step, it is an important and necessary one in the process of transforming representations about Haiti and the Dominican Republic in mainstream U.S. media and of challenging the underlying assumptions that inform governmental and nongovernmental interventions in both countries.

Therefore, we are concerned with how narrative, language, and visual and textual imagery inform the creation of knowledge about the island and its peoples. The contributions to this anthology agree with Haitian studies scholars who insist that Haiti needs new narratives. As Michel-Rolph Trouillot (1990, 2003), Gina Athena Ulysse (2015), Marlene Daut (2015), Kaiama Glover and Alessandra Benedicty-Kokken (2016), Nadège Clitandre (2011), and others have argued, there is a particular need to excavate the explicit and implicit racist and anti-black assumptions that support research about Haiti and inform geopolitical agendas in Haiti. These assumptions are most often expressed in narrative and visual representations of Haiti. These representations matter because they do political work. We want to promote narratives that validate the full humanity of Dominicans and Haitians and that avoid exceptionalism and pat abstractions—for example, that although Haitians are poor, they are "resilient" (Clitandre 2011) and that Dominicans' anti-Haitianism is both ancient and resistant to change (Martínez 2014). There is a pressing need for structural analyses that deconstruct the systems of power, especially U.S. complicity in perpetuating Haiti's underdevelopment, that sustain political cultures and a socioeconomic order rooted in authoritarianism, repression, and exclusion (Fumagalli 2015; Paulino 2016).[4]

We hope to create new narratives by situating Hispaniola's political, economic, and social trajectory squarely within Latin American and Caribbean intellectual and activist currents; by encouraging more social scientific research, particularly anthropological, historical, and sociological studies of social movements and daily life; and by fostering intellectual exchange between Dominicanists and Haitianists through conferences, translated publications, and university training.

Third, the concept of transnational Hispaniola is an attempt to create a space for engaged scholarship that speaks directly to and emerges from dialogue among members of social and cultural movements across the island. When we organized the first conference,[5] our initial idea was to gather scholars and activists to discuss whether the impact of recent and dramatic changes in Haitian and Dominican economies and migration patterns had created the conditions for a new kind of feminist movement organized around cross-class and cross-ethnic solidarity. We decided to broaden the scope of our intervention by naming the conference Transnational Hispaniola. Shared History, Shared Future: Converging Paths in the Haitian-Dominican Transborder Experience.[6]

A Brief History of Transnational Hispaniola

The first transnational Hispaniola conference was held in June 2010. The January earthquake in Haiti that year added a sense of urgency to the event, animating conversations among activists, students, and professionals from various aid and development agencies who came from Haiti, the Dominican Republic, the United States, Canada, Germany, and Norway to consider Haitian-Dominican relations in new ways. Many of the essays collected for this volume were presented at the conference Transnational Hispaniola II: Bodies, Commodities, Cultures, and Regimes of Mobility, which took place at Rutgers University in April 2012 and was organized by Carlos U. Decena, professor of Latino/a and gender and women's studies at Rutgers; Yveline Alexis, professor of history at Oberlin College; and the staff of the Center for Latino Arts and Culture at Rutgers. Building upon the insights that emerged at the first conference, the presentations at the second conference considered more closely how Dominicans and Haitians have become increasingly interconnected. At that conference, Haitian and Haitianist scholars participated more fully than at the first conference. The most recent iteration, Transnational Hispaniola III: Theories into Practice, which took place in June 2016 at the same time as the 2016 Caribbean Studies Association meetings, focused on the teaching and training of Haitian university students through modules taught by academics and practitioners. It covered topics such as economics and anthropology, political ecology, rural livelihoods, teacher training, digital humanities, human rights and the border, and media-based activism in

Haiti and the Dominican Republic. At the business meeting of the Caribbean Studies Association that year, the membership voted to form an official working group called Transnational Hispaniola, thus ensuring institutional continuity.

A Longer History of Transnational Hispaniola

Our initial search for common ground between Dominican and Haitian women prompted deeper reflections about social science research in the Dominican Republic and Haiti and about the connection between intellectual production and social change. As Maria Cristina Fumagalli (2015) has shown, Moreau de St. Mery (an eighteenth- and early nineteenth-century Creole elite from Martinique) "fully realized that, in order to be fully understood, the island of Hispaniola [had] to be approached in its entirety" (25). In the late nineteenth and early twentieth centuries, the intellectual work of *antillanistas* such as Anténor Firmin and Eugenio María de Hostos provided the foundational arguments for pan-Caribbean unity. In part as a response to the U.S. occupation of Haiti, Jean Price-Mars (1955–1986) founded a historically rooted ethnological tradition as a part of an "intellectual social formation" in conversation with Melville Herskovits in the United States, Fernando Ortiz in Cuba, and Arthur Ramos in Brazil (Yelvington 2006). The Caribbean was an exceptional region because of its potential to undo its colonial legacies by rearranging its political geography around a federation. Moreover, although Caribbean unity was a product of the island's unique history, it could be applied universally as a model of political organization that could protect smaller states against more powerful ones.

During General Rafael Trujillo's dictatorship (1930–1961), generations of scholars deployed their research to buttress the official nationalism of the regime, which elevated whiteness, Hispanic culture, and racial antagonism against Haitians as key elements of Dominican identity. The core concept of this scholarship was the *estado-nación* (the state-nation). In contrast to the previous generation's emphasis on preparing the people, the *nación*, for a pan-Antillean future, Trujillo-era intellectuals made use of their scholarship to buttress the *estado* as a civilizing, modernizing force in Dominican society. However, in the 1970s and 1980s, the pioneering scholarship of Dominican social scientists such as Franklin Franco,

Rubén Silié, Isis Duarte, Andrés Corten, Raymundo González, Roberto Cassá, Emilio Cordero Michel, María Filomena González, Orlando Inoa, and Dagoberto Tejeda fundamentally challenged research produced during General Rafael Trujillo's dictatorship and centered historical, anthropological, and sociological analyses on farmers, workers, migrants, and women. This scholarship complemented popular demands for a robust, meaningful democracy in the wake of authoritarianism and introduced new ideas that influenced, for example, musicians and visual artists to reclaim and elevate Afro-Dominican cultural practices as expressions of the people (Martínez-Vergne 2005; Mayes 2014). While the scholarship of the 1970s and 1980s was transformative, it also was insular and singularly focused on the Dominican Republic—an understandable result, given the enormity of the educational work that had to be done to redress the legacies of Trujillo-era intellectualism.

By the 1990s and the 2000s, significant changes across Hispaniola required a reconsideration of social science research. Both the Dominican and Haitian economies shifted from agriculture to export-processing industrialization, service, and tourism. Both countries experienced the feminization of poverty, the development of substantial populations who live abroad, and, as a by-product, a deepening of the countries' dependence upon remittances from their diasporas. Moreover, the significant increase of Haitian immigration to the Dominican Republic and the rise of anti-immigrant, anti-Haitian policies brought into sharp relief the structural similarities between Haiti and the Dominican Republic and the extensive political, economic, cultural, and familial networks that merged these two nations together in an interdependent, symbiotic relationship. Along with the political, economic, and social changes that had transformed Dominican and Haitian life across the island and the growth of their diasporas since the 1980s came a new generation of research from Ramona Hernández, Silvio Torres-Saillant, Emelio Betances, Bridget Wooding, Fátima Portorreal, Diogenes Abreu, Samuel Martinez, Robin Derby, and Richard Turits. This was the context in which we began our education. This kind of scholarship, which often showed how the Dominican Republic and Haiti were historically and contemporaneously connected, was productive for our research, our creative work, and our activism.

Building on these contributions, we argue that the contemporary moment requires new ways of framing questions (theory), creating knowledge (epistemology), and generating and analyzing data (methodology). Given the increasing participation of diasporic Haitians and Dominicans in producing knowledge about the island and about their immigrant communities, we sense the need to continually revisit and refine the dominant paradigms that have shaped our disciplines, paying close attention to the concepts that motivate research and drive scholarly debate.

The Transnational Hispaniola Framework

Transnationalism is one such concept. Haiti and the Dominican Republic and their respective migrant populations became symbols of the transnational in the late 1980s and the early 1990s, when this term emerged in social science research, particularly sociology, anthropology, and history. Clearly, advances in transportation (the jet airplane) and telecommunications meant that unlike an earlier generation of immigrants, Haitians and Dominicans could remain connected to home; whenever possible, these immigrants constructed lives that straddled two worlds. Scholars such as Nina Glick Schiller and Georges Fouron (1990, 2001) and Sherri Grasmuck and Patricia Pessar (1991) have argued that it was not merely technological change or free will that facilitated migrants' movements between the United States and their home countries. Rather, immigrants' ties to home were produced by structural conditions that created a wholly new migratory experience in which Haitian and Dominican immigrants sustained emotional and economic attachments to households and to entire communities.

Ramona Hernández (2002) has argued that Dominican immigration to the United States was a product of the Dominican Republic's economic ties to that country, conditioned by labor demands in the United States and by Dominican state policies that freed Dominican labor for exploitation abroad. For Hernández, if a transnational condition existed, it was an effect of advanced capitalism, characterized by the internationalization of economies and the controlled movement of labor.

In the 1990s and into the 2000s, some scholars of Dominican and Haitian immigration to the United States used the term "transnational" to capture what they viewed as a new migration process created by late capitalism and globalization. For Schiller and Georges Fouron (1990), emergent identities among Haitians living in the United States could be understood only when they are considered beyond the confines of race and ethnicity as they are constructed in the United States. In their work, transnationalism "[captured] more effectively the manner in which Haitian immigrants perceive their experience and identity than . . . descriptions of Haitians as an 'ethnic group,' as simply 'blacks' in the United States, or as part of a particular class." A transnational framework, in contrast to a diasporic one, helped researchers understand Haitian immigrants' "persisting and/ or growing identification with their country of origin [as] a strategy for both accommodation and resistance to the forces of capitalism" (342).

In this period, the concept of transnationalism, of which Haitians and Dominicans became key subjects, described and drew attention to "the emergence of a social process in which migrants establish social fields that [crossed] geographic, cultural, and political borders." Transnationalism brought attention to "populations in capital-dependent countries . . . forced to migrate to centers of capital in order to live" (Schiller, Basch, and Blanc-Szanton 1998, ix). These centers of capital could be located in the home country or abroad. Finally, the transnational framework analyzed identity formations that challenged dominant paradigms in sociological research that explained ethnic and racial identities among immigrants solely in terms of acculturation, integration, or assimilation. When scholars looked at the transnational lives of Haitians and Dominicans, they began to see how immigrants' individual and collective identities were "shaped by both the political and economic context of the country of origin and the countries of settlement" (ibid., x).

Through the framework of transnationalism, scholars sought to understand migration and individual agency in the context of globalized economies. The transnational Hispaniola framework revisits this conversation but revises the concept of transnationalism in three ways. First, as the scholars who forged this field in the 1990s themselves agreed, the transnational involved both those who moved and those who stayed. Yet the scholarship focused most of its attention on those who left Haiti and the Dominican Republic, thus elevating mobility at the expense of its counterpoint, immobility. The transnational Hispaniola framework, drawing on critical anthropological studies of mobility, endeavors to focus on the island and examine how certain local, national, and international forces create the conditions that enable some people to leave the island and keep others from leaving. Those who do not leave their country of origin still need to contend with multiscalar forces, some of which originate beyond national borders.

Second, we argue that when viewed from the Caribbean, what scholars of transnationalism often regarded as "new" in the history of migration was not so new at all. If we take seriously Trouillot's (2003) notion that globalization erupted in the Caribbean after 1492 and that the Caribbean's natural resources and its people's labor power have been central to capitalist development for over five centuries, then we can argue that cross-border and cross-regional engagements have long shaped, and continue to transform power structures, internal conflicts, gender formations, racial ideologies, and cultures of resistance in the Caribbean. Caribbean people share a deep familiarity with transborder, transcolonial, and transnational movements and their multiple impacts on household, community, and national formations.

Third, we argue that Haiti and the Dominican Republic exemplify the transnational in new ways. The island played a pivotal role in the spread of republicanism in the eighteenth century and in anti-colonial movements such as *antillanismo* in the nineteenth. Throughout the twentieth century, both countries felt the weight of economic dependence on the United States, of U.S. intervention, of occupation, and of diplomatic meddling. Our focus on the transitional ties between Haiti and the Dominican Republic draws attention back to the international economic order that continues to inform political relations between government and social formations across the island. As we noted in the first call for conference papers,

in the understanding that transnationalism is not a relatively new phenomenon, we begin from the premise that transborder and binational relations between Haitian and Dominican communities have permeated throughout history. The legacy of the social, cultural, and political realities shared by both groups has created promising spaces of dialogue, in the island as well as in the diaspora, through unifying migration experiences in the United States. Political and economic elites in both countries have, for the most part, ignored and/or tried to suppress these expressions of commonality, in favor of a more divisive political and socioeconomic discourse. However, social movements dedicated to immigrants' human rights in the U.S., Haiti, and the D.R., non-governmental organizations, and cultural figures such as Junot Díaz and Edwidge Danticat have engaged in a critical debate on the way in which Dominican and Haitian relations are often deconstructed.

As a result of a planning process that included multiple conversations with pioneering Dominican literary theorist and intellectual Silvio Torres Saillant, our collective came to understand transnationalism in the Dominico-Haitian context as a long-standing form of dual social consciousness, in sharp contrast to dominant narratives that paint highly contrasting differences between these two peoples and their cultures.

Our point of departure does not limit an understanding of transnationalism to the moments when people in Haiti interact with others in the Dominican Republic. Following in the footsteps of Sidney Mintz (1986), we maintain that a thorough understanding of the connections between the local and the global offers an understanding of changes people face and of certain ways of life they may "stubbornly" maintain, as Mintz has it (xxvi). Thus, we also use transnational to refer to empirical similarities that emerge after comparison.

Dominican-Haitian transnationalisms arise from movement not only beyond the island but also from within and across it, from the contestation and collaboration that characterize cultural and political engagement, nation-state formation, and social movements. This is a history that spans five centuries but that is ever evolving because of commercial exchange, immigrant settlement, anti-imperialist resistance and rebellion, and intertwined ethnic loyalties and identifications. This collection of essays underscores how the fates of both the Dominican and the Haitian people have been marked by a history of international intervention, supranational political interference, and economic nepotism (Candelario 2007; Garcia Peña 2016; Hoffnung-Garskoff 2010; and Ricourt 2016).

Finally, the transnational Hispaniola framework questions methodological nationalism. According to Andreas Wimmer and Nina Glick Schiller (2003), scholars who employ methodological nationalism "assume that countries are the natural units for comparative studies, equate society with the nation-state, and conflate national interests with the purposes of social science" (576). Scholars who use such a skewed approach run the risk of ignoring the role of nationalism in theory, overemphasizing the role of national boundaries in analysis, and focusing on transnational social processes within a single nation-state. Most important, as Vrushali Patil (2013) argues, "if we continue to neglect cross-border dynamics and fail to problematize the nation and its emergence via transnational processes . . . [we] will continue to confuse our categories of practice with our categories of analysis" (863). The contributors to this book and the larger community of scholars, artists, and activists who are associated with the transnational Hispaniola project advocate for intellectual, creative, and practical work that considers the nation-state as a product of transnational processes. The ultimate goal is to consider formations across Hispaniola as telling us a larger story about global dynamics and shifts in the international balance of power or maybe transformations in capital itself.

About the Chapters

This book and the transnational Hispaniola effort more broadly is an invitation to discuss research, interpretations, and creative expressions about the Dominican Republic, Haiti, and Hispaniola in its entirety. The first section, "The Historical Limits of the State in Hispaniola," focuses on structures of governance, political movements, and migrations across Hispaniola during the colonial period and into the nineteenth century. While recognizing that the historical development of Haiti and the Dominican Republic includes important differences—for example, in their histories of slavery and in the divergent developments of their peasantries—we argue that dominant narratives of Dominican history emphasize Dominican distinctness in an effort to substantiate Dominican nationalists' claims of racial and cultural purity. We seek to upset this narrative by offering new insights about moments when human action and larger processes placed Dominicans and Haitians on converging paths. Nathalie Bragadir's contribution, "Shifting Territories: The Production of Space on Eighteenth-Century Hispaniola," illuminates how historical actors living in the territory between two colonies manipulated both space and allegiance in order to pursue freedom. Bragadir's analysis shows that in the eighteenth century, the border region, much like the contemporary Haitian-Dominican border today, defied the attempts of imperialist powers to fix its boundaries.

In "The Contested State: Political Discourse during the Independence of the Dominican Republic, 1844," Fidel Tavárez revisits the Revolution of 1844 that led to the creation of an independent Dominican Republic. Tavárez argues that the national project that organized on behalf of a "Dominican people" was less unified in its outlook than previous scholars have assumed. Tavárez notes that separation from Haiti was neither inevitable nor based on the premise that Haitians and Dominicans were a diametrically opposed people. Anne Eller's selection of documents, "To Cap-Haïtien, with My Family: Dominican Passport Petitions, 1862–1863," provides an important reminder that movement across borders to nurture extensive familial ties is a long-term and well-known reality in Hispaniola. In a context in which many migrations have been erased from archives, these petitions open a window into the familial, friendship, and communal networks that bound island populations together.

Recent scholarship in Dominican literature and cultural studies complements historical perspectives that seek common ground between Haiti and the Dominican Republic. The second part of the book, "Representations of Hispaniola," explores historical traumas, the body, race, nation, gender, and sexuality in Dominican literary and media cultures. This section opens with Régine Jean-Charles's "'A Border between Geographies of Grief': River Crossings and Crossroads between Haiti and the Dominican Republic," which analyzes representations of the Haitian-Dominican border in works by Edwidge Danticat, Roxane Gay, and Évelyne Trouillot, who each exhume the historical trauma of the 1937 massacre of Haitians and Dominicans of Haitian ancestry. Jean-Charles argues that these authors understand the border as a space of violence and death but also, quite ironically and powerfully, as a space for creation and possibility. These writers insist that although the border can be imagined differently, they refuse to predict whether the border will ever be *lived* differently.

Elizabeth Russ's chapter, "'The Tam-Tam of Drums from the West': Shifting Representations of Haiti in the Later Work of Aída Cartagena Portalatín," analyzes representations of Haiti in three major works by Cartagena Portalatín: *Escalera para Electra* (1970), *Yania Tierra* (1983), and *Culturas africanas: Rebeldes con causa* (1986). Although Haiti is relatively absent in much of Cartagena's work, Russ explains that when Haiti is visible, it signals an important transformation in Cartagena's thinking about Dominican national identity. Russ shows that Cartagena eventually breaks loose from the discursive structures that define Dominican nationalism as fundamentally anti-black and anti-Haitian. Raj Chetty's contribution, "Archives of Afro-Affirmation: Post-Trujillo Journals and

Dominican Literary Blackness," provides even more context for understanding Cartagena's changing position regarding Haiti. Chetty demonstrates that in the period after General Rafael Trujillo's assassination in 1961, Dominican literary and cultural journals published works that evidenced an engagement with an Afro-diasporic world view decades before the massive wave of migration from the Dominican Republic to the United States. Chetty argues that post-Trujillo literature has been a space for considering sexuality and gender and the intersection of both with racial ideologies and racist power structures.

Elena Valdez analyzes transactional heterosexual romance as an allegory of national and transnational formations in her chapter "Transnational Romances and Sex Tourism in *Chochueca's Strategy*, by Rita Indiana Hernández; 'Emoticons' by Aurora Arias; and 'Heading South' by Dany Laferrière." Indiana, Arias, and Laferrière write about sex worker protagonists who, Valdez argues, find inclusion in the nation through the sexual economy provided by tourism. However, this incorporation is riddled with problems; namely, romance with foreigners is doomed to fail in the same way that the status of the Dominican Republic and Haiti as destinations for sex tourism undermines the national project.

Since the 1980s, Hispaniola has been a favorite destination for those seeking short-term romance in tropical landscapes because of development goals that helped shift the island's economy away from agriculture to tourism and service. The full implications of these changes are considered in the third section of this book, "The State, the Market, Bodies, and Commodities of Hispaniola." The first chapter in this section, Elizabeth Manley's "Developing an Economy of Sex: Intersecting Histories of Tourism, Beach Boys, and Masculinity in Hispaniola," connects the social and economic history of tourism with its impact on masculinity, gender identity, and heterosexual performance. Manley's analysis builds on recent research in anthropology that views sex work as contributing substantially to gender conflict and changing gender norms. Despite evidence that tourism has not produced the economic advancement that Haitian and Dominican governments have hoped for, political and business elites continue to privilege tourism as a key mode of economic development.

Kiran Jayaram's piece, "Global Capital Disguised as Sustainability in Post-Earthquake Haiti," offers a sharp critique of post-earthquake development plans in Haiti. In the wake of this human tragedy, Haiti became an example of disaster capitalism in action. Jayaram argues that the idea of sustainability has become code for the continuation of exploitative economic policies. The final selection, "Ties That Bind: *La Sentencia* and Citizenship in Contemporary Hispaniola," by April Mayes, argues that the Dominican Constitutional Court's decision to strip citizenship and nationality from thousands of Dominicans, most of whom are of Haitian ancestry, demonstrates how factions within and power brokers aligned with the Partido de la Liberación Dominicana (Dominican Liberation Party, PLD) have used anti-Haitianism to consolidate their power over the past two decades. Mayes argues that during the PLD's administration, anti-black exclusion became institutionalized in the bureaucratic mechanisms of the state, complementing and assisting the state's governance model.

The chapters in the final section of this collection, "Transnational Cultural Production," confront the complexity of putting theory into practice at the transnational level. The interview with Paul Austerlitz, "Engaged Scholarship and Engaged Creativity in the Dominican Republic and Haiti," tells the story of Dominican roots music and examines the shared traditions that unite music across the island. Even now, Austerlitz insists, music performance, dance, and ritual are liberatory practices, connected to a history of resistance that began in maroon communities during the island's early history. This section ends with Kaiama Glover and Maja Horn's chapter, "Translating Hispaniola to the Digital Realm: On Teaching Alternative Histories of the Americas." Glover and Horn, both professors at Barnard College, developed and implemented a team-taught course that brought Dominican and Haitian studies into dialogue. This experimental course provided a template for bringing Francophone and Spanish-speaking Caribbean histories into conversation. Bringing Haitian and Dominican studies together into one class created an opportunity for students to critically assess both nations in the larger context of transnational and diasporic formations. Finally, we include in the appendix several syllabi from professors who have taught courses based upon the idea of transnational Hispaniola. They represent multiple disciplines, including history, social sciences, literature, and cultural studies.

A Final Note

As a working concept, transnational Hispaniola builds upon an understanding of transnationalism as a form of dual consciousness and as a structural condition within a geopolitical landscape dominated by the United States. In the early twentieth century, Francisco Henríquez y Carvajal and Anténor Firmin communicated across colonial and national boundaries to remember another era when the possibility of ideological, economic, and political unity under the banner of *antillanismo* was tangible and, some thought, reachable in their own lifetimes. The *antillean* movement involved creating and defining new collectivities built on engagement, relation, and structural change. *Antillean* activists crossed multiple boundaries, imperial borders, and language barriers to mobilize financial resources, create political organizations, build solidarity networks, and disseminate information about their work in newspaper articles and essays. They engaged with each other as equals, rooting their fight against Spanish and U.S. imperialism in strategic alliances and serious debate about race, nation, and belonging.

According to Michael Dash, Martinican philosopher Édouard Glissant believed that "island space [is] the site of a double identity" (Dash 2003, 290). Glissant's notion of doubleness resonates with the attempt in this edited volume to exchange rigid nationalisms and their scholarly and cultural by-products for something else. The contributors to this collection believe that Haitians and Dominicans, who are so often regarded as being in opposition to each other, "do not form a pair of contradictory oppositions but are relationally involved with each other" (Dash 2003, 296). We argue that Haitians and Dominicans have long been entangled with each other, yet the narrative of that relationship has often been used as evidence of inherent cultural differences or pathology. In our historical moment, Haiti and the Dominican Republic offer new lessons about how entanglement and dual-consciousness form the basis for new ways of framing justice, effecting change, and mobilizing resistance. As the contributions to this volume demonstrate, the work ahead is difficult and points of disagreement remain, but it is also necessary and urgent.

Toward this end, we propose a new map of the island to transform Hispaniola's fractured border from a wound that memorializes violence, separation, and opposition into a gathering space for building new relationships, for relating difference, pain, and violence. On this three-dimensional map, the border becomes a *poto mitan*, the center pole. In Vodou, the *poto mitan* serves a physical and spiritual function: the center pole is a bearing structure that holds up the temple while also serving as a conduit that connects earthly and spiritual planes. Those who feed the spirits (*sèvi lwa*) construct a ritual space around the *poto mitan* by drawing symbols (*vévé*), by singing and drumming, and through dance. Most important, even though the *poto mitan* is a solid structure, it is not a fixed or static object. At the *poto mitan*, the narrative can change from failure into possibility. At the *poto mitan*, Hispaniola becomes the meeting place for a new beginning.

Notes

1. Henríquez y Carvajal (1859–1952) and the poet Salomé Ureña de Henríquez (1850–1897), his wife, collaborated with Eugenio María de Hostos (1839–1903) to establish the first secular schools in the Dominican Republic, including schools for young women and girls. Education was a key component of *antillanismo* (pan-Antilleanism), the anticolonial, pro-independence political ideology advocated by Hostos; Dr. Ramón Emeterio Betances (1827–1898), his fellow Puerto Rican and pro-independence militant; and Dominican generals Gregorio Luperón (1839–1897), Ulises Heureaux (1845–1899), and Máximo Gómez (1836–1905).

2. By the time Henríquez y Carvajal sent his letter to Firmin, the major figures who had defined the Antillean movement were dead: Jose Martí died on the battlefield in Cuba in 1895; Salomé Ureña de Henríquez succumbed to tuberculosis in 1897, the same year that Gregorio Luperón returned home to Puerto Plata, where he died from cancer; Emeterio Betances died in poverty in France in 1898; and Eugenio María de Hostos died in Santo Domingo in 1903, where he remained buried, according to his wishes, until Puerto Rico became an independent nation. See Martínez-Vergne (2005, 24–25), Mayes (2014, esp. chapter 1), and Reyes-Santos (2015, esp. chapter 1).

3. His classic study *De l'Égalité des Races Humaines* (The Equality of the Human Races) was first published in 1885 (Fleuhr-Lobban 2000). Firmin died in exile in St. Thomas in 1911.

4. A powerful example of this is The Border of Lights Collective, which commemorates the October 1937 massacre: http://www.borderoflights.org/.

5. In 2009–2010, "we" included April Mayes, then an assistant professor of history at Pomona College; Yolanda Martín, then a graduate student in sociology at the Graduate Center of the City University of New York (CUNY); Pablo Mella, S.J., then director of the Pedro Francisco Bonó Institute of Superior Studies; and Kiran Jayaram, then a graduate student in applied anthropology at Teachers College/Columbia University. Our collective has grown since then to include Carlos U. Decena, professor of gender and women's studies at Rutgers University; Yveline Alexis, professor of history at Oberlin College; and Darlene Dubuisson, instructor in anthropology at CUNY.

6. We used the term Hispaniola to avoid generating controversy, but we ended up creating other tensions. Since we wanted to emphasize what these two countries shared, we needed a term that captured the island's totality. We rejected "Quisqueya" because of its association with the Dominican national anthem, and we felt it too provocative to use "Haíti," even though "Ayiti" was the term indigenous populations used for the island.

According to a letter sent by the president of the Dominican Geographic and Historical Society in 1931, "Hispaniola" is the incorrect Latin neologism of "La (Isla) Española," "The Spanish Island," the name Christopher Columbus gave to the first Spanish colony in the Americas. Pedro Mártir de Anglería, lacking a proper Latin term for the island, translated "La Española" as "Hispaniola." Much to the chagrin of Dominican geographers and historians, the United States Geographical Society adopted "Hispaniola" for use on all official maps in 1931 (Consejo Nacional de Educación 1931, 162–184). Upon hearing the announcement that a third transnational Hispaniola conference would be held in Port-au-Prince, several Haitian scholars refused to participate because of the word Hispaniola. For a thorough explanation from a Haitian scholar who accepts the name Hispaniola, see Doucet (2011).

Works Cited

Candelario, Ginetta. 2007. *Black behind the Ears: Dominican Identity from Museums to Beauty Shops*. Durham, NC: Duke University Press.

Clitandre, Nadège T. 2011. "Haitian Exceptionalism in the Caribbean and the Project of Rebuilding Haiti." *Journal of Haitian Studies* 17 (2): 146–153.

Consejo Nacional de Educación. 1931. "¿Debe Cambiarse el nombre de la Isla?" *Revista de Educación. Órgano del Consejo Nacional de Educación* 3 (12): 162–184.

Dash, Michael J. 2003. "Anxious Insularity. Identity Politics and Creolization in the Caribbean." In *A Pepper-Pot of Cultures: Aspects of Creolization in the Caribbean*, edited by Gordon Collier and Ulrich Fleischmann, 287–299. Amsterdam & New York: Editions Rodopi.

Daut, Marlene. 2015. *Tropics of Haiti: Race and the Literary History of the Haitian Revolution in the Atlantic World, 1789–1865*. Liverpool: Liverpool University Press.

Doucet, Rachelle Charlier. 2011. "Haïti, Quisqueya ou Bohio: Comment donc appeler cette île?" *AlterPresse*, July 15. http://www.alterpresse.org/spip.php?article11280#.WYeVpneGPdQ.

Firmin, Anténor. 1910. *Lettres de Saint Thomas. Études sociologiques, historiques et litteraires*. Paris: Girard & Brière.

Fleuhr-Lobban, Carolyn. 2000. "Anténor Firmin: Haitian Pioneer of Anthropology." *American Anthropologist* 102, n.s. (3): 449–466.

Fumagalli, Maria Cristina. 2015. *On the Edge: Writing the Border between Haiti and the Dominican Republic*. Liverpool: Liverpool University Press.

Garcia Peña, Lorgia. 2016. *The Borders of Dominicanidad: Race, Nation, and Archives of Contradiction*. Durham, NC: Duke University Press.

Glissant, Édouard. 1989. *Caribbean Discourse. Selected Essays*. Translated by J. Michael Dash. Charlottesville: University Press of Virginia.

Glover, Kaiama L., and Alessandra Benedicty-Kokken. 2016. "Editors' Introduction." In *The Haiti Exception: Anthropology and the Predicament of Narrative*, edited by Alessandra Benedicty-Kokken, Kaiama L. Glover, Mark Schuller, and Jhon Picard Byron, 1–14. Liverpool: Liverpool University Press.

Grasmuk, Sherri, and Patricia Pessar. 1991. *Between Two Islands: Dominican International Migration*. Berkeley: University of California Press.

Hernández, Ramona. 2002. *The Mobility of Workers under Advanced Capitalism. Dominican Migration to the United States*. New York: Columbia University Press.

Hoffnung-Garskof, Jesse. 2010. *A Tale of Two Cities: Santo Domingo and New York after 1950*. Princeton, NJ: Princeton University Press.

Martínez, Samuel. 2014. "The Price of Confrontation: International Retributive Justice and the Struggle for Haitian-Dominican Rights." In *The Uses and Misuses of Human Rights. A Critical Approach to Advocacy*, edited by George Andreopoulos and Zehra F. Kabasakal Arat, 89–115. New York: Palgrave Macmillan.

Martínez-Vergne, Teresita. 2005. *Nation & Citizen in the Dominican Republic, 1880–1916*. Chapel Hill: University of North Carolina Press.

Mayes, April J. 2014. *The Mulatto Republic: Class, Race, and Dominican National Identity*. Gainesville: University Press of Florida.

Mayes, April, Yolanda C. Martín, Carlos Ulises Decena, Kiran Jayaram, and Yveline Alexis. 2013. "Transnational Hispaniola: Toward New Paradigms in Haitian and Dominican Studies." *Radical History Review* 115 (Winter): 26–32.

Mintz, Sidney. 1986. *Sweetness and Power: The Place of Sugar in Modern History*. New York: Penguin Books.

Patil, Vrushali. 2013. "From Patriarchy to Intersectionality: A Transnational Feminist Assessment of How Far We've Really Come." *Signs: Journal of Women and Culture* 38 (4): 847–867.

Paulino, Edward. 2016. *Dividing Hispaniola: The Dominican Republic's Border Campaign against Haiti, 1930–1961*. Pittsburgh: University of Pittsburgh Press.

Reyes-Santos, Alaí. 2015. *Our Caribbean Kin: Race and Nation in the Neoliberal Antilles*. New Brunswick, NJ: Rutgers University Press.

Ricourt, Milagros. 2016. *The Dominican Racial Imaginary: Surveying the Landscape of Race and Nation in Hispaniola*. New Brunswick, NJ: Rutgers University Press.

Schiller, Nina Glick, Linda Basch, and Cristina Blanc-Szanton. 1998. "Towards a Definition of Transnationalism. Introductory Remarks and Research Questions." In "Towards a Transnational Perspective on Migration: Race, Class, Ethnicity, and Nationalism Reconsidered," edited by Nina Glick Schiller, Linda Basch, and Cristina Blanc-Szanton. Special issue, *Annals of the New York Academy of Sciences* 645 (July): viii–xiv.

Schiller, Nina Glick, and Georges Fouron. 1990. "'Everywhere We Go, We Are in Danger': Ti Manno and the Emergence of a Haitian Transnational Identity." *American Ethnologist* 17 (2): 329–347.

———. 2001. *Georges Woke Up Laughing: Nationalism and the Search for Home*. Durham, NC: Duke University Press.

Trouillot, Michel Rolph. 1990. "The Odd and the Ordinary: Haiti, the Caribbean, and the World," *Cimarrón* 2 (3): 3–12.

———. 2003. *Global Transformations: Anthropology and the Modern World*. New York: Palgrave Macmillan.

Ulysse, Gina Athena. 2015. *Why Haiti Needs New Narratives: A Post-Quake Chronicle.* Middletown, CT: Wesleyan University Press.

Wimmer, Andreas, and Nina Glick Schiller. 2003. "Methodological Nationalism, the Social Sciences, and the Study of Migration: An Essay in Historical Epistemology." *International Migration Review* 37 (3): 576–610.

Yelvington, Kevin. 2006. *Afro-Atlantic Dialogues: Anthropology in the Diaspora.* Santa Fe, NM: School of American Research Press.

1

The Historical Limits of
the State in Hispaniola

1

Shifting Territories

The Production of Space on Eighteenth-Century Hispaniola

NATHALIE BRAGADIR

The sites and sights of the borderlands (as places simultaneously resistant to "others" and places of expressed resistance) provide territories where these two conditions can be juxtaposed. These are places where the act of mapping—of "taking measure"—can permit the speculation of alternative blueprints through which the essential connections between body and land are reshaped.

Teddy Cruz, *Architecture of the Borderlands*

For instance, a man is living in the state of Mississippi today, a cutoff occurs tonight, and tomorrow the man finds himself and his land over on the other side of the river, within the boundaries and subject to the laws of the state of Louisiana! Such a thing, happening in the upper river in the old times, could have transferred a slave from Missouri to Illinois and made a free man of him.

Mark Twain, *Life on the Mississippi*

In the colonial archives of Sevilla and Aix-en-Provence and in the national archives in Santo Domingo, entire catalogs are devoted to "Border Affairs" between Saint Domingue and Santo Domingo. The archives have a way of speaking for themselves: the sheer number of documents alone indicates that this island's colonial history centered on territorial claims. The French and Spanish diplomatic correspondence over border issues in Hispaniola during the eighteenth century shows that during this period, colonial authorities could not effectively isolate one side of the island from the other. Paradoxically, bilateral attempts to delimit a border, whether on the island or across the Atlantic, reveal a series of important dialogues— sometimes cooperative, sometimes confrontational—between France and Spain. This chapter provides a glimpse into the history of the border in Hispaniola and argues that the official treaties and mapping practices regarding the border reveal a volatile reality that created anxiety for officials on both sides as France and Spain pursued territorial possession. My analysis of the mapping and spatial practices during the creation of the colonial border reveals how status and racialized subjecthood centered on territorial possession and sovereignty. Whether they were actively crossing the border themselves or having the limits redrawn around them, people have been crossing this border since its inception. Some had the power to transform their status through adopting a new allegiance, but others who were not so fortunate found themselves constrained by the border and without access to their freedom or their property.

Pierre Ravel, a French freeman of color, is an example of the latter. He was arrested in 1768 by Spanish commander Nicolás de Montenegro for encroaching on Spanish territory near the border town of San Rafael. Because the French made only a feeble effort to arrange for his freedom, he was held for almost two years in the prisons of San Rafael and Santo Domingo. Calling himself a "loyal vassal among all nations,"[1] Ravel was indignant about the fact that he had remained imprisoned for so long. Ravel said, "From the first step of my tragedy I have been treated as a criminal."[2] Why was he held responsible for a boundary issue that should have been settled between French and Spanish sovereigns? Why should he, as a Frenchman, have to ask permission of the Spanish side to purchase a piece of property sold to him by another person of French nationality? Ravel explained his position in testimony before the *audiencia* in Santo Domingo, the Crown's appellate court in the colonies:

> When a Frenchman wishes to acquire a certain property from a master or lord, he will only do so on French domain, not Spanish, whose limits should be known by the respective lords of both nations, and in the case that some error should occur, he who bought the property in good faith, acquiring the title from its legitimate sovereign, should not be the victim.[3]

Ravel's predicament revealed how these states' inability to define and police firm boundaries between their territories created unpredictable and dangerous consequences for those who lived in this contested space. In his attempt to settle in highly contested territory away from Spanish authority, Ravel realized too late that contact with both sides was necessary for his survival.

The notion of the borderland—not just the border—is crucial in analyzing Ravel's case. Establishing the borderland as the starting point eventually leads to the social networks that reach across it. The limits of the border that were established in the French and Spanish maps and treaties by officials in capitals (on the island or in Europe) were far from recognized on the ground (Fig. 1.1). Defining the unit of analysis as the contested region that eventually became a border has the potential to deepen our understanding about imperial authority and power in daily life. Border studies scholars Michiel Baud and Willem van Schendel (1997) see this dynamic as a paradox:

> From the perspective of national centers of authority, the border between countries is a sharp line, an impenetrable barrier. But from the perspective of the border, borderlands are broad scenes of interactions in which people from both sides work out everyday accommodations based on face-to-face relationships. (216)

Sven Tägil notes another paradoxical quality: borders act simultaneously as dividers and connectors. He writes, "Boundaries separate people . . . and the separating qualities of boundaries influence interaction between them." In his discussion about the U.S.-Mexico border, Stanley Ross also views the border as "a region where two civilizations face each other *and overlap*" (quoted in Baud and van Schendel 1997, 216; italics in original). In other words, while borders create political, social, and cultural divides, they also reveal the existence of networks of communication across them.

Every border has a different history, and Hispaniola's particular history of slavery greatly influenced the groups who became most associated with the border region and the ways border figures—maroon slaves, free people of color, military officials, and contrabandists—identified with one side or the other. Toward the end of the eighteenth century, Saint Domingue, the French side, was the more powerful because of a booming economy based in slavery and sugar production. On the eve of the Haitian Revolution, more than 180,000 people lived in Saint Domingue, 90 percent of whom were enslaved. Meanwhile, the Spanish side to the east, which was composed mostly of cattle ranchers, or *hateros*, was poorer and had a population about half the size of its neighbor, 15 percent of whom

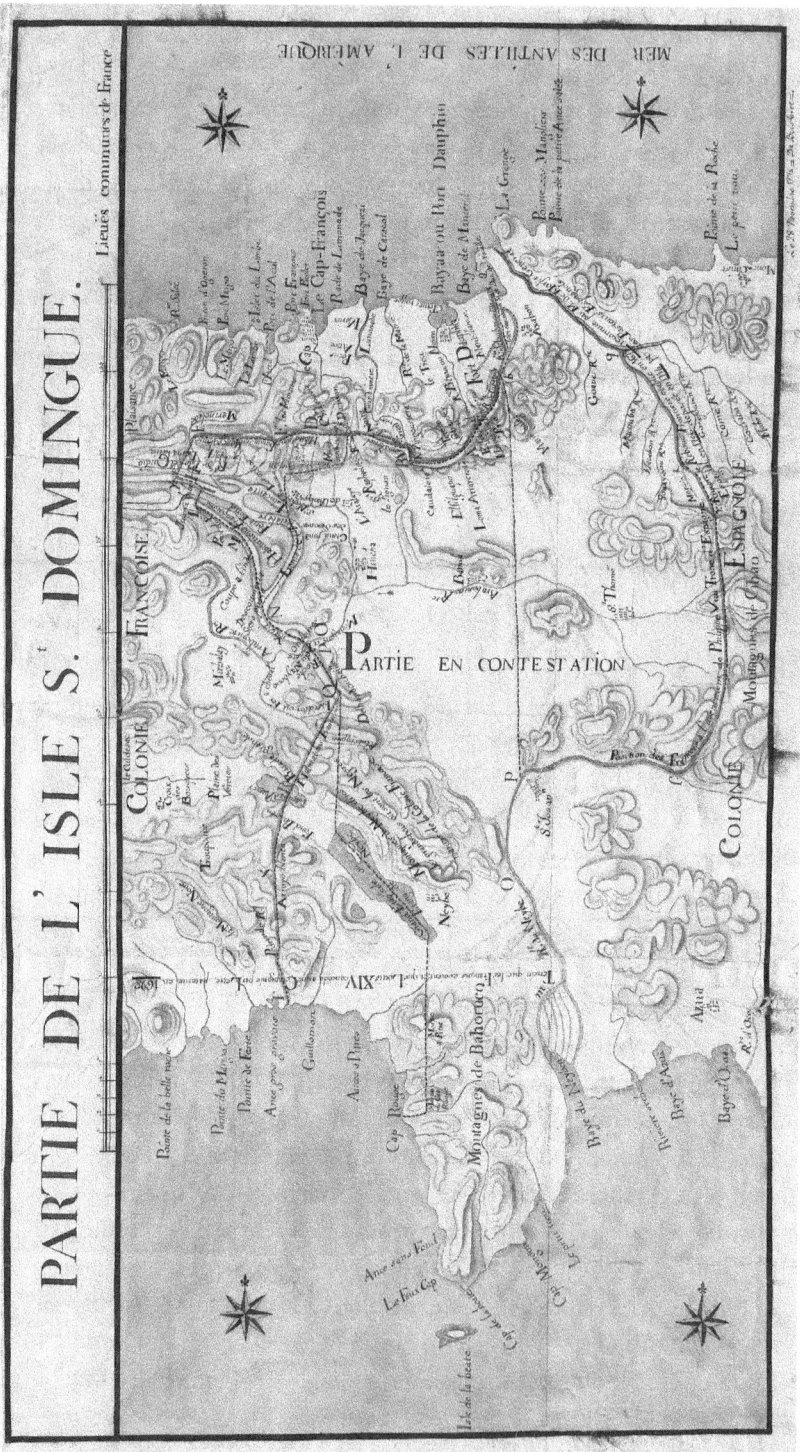

Figure 1.1. *Partie en Contestation* (area in dispute), map of the island of Saint Domingue, 1776, by De Boisforêt. Estado Mapa 72, Archivo Histórico Nacional, Madrid, Spain.

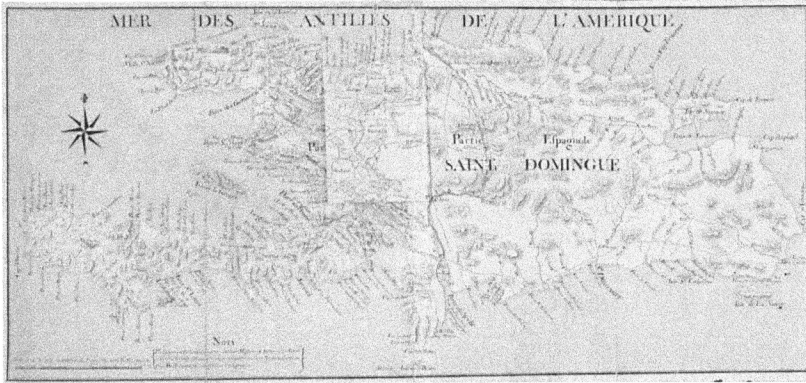

Figure 1.2. Map of the island of Saint Domingue with alternative border, 1772, by De Boisforêt. Collection Moreau de St. Mery. Archives Nationales d'Outre Mer, Aix-en-Provence, France.

were enslaved. Maroon communities of escaped slaves from both sides of the island occupied the still relatively unknown territory of the border region, which was also inhabited by freed people of color who made their living by buying and selling contraband goods that included cattle from the Spanish side and agricultural and manufactured items from the French side. These border subjects were a source of constant anxiety for the French and Spanish officials. They threatened the very core of colonial power with their illegal settlements and trafficking in contraband. These cross-border practices had the potential to undermine the colonists' all-important claims to territory and possession (Fig. 1.2).

The anxiety over this zone is revealed in the Spanish use of the term *tolerancia*, abbreviated from *raya de tolerancia* (line of tolerance), to define the region that separated Saint Domingue from Santo Domingo. This term occurs frequently in the Spanish correspondence but does not appear in the French documents. "*Raya de tolerancia*" seems to have signaled the Spanish Crown's concerns over French incursions into Spanish territory, since the borderline often shifted from west to east. The complicated process of possession was the most important method of proving ownership of territory because it could be argued based on fact (and evidence) rather than on entitlement. Lauren Benton (2010, 7) has claimed that in imperial disputes over territory, rituals of possession on the ground, such as forts, markers, cultivation of land, and public declarations, were more effective methods for proving land sovereignty than diplomatic treaties and maps.

On an island divided by a contested border area whose topography was still largely unknown, these rituals were essential to establishing some kind of separation.

Perhaps the most important and effective proof of possession was the occupation and cultivation of land by settlers. French authorities and French settlers, it appears, purposely selected land in spaces that risked being destroyed by the Spanish troops. If cultivation meant proof of possession, it was in the best interest of the French to cultivate land in contested territory. The Spaniards, therefore, whose main economy was based primarily on grazing cattle over vast, often unmarked tracts of land, would be at a clear disadvantage to the French coffee growers and sugar growers, whose cultivation of the land was much more obvious and permanent. Because the demarcation of the border was constantly changing, the inhabitants of the borderland—mostly contrabandists, *hateros*, escaped slaves, free people of color, and immigrants from the Canary Islands (or *yslenos*)—found ways to thwart the rules and limitations of this border. Subject to violent and prohibitive codes and practices, they felt loyal to neither Spain nor France. In fact, they used the lack of territorial possession at the border to subvert colonial authority.

Paying close attention to claims of allegiance in colonial Hispaniola is extremely revealing. The precarious, almost nonexistent control French and Spanish authorities exerted over this region is demonstrated in the fluidity with which residents changed their allegiances from one sovereign power to the other and their willingness to challenge the allegiance of others with whom they had disputes. Moreover, the apparent failure of either the French or the Spaniards to obtain the loyalty of subjects living in the area made it more difficult for them to fix subjecthood on residents and then assign inherent qualities to colonial subjects that would eventually define differences between colonial regimes as natural and predestined.

Two striking examples of the ability of borderland residents to alternate allegiances involve Isidro and Nicolás, two freemen of color living in the border region in 1729 whose individual settlements created havoc among the French and Spanish imperial powers. Nicolás, whom Spanish authorities noted had been raised among the Spaniards and was living on land deemed Spanish territory, was now claiming to be French. This switch in allegiance had enormous consequences in the highly contested border region. If Nicolás was accepted as French, as he claimed he was, then the land he was occupying could fall under French jurisdiction. In an apoplectic letter sent from the capital in Santo Domingo to Senor Maestro de Campo Manuel Caravallo on the Spanish border, Don Francisco de la Rocha Ferrer issued a directive:

> Under no circumstance let it be permitted that the French inhabit, ride, or overstep one hand span further from what has been presently tolerated, and that those who are found be taken to this city [Santo Domingo], and that those who resist be killed and that the slaves who are found be taken to this city to be confiscated by order of the king.[4]

These were moot threats, however, as the poorly marked border provided little protection for the weaker and poorer Spanish sovereignty. Because the two sides could not agree on which natural markers—such as rivers, mountains, and forests—to use to demarcate French and Spanish claims, claims made by border residents such as Nicolás carried weight and were cause for concern. For the purpose of establishing border limits, both the French and Spanish officials attempted to claim these border inhabitants as theirs. However, the subjects could easily pass as either and strategically claimed one allegiance or the other when the situation demanded it.

In that same year of 1729, another free person of color and border resident named Isidro became a problem for French authorities. In a letter to the Spanish governor, the French cavalier de Rochelar, who was supervising troops on the ground that patrolled the border, wrote that it had come to his attention that the Spaniards were now claiming the territory of Petit Fondo, a region in the southern borderland by Neyba. According to Rochelar, this had never previously been contested territory due to French hunting activities and because of Isidro's settlement (who, according to French authorities, had always been regarded as "French"). Isidro's children, Rochelar claimed, had been baptized among the French. However, because of territorial disputes in the area, Isidro said that he was loyal to Spain:

> The property of one freeman of color named Isidro was so established among us, where he had many children baptized, that we saw him as French, and who afterwards attempted to become Spanish in order to plausibly dispute us this land.[5]

Isidro, Rochelar insisted, had always "belonged" to the French. With this declaration, Rochelar also claimed Isidro's land as French territory.

Even the Spanish inhabitants of the region, Rochelar added, recognized Isidro as "French." According to Rochelar, if Isidro's Spanish neighbors accepted his Frenchness as fact, the Spanish Crown should do so as well and cease its attempts to assert itself in Petit Fondo. Isidro appears to have been trying to cope with a changing situation. Rochelar's argument that Spanish residents in the area knew Isidro and could confirm his loyalty to France suggests that the region was slowly turning into Spanish territory as defined by possession through settlement. Isidro's allegiance to Spain may have been his only means of securing and protecting his possessions as the Spanish population grew and undermined French claims to Petit Fondo. His becoming "Spanish" would have secured his status in this evolving and conflicted situation that apparently favored Spain. Allegiance, it appears, followed people and then determined which side could claim control over space.

This rivalry at the line of tolerance differed considerably from the other border Spain and France shared in the metropole. In his study of the Pyrenees region between France and Spain, Peter Sahlins (1989) analyzes a well-known seventeenth-century European genre of literature that contrasted the national characteristics of the French and Spaniards:

> The temperament of the Spaniards is hotter and more humid, and their color darker; that of the French is colder and less humid; their skin is softer and whiter. French women are more fertile than Spaniard [women]. . . . The French speak with more ease, the Spaniards keep quiet and know how to dissimulate better. (109–110)

This genre reveals a long-standing tradition of competition and comparison between the populations of the two sovereignties. The French and the Spanish nations had a long and complicated history of rivalries and alliances with each other that was constantly changing in the metropole and in the colonies—and not always simultaneously. This made it very difficult for the inhabitants of Hispaniola to know how to relate to each other, should they interact as sworn enemies, as rivals, or as neighbors? The constant push and pull between France and Spain in Europe provided a template for the two nations' interactions on Hispaniola and for the conflicts between Saint Domingue and Santo Domingo.

However, the back and forth over allegiance in the cases of Isidro and Nicolás were markedly different from those of the European border region. The "essence" of nationality had not yet emerged as a major issue in disputes such as those involving Isidro and Nicolás; only territory and possession manifested in the form of allegiances mattered to the French and Spanish states. On Hispaniola, allegiance to one imperial regime or the other was a calculated decision residents made in response to shifting political and economic circumstances. The border between French and Spanish colonies in the Caribbean did not demarcate the "natural" differences between the French and the Spanish, as the Pyrenees did in Europe. Instead, the Hispaniola case shows how territory and possession followed claims of allegiance instead of creating them.

The mapping of the border was an attempt by colonial authorities to demarcate territorial jurisdictions and fix their presence. But to what extent could they impose their jurisdiction over the colonists? When Pierre Ravel arrived at his recently purchased plot of land by the mouth of the Río Grande in the parish of Santa Rosa, his only proofs of property were a title and a map drawn by a French cartographer, Monsieur Paris; both had been "measured and marked" (*medido y amojonado*).[6] Yet as the two years Ravel spent in jail prove, his properly delineated map was useless because he was a Frenchman who was asserting his rights in Spanish territory. Indeed, both French and Spanish authorities agreed that maps could not be trusted as truthful representations of the border region's topography because officials assumed that cartographers were biased in favor of their respective governments. Instead, authorities regarded natural landmarks as permanent enough to demarcate territorial possession. But even the assumed objectivity and stability of natural fixtures were subject to the weight of territorial contestation.

In understanding this conflict between geography and cartography, Michel de Certeau's (1984) comments on physical landmarks are refreshingly evocative.

To whom does [the frontier] belong? The river, wall or tree makes a frontier. It does not have the character of a nowhere that cartographical representation ultimately presupposes. It has a mediating role. So does the story that gives it voice: "Stop," says the forest the wolf comes out of. "Stop!" says the river, revealing its crocodile. But this actor, by virtue of the very fact that he is the mouthpiece of the limit, creates communication as well as separation; more than that, he establishes a border only by saying what crosses it, having come from the other side. He articulates it. He is also a passing through or over. In the story, the frontier functions as a third element. It is an "in-between"—a "space between," *Zwischenraum*, as Morgenstern puts it. (126)

De Certeau claims that although natural landmarks have the ability to create borders, the limits are articulated and come alive only when such landmarks are crossed. A border thus encompasses a mediation and passing through in its very definition.

> Created by contacts, the points of differentiation between two bodies are also their common points. Conjunction and disjunction are inseparable in them. Of two bodies in contact, which possesses the frontier that distinguishes them? Neither. Does that amount to saying: no one? (127)

De Certeau's musings suggest the dual quality of borders. They express limits—boundaries—and the movement toward, through, and over those limits. This explains why borders are fundamentally contested spaces and why they provoke anxiety in state powers that want to assert their hegemony. This was notably the case among state officials on Hispaniola.

Hispaniola's maps changed constantly. Depending on whose map you read, rivers and other natural markers could disappear entirely or mysteriously change position according to the claims of colonial authorities. In response to the questionable information maps provided, colonial officials agreed to place border markers, or *guardarrayas* and *mojones*, but these soon became another contested issue between France and Spain. Markers could easily be tampered with and displaced. The weaker Spanish side was especially indignant whenever the French placed markers; they claimed that they were constantly encroaching on Spanish territory. French settlers could easily remove boundary stones to extend the boundaries of their property. The removal of one *mojón* in 1785, in fact, caused so much uproar among Spanish officials that its documentation fills an entire folder in the Archivo General de la Nación in Santo Domingo, entitled, "Destrucción francesa del mojón 174" (French Destruction of Marker 174). Juan Gapy, a French freeman of color who was attempting to settle in the border region, destroyed the marker. The anger over this action is documented in this excerpt from a letter from the Spanish general Gaspard de Leoz y Echalas to the governor of Santo Domingo, Joaquin Garcia y Moreno which refers to the event as the crime so irreverently committed by Juan [Gapy], not only in trespassing upon our territory, but also in having the audacity to destroy and remove the boundary stone 174, whose permanence was so solidly established in the treaties between our Sovereigns.[7]

The fury over the ease with which one person removed a marker that had been made "permanent" in the maps and treaties between both nations was palpable: the materiality of the border could be tampered with and completely erased without warning. The Spanish border commander Gaspard de Leoz y Echalas and his counterpart, French border commander Compte de Choiseul, who were friends even though they were from rival nations, organized an expedition to the area to resolve the problem. Choiseul was able to resolve the issue easily with Leoz y Echalas; he placed the blame on the French cartographer Boisforêt for misrepresenting the limits (Fig. 1.3). Gapy then set fire to his own house (it is unknown whether he was coerced into doing so) and left the region. The *mojón*, however, was never rebuilt because the area where it was located was so remote. The issue was ultimately resolved in Spain's favor after the French and Spanish commanders amicably resolved the dispute. The real defeat, however, was suffered by the French freeman Jean Gapy, who lost his property and was forced to leave the region.

This glimpse into the construction and easy removal of parts of the border gives a very different impression from an abstract line drawn on a map or from a vague verbal reference to the "*tolerancia*" or other such border terminology French and Spanish officials used in their diplomatic correspondence. The removal of *mojón* 174 precipitated an intense debate over the materiality of the border that was recorded in an *itinerario manual de la frontera* (manual itinerary of the border) that described the extremely complicated process of demarcating boundary lines:

> A single boundary Stone, Pyramid, Rock or Boulder is given a number, each one following the next in a line, name of the Property and Owner without an intermediary where it could be seen that No. 174 was recorded as a single artificial boundary stone, of those that should have been confirmed as a combination, and that No. 132 is a rock, and 133 an inaccessible boulder, and without doubt as big as the Palace of Santo Domingo, where the Viscount also erroneously mistakes one site for another, after the *prácticos* informed him that they had not seen 132 during their Rounds.[8]

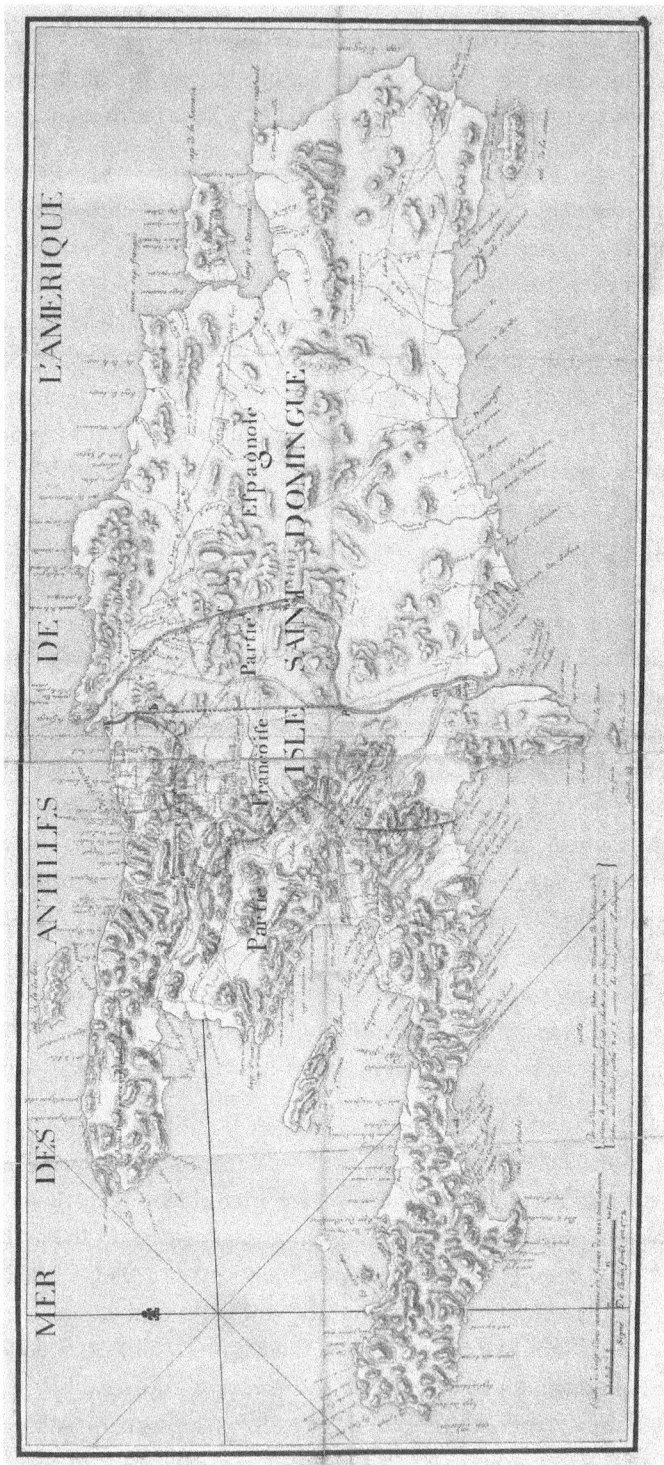

Figure 1.3. *Plano de los límites provisionales según el acuerdo [de Aranjuez] de 1772* (with two borders) (Plan of the provisional limits according to the agreement of 1772), by De Boisforêt. Estado Mapa 73, Archivo Histórico Nacional, Madrid.

This description demonstrates the process by which a border was drawn, from marker to pyramid to mountain to rock, each one labeled with a number that would then be transferred to a map. Making a boundary involved both natural and artificial markers, and the artificial ones—like number 174—were the easiest to move. A *peñasco* (boulder) like number 133, although it was "as big as the Palace of Santo Domingo," would be useless, however, because its inaccessibility meant that it could easily be overlooked by the *prácticos*—who were responsible for making the rounds and ensuring that the border markers were in the right place. A border, therefore, consisted of both natural and manmade markers. The locations of these markers were verified by human monitors. The act of placing a *mojón* was a deliberate ritualistic act, as Leoz y Echalas described it:

> In the same act of placing any boundary stone, or carving out a firm rock, the *prácticos* would materially inspect it for its security, and do the same for the next one, and they would clear out a dense forest to form a small plaza and mark the thickest trees closest to the rock.[9]

Placing a border marker involved clearing the nearby area to create a small plaza around the rock or the artificial *mojón* and marking the biggest trees immediately surrounding it. The act of demarcating the border both used and transformed the natural topography of the area. To think about the elements that constituted the making of a border is as compelling as it is revealing. Leoz y Echalas described the process in more detail:

> Along the length of the border we took special care ([in order to obtain] the most steady and accurate results possible) to use the natural rocks and boulders that we would find already fixed in the land as boundary markers, and sometimes [we] preventively removed a stone that had already been engraved in the Cabeza de los Negros, to avoid confusion: I infer that from this practice originated the error of the Viscount in thinking that we had arrived at the point in question with the engraved stone, *which would have been very toilsome for the slaves* for the large distance from which it came and uncertain and unknown to us, until we came to that point. (my emphasis)[10]

In this letter, Leoz y Echalas attempted to explain the misunderstanding that had arisen over one particular misplaced border marker in the region of Cabeza de los Negros. The letter mentioned that it would have been too difficult for slaves to carry the marker for such a long distance. While it remains unclear if enslaved labor was used to demarcate the entire border of Hispaniola, this letter documents the presence of slaves as boundaries were being demarcated. Thus, both slaves and free people of color were constantly interacting with the materiality of the border by the acts of placing the markers and removing them, as was the case with the freed Frenchman Jean Gapy.

The ease with which the border markers could be tampered with, misplaced, and replaced fueled the constant contestation of territory in the border region. Numerous bilateral expeditions were sent to the border to provide proof of possession. These usually consisted of an international crew of military officials, cartographers, engineers, *prácticos*—and, of course, slaves who carried food and equipment. However, these expeditions rarely achieved significant results. Other factors, then, were as essential as demarcation or verification to the process of stabilizing the border. On Hispaniola, the return of runaway slaves, as agreed in bilateral treaties, proved particularly effective in the diplomatic negotiations between both sides of the island (Fig. 1.4).

In December 1771, border commander Miranda received a memorandum from José Solano, the president of Santo Domingo, that issued special instructions to observe the 1762 treaty, the most recent one between the two nations. Solano specified that

> fugitive slaves being reclaimed by their legitimate master and barring any other crime except flight, should not be corporally punished. Should those slaves have already entered into a marriage contract, they may remain in the nation where they were married and pay their masters in the other nation a fair price that will be valued in good faith for a Spaniard and a Frenchman; that this will be executed in the same manner regarding the children, should their mothers be legitimately reclaimed.[11]

Despite President Solano's concern that the treaty be followed to the letter, the reality was that the majority of fugitive slaves on the island regularly crossed the border from Saint Domingue to Santo Domingo, as ninety percent of the French side of the island was enslaved versus fifteen percent of the Spanish side. The agreement that fugitive slaves who had married on Spanish soil would be allowed to stay as long as the owner was recompensed created an incentive for fugitive slaves from the French

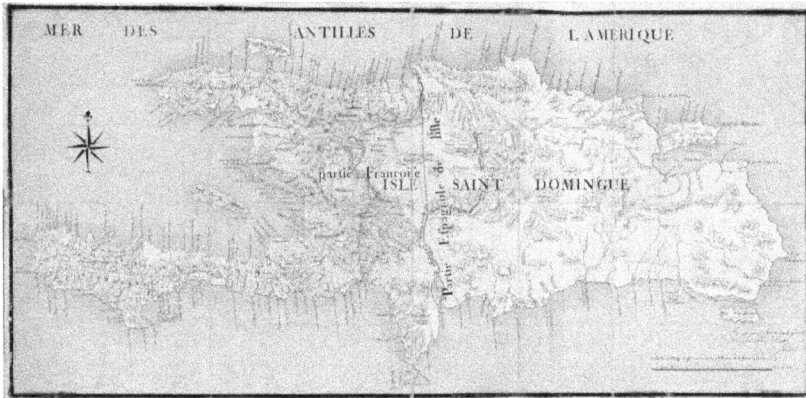

Figure 1.4. *Plano de los límites provisionales según el acuerdo [de Aranjuez] de 1772* (with multiple borders) (Plan of the provisional limits according to the agreement of 1772), by De Boisforêt. Collection Moreau de St. Mery, Archives Nationales d'Outre Mer, Aix-en-Provence, France.

side to marry on Spanish soil and swear allegiance to the Spanish Church and Crown. The French lamented the fact that Spanish priests performed marriages for slaves, thus converting them to Spanish subjects and providing them asylum. The French were unable to prevent these practices, however, as it was the only leverage the weaker Spanish side had over the French, who frequently attempted to transgress the border. The weaker Spanish side would often repeat the phrase *"ni una palma,"* to indicate that they would prevent the French settlers from crossing "even a palm of the hand," a Spanish standard unit of measurement adopted from the Romans, onto to their territory, but in actuality they were forced to endure it more often than not.

The Spanish welcomed any inhabitants who could contribute to their dwindling population, and the 1762 treaty demonstrates considerable tolerance and protection of runaway slaves from the French side. In fact, in 1763, a French officer named Bertrand sent a letter to the Spanish president that implored the Spaniards to stop branding runaway slaves, as the branding meant that French slaves could not be returned to their original owners. Bertrand's insistence can be sensed even through a Spanish translation of the letter:

In sum: the continuation of the brand authorizes larceny [and] confuses the French slaves with those of the Spaniards[.] Its suspension is of ultimate consequence in favor of the French colony and the flight of its slaves and their restitution.[12]

The Spaniards, however, professed (probably false) indignation that the French were accusing them of "Hispanifying each other" (*españolizando los unos y los otros*).[13] On Hispaniola, the rebranding of fugitive slaves thus contributed to the precarious nature of sovereign allegiance and identity. The Spaniards insisted (disingenuously) that they would never illegally tamper with the brand of a French refugee slave in order to prevent restitution. Bertrand described the scope of the French problem with brands:

> Either the slaves are introduced legitimately . . . or the introduction is illicit or through contraband. Or in brief the slaves have introduced themselves through their escape of our colonies. . . . Countless slaves encountered in these parts [became] fugitives from their masters' homes before they [were] branded. Countless others have burned off their brands.[14]

French officials' inability to prove whether a slave had originally come from the French side was a source of constant frustration to them. But what is even more striking is the language French officials used when they described the process of discerning the allegiance of fugitive slaves. The border allowed for the existence of such terms as "*españolizar*," which described the possibility that an island resident could change allegiance from French to Spanish or vice versa. In some instances, shifting allegiances was a weapon free people of color used to assert what little agency they could in constantly changing circumstances. Changing sides could also result in new oppression when the two nations exchanged runaway slaves, and the branding of an enslaved person could replace a French master with a Spanish one.

The last treaty signed between the two sides of Hispaniola before the slave uprising of Saint Domingue was the Treaty of Aranjuez (1777). The treaty was the direct result of Pierre Ravel's border transgression. That act triggered a yearlong expedition that involved border commanders Choiseul and Leoz y Echalas, the cartographer Boisforêt, and many *prácticos* and slaves. The treaty made no mention of any previously documented boundaries between the two colonies, however. It focused on returning runaway slaves and coast guard deserters and on prohibiting the sale of slaves and animals across the border without a permit.

Like the 1762 treaty, this treaty explicitly involved the return of maroon slaves. It addressed the complex issues of how to identify the allegiance of fugitive slaves and how the marriage of two slaves on one side of the border would make them legal subjects of that nation. It stated: "When it is unclear if the refugee slave is Spanish or French, he will be held in prison until the *property* has been proven" (reprinted in Davenport 1937, 125; my emphasis).[15] Allegiance in this case was determined by a double definition of belonging: as a sovereign subject and as human property. The ease with which runaway slaves or freed persons of color could transform their status by claiming allegiance to whichever power seemed more convenient and useful was a frequent preoccupation of French and Spanish officials. The various treaties and stipulations concerning the border region evidence this concern among colonial authorities. French and Spanish officials frequently complained about how people living in contested areas used ambivalence to their advantage, reshaping their "sovereign allegiance" because they wanted to claim land or freedom from enslavement.

In his study of the border between France and Spain, Peter Sahlins (1989) argues that national identity appeared in regions European powers had colonized before that concept emerged in Europe in the nineteenth century. For Sahlins, this process began when colonial officials defined the physical boundaries of a regime's reach and claimed the people living within that space as members of a new entity. As a result, in countries such as France and Spain, "nationality took on, the principles of *jus sanguinis* aside, a territorial dimension" (276).[16] Sahlins argues that a sense of difference in the French-Spanish borderlands—of us versus them— complemented the practice of defining belonging, which often took place when the state established and defended territorial boundaries.

What took place in Hispaniola in the eighteenth century both confirms and expands Sahlins's insights. The struggle to define colonial boundaries on Hispaniola demonstrates that residents could transform, adjust, and replace their allegiance of individuals as they negotiated their access to property, their freedom from enslavement, and their autonomy.

For colonial regimes, mapping and boundary-making rituals performed on the ground were attempts to establish power and presence in the context of volatile and constantly changing circumstances. They were exercises in the consolidation of power that almost always failed (Fig. 1.5). As colonial authorities drew sharper lines between subjects and invested border residents with certain rights and duties, they created more

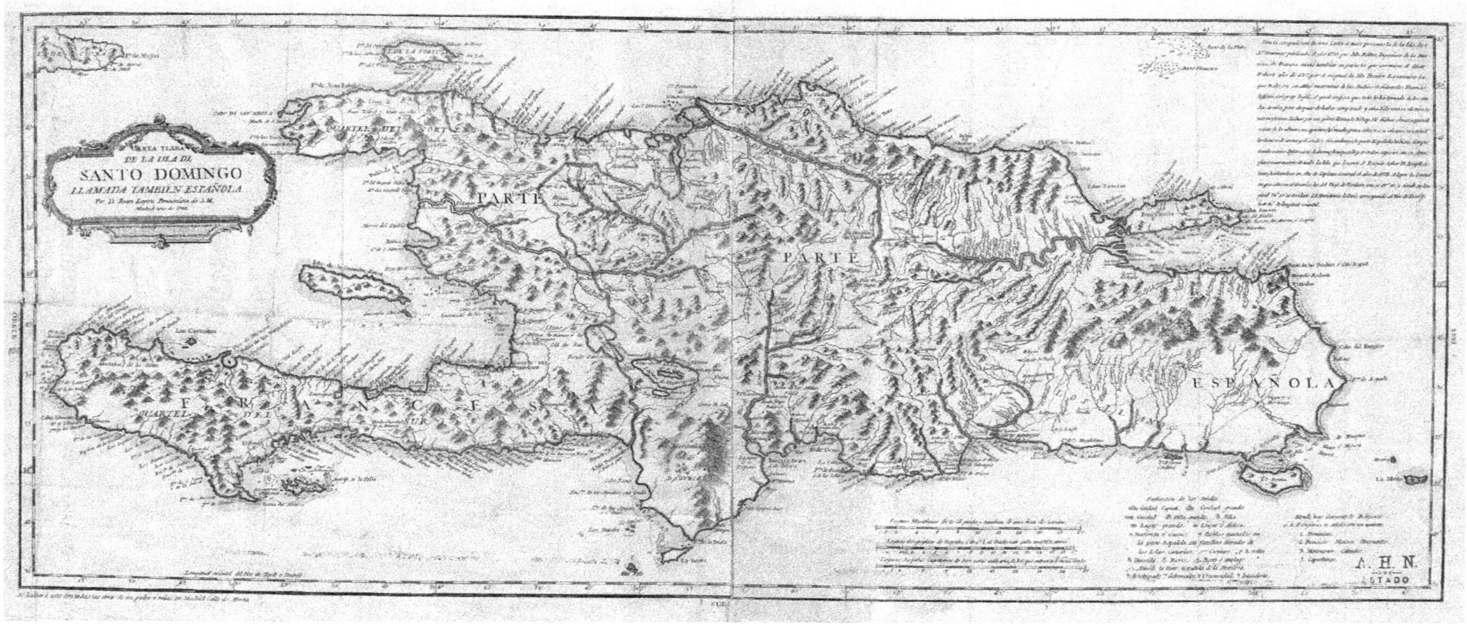

Figure 1.5. Copy of the De Boisforêt map favoring Spanish claims, 1784, by D. Juan López. Estado mapa 68, Archivo Histórico Nacional, Madrid.

opportunities for border residents to manipulate or avoid the new rules altogether. On Hispaniola, as elsewhere across the Atlantic, slavery and colonialism troubled the link between territory and subjecthood. People moved their bodies and their communities across colonial boundaries, especially from east to west, in order to transform their status. In the process, they not only asserted claims to one crown over the other, they also gave expression to a distinct sense of autonomy.

These unique tensions and possibilities at the border formed complex dynamics that resulted in constant negotiations over the relationship between individuals' allegiance to state power and the state's ability to assert territorial possession through the settlement of residents and their adherence to the colonial regime. However, in my emphasis on the possibilities for change, I do not mean to present a utopian vision of the border as a place where inhabitants could live in relative freedom from the state. What began to emerge on this island was an idea of sovereign allegiance and status constructed by race, language, and territory that would be— and still is—contested. Even to this day, citizenship based on blood (*jus sanguinis*) and on birthright (*jus soli*) remains heavily debated on the island. The present-day struggles between the Dominican state's belief in its right to sovereignty and the basic human right of Haitian migrants and their Dominican-born children to a nationality must be viewed in conjunction with the longer history of their shared borderlands.

Notes

1. "*Fiel y leal vasallo entre todas las naciones.*"
2. "*Desde el primer paso de mi tragedia he sido tratado como un facineroso.*"
3. "*Quando un particular Frances pide a los señores o merced de alguna posesion, no entiende pedir sino en los dominios de la nacion Francesa, y no de la Española, cuyos limites deven saberlos los señores gefes respectivos, y en tal caso de incurrir en algun error, no debe ser la victima el particular que entró en su posesion con buena fe, titulo adquirido de su legitimo soberano.*" Santo Domingo 1018, Archivo General de Indias, Seville.
4. "*Que por ningun acontecimiento permitan, que los franceses, pueblan, monteen, ni se propasen un palmo mas adelante de lo que les estaba tolerado al tiempo, que tome possession deste Govierno, y que a los que encontraran, los prendan y remitan a esta ciudad, y si hizieran alguna Resistencia los maten y que los negros que encontraran me los remitan a este ciudad donde los confiscare por de S.M.*" Don Francisco de la Rocha Ferrer to Senor Maestro de Campo Manuel Caravallo, Santo Domingo, February 17, 1730, Santo Domingo 17/02491, Archivo General de la Nacíon, Santo Domingo.

5. *"El establecimiento de un negro nombrado Isidro tan antiguo entre nosotros, a donde ha tenido muchos hijos Baptizados, que lo miravamos por frances, y a quien despues de atrahido hazerse español por el devil titulo de tener alguna apariencia de razon de disputarnos este terreno."* Cavalier de Rochelar to Governor Francisco de la Rocha y Ferrer, Petit Goave, May 11, 1730, Santo Domingo 17/02491, Archivo General de la Nacíon, Santo Domingo.

6. Ravel, testimony to the Royal Audiencia of Santo Domingo, March 30, 1730, Santo Domingo 1018, Archivo General de Indias, Seville.

7. *"El hecho criminal en que tan irreverentemente ha contrabenido dicho Juan Gapito, no tan solo en anvanzar nuestros terrenos, sino tambien teniendo la osadia de destruir y quitar la piedra en que se haya parado el citado numero 174, tan solidamente encargado su permanencia en los tratados convenidos entre Nuestros Soberanos."* Commander Gaspard de Leoz y Echalas to Colonel Joaquin Garcia y Moreno, March 10, 1785, Santo Domingo 17/02493, Archivo General de la Nacíon, Santo Domingo.

8. *"Se explica por números si es simple Mojón, Pirámide, Peña o Peñasco, con el rumbo a que se sigue la linea desde cada uno, nombre del Terreno y del Habitante sin mediador donde le habia alli se ve que el No. 174 era notado como simple Mojón artificial, de los que debían asegurarse con mezcla, y que el No. 132 es una Peña, y el 133 un Peñasco inaccessible, y sin duda tan grande como el Palacio de Santo Domingo, donde tambien se equivoca el Señor Vizconde en la cita que hace del uno por el otro, sobre haver dado parte los Prácticos que no vieron el 132 de sus Rondas."* Commander Gaspard de Leoz y Echalas to Colonel Joaquin Garcia y Moreno, March 10, 1785, Santo Domingo 17/02493, Archivo General de la Nacíon, Santo Domingo. Prácticos were usually free people of color who lived in the border region but owned no property. They were considered to be vagabundos. They were indispensable because of their familiarity with the region, but their status as vagabonds created anxiety for state officials.

9. *"En el mismo acto de colocar cualquier Mojón, o graver una peña firme se hacia que los Prácticos la reconociesen materialmente para su seguridad, y vicita en lo sucesivo, y donde havia Bosque espeso se despejaba el contorno formando una pequeña Plaza, y se marcaban los Arboles gruesos mas inmediatos en la Piedra."* Ibid.

10. *"Pues como en toda la Frontera tubimos especial cuidado (para la mayor estabilidad y exactitud de esta obra) en aprovechar para Mojones las Peñas y peñascos naturales que hallábamos apropócito fixos en el terreno, y algunas veces llevar de prevención en la Cabeza de los Negros una Piedra ya labrada, por no hallarse en todas partes: infiero que de ésta práctica haya nacido la Equivocación que padece dicho Señor Vizconde en creher que llegaremos al punto de que se trata con la Piedra gravada, que huviera sido muy penoso a los Negros por la grande distancia de donde venia quasi incierto, y desconocido para nosotros, hasta que llegamos a el."* Ibid.

11. *"Siendo reclamados los negros fugitivos de que habla debidamente por sus legitimos dueños y precediendo. Las correspondientes cauciones de no tener otro delito que el de la fuga, y de no ser castigados corporalmente. En cuyo caso tendrá lugar el que los esclavos que hayan contrahido matrimonio se queden en la nacion donde se hayan casado pagando a los dueños de la otra nacion el justo precio que se tasará de buena fe por un español, y un francés; que esto se executaría del mismo modo respecto de los hijos, si sus madres*

huviesen sido lexitimamente reclamados." President Jose Solano to Border Commander Miranda, Santo Domingo, December 5, 1771, Santo Domingo 1018, Archivo General de Indias, Seville.

12. "*Breve: la continuación de la Estampa authoriza el Latrocinio, confunde los negros de Franceses, con los de los Españoles, su suspención es de la ultima consequencia a fabor de la Colonia Francesa de la fuga de sus negros y su restitución.*" French border commander Bertrand to Governor Manuel de Azlor of Santo Domingo, June 5, 1763, Santo Domingo 17/02492, Archivo General de la Nacíon, Santo Domingo.

13. Ibid.

14. "*O los Negros han sido introducido legitimamente . . . o tal introduccion ha sido ilicita o por contrabando. O en fin los negros se han introducido ellos mismos por su fuga de nuestras Colonias. . . . Quantos negros se hallan en esta parte fugitibos de las casas de sus Amos antes de haverlos marcado. Quantas otros que han quemado su estampa.*" Ibid.

15. "*Quand il sera douteux si le nègre est Espagnol ou Français, il sera détenu en prison jusqu'à ce la proprieté on ait été prouvée.*"

16. *Jus sanguinis*, or the right of blood, is based on the principle that state citizenship or membership to a nation is determined by ethnic or cultural origin. This contrasts with *jus soli*, or the determination of citizenship by right of soil, or place of birth.

Works Cited

Baud, Michiel, and Willem van Schendel. 1997. "Toward a Comparative History of Borderlands." *Journal of World History* 8 (2): 211–242.

Benton, Lauren. 2010. *A Search for Sovereignty: Law and Geography in European Empires, 1400–1900.* New York: Cambridge University Press.

Cruz, Teddy, and Anne Boddington, eds. 1999. "Architecture of the Borderlands." Special issue, *Architectural Design* 69 (7–8).

Davenport, Frances. 1937. *European Treaties Bearing on the History of the United States and Its Dependencies.* Volume 4. Washington DC: Carnegie Institute of Washington.

De Certeau, Michel. 1984. *The Practice of Everyday Life.* Berkeley: University of California Press.

Sahlins, Peter. 1989. *Boundaries: The Making of France and Spain in the Pyrenees.* Berkeley: University of California Press.

2

The Contested State

Political Discourse during the Independence of the Dominican Republic, 1844

FIDEL J. TAVÁREZ

On February 23, 1844, just a few days before the Dominican Republic declared its independence, the *Ayuntamiento* (city council) of Santo Domingo met to discuss some of the pressing issues the city was confronting. Although important officials like Domingo de la Rocha, the *corregidor* (mayor), and other locally appointed *regidores* (aldermen) participated in these discussions, there was nothing unusual about this meeting. What is particularly telling, however, is how the secretary in charge of recording the minutes of this session chose to label the political community to which the inhabitants of Santo Domingo belonged. This time, secretary Pedro A. Bobea indicated that the session was taking place "in the city of Santo Domingo on February twenty-third of eighteen forty-four, forty-first of independence and second of the regeneration."[1] In this short but telling heading, Bobea alluded to the revolution that had culminated with the independence of Haiti in 1804 and to the political unrest of 1843 that had overthrown the long regime of Haitian president Jean-Pierre Boyer. Therefore the *Ayuntamiento* of Santo Domingo commemorated 1804 as the year of its independence and 1843 as the year of its republic's regeneration of liberty. Nothing in the record of the *Ayuntamiento* contradicts the fact that these officials from Santo Domingo were nation building, as it were, on behalf of Haiti.

However, this allegiance changed just eleven days later, when Bobea indicated that the session he was recording had taken place "in Santo Domingo on March sixth of eighteen forty-four, [year] 41 and first of the Patria." On this occasion, Bobea commemorated both the independence of Haiti from France in 1804 and the separation, although he might have perceived it differently, of the Dominican Republic from Haiti, which political leaders from Santo Domingo had orchestrated about a week earlier on February 27, 1844. It took Bobea until March 23 to finally recognize Dominican independence and to settle on "year first of the patria" as the most appropriate heading.[2] The important point is that even though Bobea decided to commemorate Dominican independence exclusively on March 23, just a few weeks earlier, on March 6, he had not yet registered that the eastern portion of the island had separated itself from the Republic of Haiti on February 27.

Why did it take Bobea almost a month to recognize that the eastern portion of the island had declared its independence as a separate Dominican nation-state? It is possible that he initially conceived of February 27 as a kind of internal political battle that culminated with the establishment of a Haitian confederated state by which the eastern, Spanish-speaking portion of the island would enjoy a certain level of autonomy. By celebrating both Haiti's independence of 1804 and Santo Domingo's independence from Haiti forty years later, he seemed to accept the Haitian state as legitimate even while praising the political autonomy the inhabitants of the eastern portion of the island gained in 1844. In a nutshell, Bobea's dual commemorations suggest that Dominican independence was not a foregone conclusion, even for the political leaders of the *Ayuntamiento* of Santo Domingo. In fact, Bobea, like most Dominican political leaders of the time, did not conceive of February 27 as a definitive and foundational moment for the Dominican nation-state. Nor did he see the events of February 27 as an inevitable collision between two incompatible peoples.

Bobea's dual commemorations do not sit well with the extant historiography of Dominican independence. Historians have largely agreed that Dominican independence was driven by ethnic nationalism (Troncoso Sánchez 1974; Avelino 1995; Balcácer and García 1992; Pérez Memén 1992). According to the dominant narrative, on February 27, 1844, Dominicans liberated themselves from the 22-year-long "Haitian domination" (Moya Pons 1972). Dominican patriots completed their magnanimous mission at the Puerta de la Misericordia at eleven o'clock at night on February 27, when Matías Ramón Mella, the Padre de la Patria (Father of the Nation), fired a loud *trabucazo* (blunderbuss) to celebrate the victory. As the narrative would have it, although a few politically ambitious men later threatened the existence of an independent Dominican state,

they joined the independence movement because they, like all Dominicans, recognized incompatible cultural differences between Dominicans
and Haitians.[3] According to this narrative, nationalist fervor took hold
as Dominicans overthrew the Haitian regime because it had purportedly
violated Dominicans' right to govern themselves.

National narratives of independence often herald the grand deeds of
a people who are supposedly bound together by a desire for a common
homeland. As historian Pedro San Miguel remarks, "ensconced in the
sphere of myth," these narratives of homogeneity "have become a sort
of sacred history" (San Miguel 2005, 2). The historiography of Dominican independence is certainly no exception. The dominant narrative of
the Dominican foundational moment assumes that those who supported
independence had a common cultural and political identity that was distinct from that of Haitians. Cohabitation under the rule of one state was
thus impossible.[4] This assumption has significant implications, for it has
contributed to the creation of the Haitian "other" and has become a com-
memorative history that uncritically condones present-day nationalist
sensibilities. This chapter questions the nationalist myth that has rendered
Haiti incommensurable with the Dominican Republic. As Bobea's chronology suggests, Haitian independence loomed large in the imagination
of Dominican political leaders not as a moment of terror but as an event
of liberation against European imperialism.

This chapter scrutinizes Dominican "sacred history" by investigating
the meaning independence had for the different historical actors who participated in the creation of the Dominican state. It questions whether Dominican independence occurred solely because of irreconcilable differences in culture between Haitians and Dominicans. In other words, were
all of the political leaders of and participants in the Dominican movement
for independence driven by nationalist fervor and a sense that Dominicans were culturally incompatible with Haitians? A close analysis of the
earliest documents the Junta Gubernativa produced and the speeches
and writings of Dominican political leaders suggests a more complicated
story, one that features competing political ideologies at a time when contemporary actors were defining the nature, function, and shape of the
nation-state.

To be sure, some political leaders did in fact deploy the romantic/
ethnic concept of nation that the nationalist historiography accepts uncritically (Palti 2009). These romantic men, especially those connected

to La Trinitaria secret society, advocated for complete Dominican independence well before February 27, 1844. This chapter will be largely concerned with reconstructing the intellectual development of this kind of ethnic nationalism among Trinitarios. But it will be equally concerned with reconstructing the intellectual development of a set of political leaders who did not hold that the nation had a cultural essence. For these men, whom I call separatists, the nation was a political association based on will and intention rather than on shared heritage. This concept of nation accepted people of all languages and cultures as long as they chose to be part of the community and pledged to fulfill the duties that accompanied inclusion. For separatists, the nation was always an unstable and fluid collectivity rather than a community that was determined naturally by birth, as it was for romantics; inclusion in the nation was a process that required constant affirmation and fulfillment of duties (Herzog 2003).[5]

Therefore, it is not sufficient to assert that Dominicans could no longer cohabitate with Haitians because they felt culturally incompatible with their neighbors. Instead, we must account for the manifold tactics of legitimation the first generation of Dominican political leaders deployed. Most importantly, we must account for the intellectual fault line between separatists and Trinitarios. The main contention of this chapter is that Dominican independence must be understood as an intellectual civil war of sorts and not as a product of a people who had gained a unified national consciousness against Haiti. This chapter thus questions the Dominican national myth that plays into anti-Haitian sentiment and opens space for a more balanced account of the Dominican Republic's foundational moment.

The chapter is divided into three parts. The first section reconstructs the events that led to the Dominican declaration of independence, paying particular attention to the political unrest in the Republic of Haiti from 1842 to 1844 and to the competing visions of independence Trinitarios and separatists advanced. The second section focuses on the efforts of separatists and Trinitarios to consolidate an independent Dominican state aligned with their respective ideals. Although separatists dominated politics during the first few months of independence, Trinitarios launched a short-lived coup against the separatist government in June 1844. Even though the Trinitarios failed to retain power, an examination of how they sought to dismantle the separatist project and implement their own vision of the Dominican Republic brings the two competing visions of an independent Dominican state into sharp relief. The third section discusses the competing constitutional models that separatists and Trinitarios designed, revealing that they embodied opposing visions of what the nation was and how the state should function. The chapter concludes with some tentative reflections about why recovering this contested history is important, even necessary, in the present.

Competing Visions of Independence

After twenty-two years of unification with the Republic of Haiti, the Spanish-speaking side of the island of Hispaniola declared its independence as the Dominican Republic on February 27, 1844. Despite current nationalist myths, the events leading to Dominican independence were not the natural result of simmering grievances against a purportedly foreign repressive power. People of African descent, both enslaved and free, had welcomed Haiti's radical anti-slavery, and many Creole political leaders had supported the unification of the island under the Republic of Haiti in 1822. In fact, soon after José Nuñez de Cáceres declared the secession of the Estado Independiente del Haití Español (Independent State of Spanish Haiti) from Spain in 1821, he decided to unify the Spanish-speaking side with Haiti in April 1822, claiming that the unification would be "the last episode that will take place in the political theater of our island" (Coiscou Henríquez 1973, 317). In many ways, then, the events of 1844 were a clear departure from the unification project of 1822. The goal of this section is to explain why political leaders of the east lost faith in the Haitian Republic and why the independence movement opened space for divergent political projects.

The Dominican project for independence gained momentum after a strong earthquake decimated the northern cities of Santiago de los Caballeros and Cap-Haïtien on May 7, 1842 (Moya Pons 2008, 260). By September 1842, Jean-Pierre Boyer, president of the Republic of Haiti, had become very ill, and a southern organization known as the Society for the Rights of Man and the Citizen took advantage of the opportunity to denounce the president. A libel known as the Praslin Manifesto (or the Les Cayes Manifesto) accused Boyer of perpetrating a series of injustices (Moya Pons 2008, 260–262). When the opposition's most notable leader, Charles Hérard Aîné, overthrew Boyer in March 1843 and became the new president of Haiti, he initiated the constitutional reform that was to spark Dominican independence. Some Trinitarios joined separatists in supporting the reform movement, but this alliance was a convergence of convenience rather than an ideological confluence. The Trinitarios' support for reform eroded when Hérard took power and openly attacked Juan Pablo Duarte as an inexperienced ideologue. While Duarte fled to Curaçao, other Trinitarios, including Francisco del Rosario Sánchez, Matías Ramón Mella, and Vicente Celestino Duarte, stayed in Santo Domingo to coordinate Dominican independence. In contrast, leaders such as Buenaventura Báez, who would soon join the separatist cause, became representatives in the constitutional assembly that drafted the new Haitian constitution of 1843.

To fully grasp the situation that political leaders in Santo Domingo faced in 1843 and 1844, it is necessary to understand a few things about the social, institutional, and intellectual background of separatists and Trinitarios. It is most important to keep in mind that while the Trinitarios generally had little connection to the Haitian state, separatists were deeply involved with the Haitian government during the "Haitian occupation" of 1822–1844. Their distinct relationships to the Haitian state shaped how these two groups approached political reform. Whereas separatists focused on achieving political reform through legal means (initially accepting the Haitian government as legitimate), Trinitarios aimed to subvert the Haitian state by proclaiming its illegitimacy. Consequently, Trinitarios began advocating for independence in the 1830s, while separatists did not join the independence movement until the political crises of 1843 delegitimized and destabilized the Haitian government.

The efforts of Trinitarios to make Dominican independence a reality dated back to 1835, when Juan Pablo Duarte and José María Serra circulated pamphlets condemning foreign rule over Dominicans. Duarte and Serra formalized their revolutionary vision in 1838 when they founded a revolutionary secret society known as La Trinitaria (Zabala 2005). Duarte and Serra also created a theater group, La Dramática, which staged revolutionary plays to spread nationalist fervor, and another activist organization, La Filantrópica, whose purpose was to raise funds for the revolution. The Trinitarios were primarily members of a small urban bourgeoisie who were negatively affected by some of the policies of the Haitian government (Moya Pons 2008, 258). This young generation of Creoles found inspiration in what we could call liberal romanticism, an intellectual inclination defined by the idea that nations existed prior to the state and that a responsible government would preserve the sovereignty of that nation.

The romantic ethos of the Trinitarios is apparent in their pledge statement (*juramento*), which advocated independence from Haiti and from any other "foreign" country:

> I swear by my honor and consciousness, in the hands of our president Juan Pablo Duarte, to cooperate with the definitive separation from Haiti and to implement a sovereign and independent republic free from any foreign dominion, by offering my life, wealth and presence. (Henríquez y Carvajal quoted in Balcácer and García 1992, 74)

Committed above all to achieving national independence, the Trinitarios considered that only members of the Dominican nation could legitimately govern "their" territory. In the same vein, Duarte asserted that "if Spaniards have their Spanish monarchy, France theirs and even Haitians have constituted the Haitian Republic, why should Dominicans be subjected to France, Spain or Haitians without thinking of constituting themselves as others have?" (quoted in Serra 1887, 23) Trinitarios thus supported Dominican independence not primarily in reaction to Haitian despotism but because national independence represented the ultimate realization of the Dominican nation.

In contrast to Trinitarios, separatists became revolutionaries only as the Haitian polity crumbled in 1843. Separatist leaders included experienced politicians who had previously served as officials of the Haitian government and who participated in the Haitian constitutional assembly of 1843. For instance, Tomás Bobadilla, the first president of the Dominican Junta Central Gubernativa, held official positions under the Spanish monarchy and the short-lived Independent State of Spanish Haiti that José Nuñez de Cáceres created in 1821. After that, he served in the Haitian government in numerous capacities. In 1822, after the unification of the island, President Boyer appointed Bobadilla to the post of fiscal del Tribunal del Seybo (district attorney of the Court of El Seybo) and as a member of the Comisión de la Instrucción Pública (Committee on Public Instruction). In 1830, Bobadilla assumed the position of *defensor público* (public defender), and a year later he was named *notario público* (public notary). In his last show of commitment to the Haitian government, Bobadilla served on the investigative committee created in 1842 to halt the reformist movement Charles Herard had initiated (Rodríguez Demorizi 1938, 3–12). Bobadilla is just one example of the many separatists who were committed to preserving the law; indeed, many were trained jurists.

Keeping the distinct trajectories of separatists and Trinitarios in mind, let us return to the political moment of 1843–1844. As political turmoil swirled around Haiti and as Trinitarios plotted a revolution, separatists initiated their own independence project. Buenaventura Báez and other separatists who traveled to Port-au-Prince in November 1843 to partici- pate in the constitutional assembly also met secretly with French consul Nicolás Levasseur in Haiti's capital. They reached an agreement called the Plan Levasseur, which specified that as of April 1844, France would support Dominican independence in exchange for the Bay of Samaná (Rodríguez Demorizi 1996). The Plan Levasseur, however, did not come to fruition, because on January 16, Trinitarios, joined by separatist leader Bobadilla (who had been ousted from the constituent assembly of 1843), drafted a manifesto calling for the creation of a Dominican state.[6]

No document better illustrates the discursive battle between Trinitar- ios and separatists than the Separation Act of January 16, 1844, or, as it is known in Spanish, the "Manifestación de los pueblos de la parte del este de la isla antes española o de Santo Domingo, sobre las causas de su separación de la república haitiana" (quoted in Rodríguez Demorizi 1957, 30). While some historians assert that only Tomás Bobadilla authored the document, others believe that some Trinitarios, including Francisco del Rosario Sánchez, contributed to its creation (Balcácer 1995, 65).[7] Regard- less of who was initially responsible for writing it, the document was prob- ably altered during the revolutionary meetings held shortly before it was signed. Although the Separation Act mainly reflected the political views of separatist political leaders, a discursive ambiguity is evident in the distinct definitions of Dominican nationality that the document conveys.

The document first describes the Dominican nation as a political com- munity determined by people's adherence to the separation cause. The document begins: "DOMINICANS! (Understood by this name all the sons of the eastern portion and also those who wish to follow our path)" (Rodríguez Demorizi 1957, 36). The words in parentheses welcome people to join the Dominican nation through individual volition. The plural and processual character of this definition differs significantly from the ro- mantic nationalism of Trinitarios. This separatist vision constructs Do- minican nationality not as a cultural essence or even as a mere function of place of birth but as the consequence of an individual's desire to join the separatist cause to create a new political community.

Later, the Separation Act defines the Dominican nation as a distinct and unique cultural community. In a passage that clearly articulates the ethos of romantic nationalism, the document states that separation from Haiti was necessary because the inhabitants of the different sides of the island did not share the same customs. The document says that "because of differences in customs and the rivalry that exists between one group [Dominicans] and the other [Haitians], there will never be perfect union and harmony" (Rodríguez Demorizi 1957, 35). This definition espouses the belief that similarity in customs is a necessary precondition for co-habitation in one state. Indeed, this definition cannot fathom cultural difference within the nation. In this Trinitario ideal, the constituency of the Dominican nation was predetermined and was not readily subject to modification.

Despite this Trinitario discursive intervention, the document exposed the foundational elements of the separatist discourse: the notion of Haitian tyranny. Bobadilla buttressed the separatist project by referring to the natural law notion of *derecho de gentes* (law of nations), which stipulated that political communities had the right and duty to overthrow governments if they proved to be despotic. The manifesto proclaimed that

> we believe that we have heroically demonstrated that the evils of a government should be tolerated while they are bearable, instead of making justice abolishing forms; but when a large series of injustices, violations, and slanderous accusations together denote an intention to reduce everything to despotism and the darkest tyranny, it is the sacred right and duty of *pueblos* to overthrow that government and provide new guarantees that secure future stability and prosperity. (Rodríguez Demorizi 1957, 29)

This passage implies that had the Haitian government not been despotic, separation would have been unnecessary. The manifesto stated that during the 1822 unification of the island, "no Dominican received them [Haitians] without conveying a desire to sympathize with their new co-citizens." However, "if the eastern part was considered to be incorporated voluntarily to the Haitian Republic, it should have enjoyed the same benefits as those it was united with" (Rodríguez Demorizi 1957, 30, 34). The contradictions between the premise of the right of voluntary association under political equality and separatists' perception of political inequality powerfully justified the separatist independence project.

The Separation Act also claimed that in hindsight Haitian rule had been illegitimate from the beginning. Since representatives of the east had not participated in the drafting of the 1816 Haitian constitution, the inhabitants of the east were subjected to a "bastard constitution." This, in turn, was a "scandalous usurpation."[8] Furthermore, Haitian rule was illegitimate because

> it is very certain that if the eastern part should belong to another power other than its own sons, it would be to France or Spain, and not to Haiti, because we, the people of the east, have a greater claim to govern the people of the west [Haiti] if we take into account the first years of the discovery of the immortal Columbus. (Rodríguez Demorizi 1957, 34)

It seems odd that a separation act proclaiming national independence would include such a statement. But those who dismiss this passage as the creation of the "vicious" politician Bobadilla (who supposedly wrote this document to fulfill his selfish political and economic interests) miss a key point. Because Bobadilla did not share the romantic nationalist idea that "ethnic" Dominicans had the right to form an independent state to preserve national sovereignty, he did not—in fact could not—consider an independent state to be necessary as long as the ruling government was not despotic (as the Haitians had ostensibly been). This perspective clarifies the meaning of the Plan Levasseur. Separatists were not concerned with national sovereignty as a goal in and of itself; rather, their main concern was to become part of the civilized world, the international community of states, and to preserve the natural rights of the inhabitants of Santo Domingo.

Even though the Separation Act was closely aligned with the separatist ideology, Trinitarios, as we shall see, continued to engage in activities that supported their program of romantic and ethnic nationalism. Consequently, from the very beginning, the newly created Dominican nation-state was suffused by tension and ideological differences between separatists and Trinitarios.

Consolidating the State

Solidarity between Bobadilla and Trinitarios did not last much beyond the February 27, 1844, celebration of independence. Defining the function, shape, and constitution of the Dominican state proved to be more difficult than any political leader initially envisioned. Relations between Trinitarios and separatists soured after the first armed confrontations with Haiti's 30,000 troops, which were deployed in March and April 1844 to quell the revolution in the east. Unexpectedly, Dominican victories in battles fought on March 19 and 30 only widened the divide between Trinitarios and separatists. Separatist general Pedro Santana believed that his relatively small contingent of peasants armed with knives and machetes was no match for Haiti's large professional army. He consistently pleaded for weapons from the Junta Gubernativa Provisional. Given his perceived dire circumstances, Santana urged Bobadilla to accelerate discussions with France to cede the Bay of Samaná in exchange for weaponry; he also rejected Duarte's argument that he needed to organize an offensive against the Haitian army.

Duarte, a romantic patriot, believed that nationalist fervor alone was enough to defeat the supposedly unmotivated Haitian army. Duarte and his Trinitario partisans grew increasingly frustrated with the separatist Junta Gubernativa's repeated efforts to place the Dominican state under French protection. On March 8, 1844, the Dominican junta condoned the ceding of the Bay of Samaná to France in exchange for weapons, munitions, money, and official recognition as a legitimate nation-state (Campillo Pérez 1994, 49). On June 1, the separatist junta reasserted its desire to receive protection from France in exchange for Samaná (Campillo Pérez 1994, 107). On this occasion, even Duarte, who had recently joined the junta, signed the request for French protection. Eight days later, frustrated by Santana's inaction and the junta's desire to establish a French protectorate, Duarte joined other Trinitarios in staging a coup against the separatist junta.

Following the Trinitario coup of June 9, Duarte aggressively opposed the repeated attempts of separatists to secure military support from France in exchange for the Bay of Samaná (Balcácer and García 1995, 122). Worried about the specter of a powerful French influence in the Caribbean, the British government had protested the plan to cede the Bay of Samaná to the French government. On June 18, the new Trinitario-led Junta responded with a letter assuring the British government that they did not intend to give away the peninsula of Samaná to the French (Campillo Pérez 1994, 119).[9] The letter asserted that "the peninsula and bay of Samaná belongs to our territory, and Dominicans, as a free and sovereign people, have the entire disposition of what is theirs." Separatists would have certainly agreed. However, Trinitarios went further and assured Britain that it did not need to worry about a foreign occupation of the Bay of Samaná because "the entire [Dominican] nation opposes any foreign intervention in our politics" (Campillo Pérez 1994, 117–118). For Trinitarios, national sovereignty and independence were end goals that would guarantee the political liberty of the Dominican nation.

Reversing the separatist embrace of "all those who wish to follow our path," the Trinitario coup threatened separatist leaders with French surnames, whom Trinitarios now categorized as foreigners. On June 13, a group of military generals from northern towns addressed the junta, condemning José Maria Imbert, the separatist general of the district of Santiago, for imprisoning two lieutenant colonels. These northern Trinitario military leaders, Mella among them, proclaimed that "the arbitrary authority of the outlaw Rivière [former Haitian president Charles Herard] is replicated in General Imbert, an impotent commander, a foreigner unworthy of stepping into our territory, and a man who is undoubtedly the scum of society" (Rodríguez Demorizi et al. 2006, 212–213). The Trinitario generals' sudden attack perplexed José María Imbert, who believed he had proved himself worthy of Dominican citizenship through his extensive contributions to the war against Haiti. That same day, Imbert wrote a letter to Eustache de Juchereau de St. Denys, the French consul in Santo Domingo, that expressed a deep concern about the anti-French actions that had been proliferating in the northern region of the Cibao. Speaking in confidence, Imbert protested that among "the few French in this part of the island, all have embraced the Dominican cause with ardor and have contributed in all ways to its success to make it triumph . . . Without them [the French leaders,] the city of Santiago and with it the entire Dominican territory, even the citadels of Santo Domingo, would have fallen defenselessly into the hands of the enemy. Before, we were eulogized, raised to the clouds. I was called the savior of Santiago" (quoted in Rodríguez Demorizi 1996, 154–156). The romantic nationalist policies of the Trinitarios took Imbert off guard; he rationalized the sudden accusation and dismissal as an ill-intended maneuver.

The Trinitario Junta that Sánchez commanded responded to the northern generals' protests against French delegates by sending Duarte to the north on June 18 to replace municipal officials from the department of Santiago who were alleged foreigners. These included Delorve, Rocha, and Mena. However, Duarte left Imbert undisturbed. In an effort to avoid appearing despotic and to keep the peace, the nationalist junta transferred the purportedly French officials to positions in Santo Domingo, where they could be closely monitored. The junta commanded Duarte to reestablish the municipal jurisdictions of *pueblos* and to hold elections. This is how the Trinitarios secured their alliance with northern political leaders (Rodríguez Demoriziet al. 2006, 214–216). Duarte's mission to the north proved to be more politically significant than he anticipated. On July 4, Mella and other military leaders of the north proclaimed Duarte president of the Dominican Republic (although Duarte asserted in a letter addressed to citizens of Puerto Plata that he had been elected by the people) (Rodríguez Demorizi, Larrazábal Blanco, and Alfau Durán 2006, 86–87). Sánchez, who continued to preside over the Junta in Santo Domingo, warned that the politically ambiguous situation of having two concurrent governing bodies weakened Trinitario rule. Sanchéz's concern proved to be correct. On July 12, Pedro Santana marched his troops into Santo Domingo, staged a coup, and named himself the president of the Junta, putting an end to the Trinitarios' month-long political control of the state (Moya Pons 2008, 291–294).

Santana's takeover signaled separatist control of the state for years to come. He moved quickly to secure French support and laid the foundations for a centralized government that was unified under one constitution. On the day of the coup, he also sent a letter to the French consul of Santo Domingo, St. Denys, reaffirming that the Dominican government wished to place itself under French protection (Campillo Pérez 1994, 150). Twelve days later, on July 24, Santana issued a decree outlining the process for electing representatives of a constituent congress that would write the first Dominican constitution. In its first sentences, the decree clearly outlined the separatist vision for the Dominican state by affirming that "after getting rid of the Haitian yoke, the first duty [of representatives of the constituent assembly] is to call the *pueblos* so that by exercising their sovereignty they form a political constitution and draw the government that best suits them according to the principles already outlined in the 16 January manifesto." The new Dominican state was to be legitimately formed through the exercise of the "will of the *pueblos*." Article #11 of this decree stipulated that once electors determined who was to be president of the electoral assembly, the votes would be burned, "hereby concluding the work of corregidores, their adjuncts, and the judges of the peace or their substitutes" (quoted in Rodríguez Demorizi 1980, 119, 121).

Another fundamental component of Santana's state was his strong attack on the Trinitario project. As paradoxical as it may seem to Dominicans today, on August 22, Santana declared that Duarte, Mella, and Sánchez, the three men who are known today as the Padres de la Patria, were actually "traitors of the Patria." Santana charged them with conspiring against the Dominican state by creating a parallel presidency in the northern region of the Cibao. The extant historiography often characterizes Santana's accusation against the Padres de la Patria as a sign of his greed. In this narrative, Santana chose to harm the nation to advance his personal ambitions and political interests. These nationalist narratives reverse the accusation of treason, labeling Santana and other separatists as politicians of bad character who betrayed the national cause. By personalizing this issue, the historiography too often ignores what was at stake politically. According to Santana's conception of the state as a political community held together by the "will of the *pueblos*," Duarte threatened the sovereignty of the *pueblos* by unilaterally assuming the position of the presidency without elections. Santana was committed to establishing a government through the will of the *pueblos*, even if with a limited electorate. Hence, he condemned Trinitario actions for usurping the "sovereignty of *pueblos*," which "inspired a general subversion in the established order and principlés." According to Santana, Duarte's illegal presidency caused national "division and civil war" and made "people arm themselves against each other" (Campillo Pérez 1994, 150).

Trinitarios counterattacked by affirming that ceding any portion of Dominican territory violated Dominicans' natural right to possess their territory and subjected Dominicans living in the ceded territory to "enslavement" and foreign rule. Santana dismissed the accusations as "slanderous" propaganda that claimed that "the country had been alienated to a foreign nation in order to reinstitute slavery" (quoted in Campillo Pérez 1994, 150). He provided assurances that those who had previously been chattel slaves would not be enslaved once again. Tellingly, Santana ignored the broader Trinitario accusation that rule by a foreign power constituted a form of enslavement. Santana's reply clearly conveys that what he was concerned about was not that the Padres de la Patria spread the notion that the separatist government intended to annex the country to a foreign power—this he would have never denied—but that the Dominican Republic would be annexed in order to restore chattel slavery. The phrase "in order to reinstitute slavery" adds a qualifying component that cannot be ignored. What was significant for Santana was not the action of ceding parts of Dominican territory, but the Trinitario accusation about his alleged intention to reinstitute chattel slavery.

The separatist junta's vehement desire to position itself against slavery was not new. In the Separation Act, Bobadilla had already proclaimed that slavery was forever abolished in the new republic. The junta again issued a resolution repudiating slavery on March 1 (Rodríguez Demorizi 1957, 46–47). Then, on July 17, 1844, shortly after Pedro Santana had purged the Trinitarios from the government, the Junta issued another decree that condemned slavery and specified that "slaves that set foot in the territory of the Dominican Republic will be considered and set free immediately." This decree further stated that whoever engaged in the trafficking of slaves "without distinctions of class or status . . . will be considered a pirate and tried and punished with the death penalty." The separatists' concern with establishing their vehement opposition to slavery stemmed from their need to discredit the Trinitarios' accusations that placing the Dominican state under the protection of France would threaten the principle of liberty. What made this a particularly volatile issue was the fact that powerful owners of cattle ranches such as Pedro Santana depended on a military force made up of large contingents of peasants of color. It is thus not surprising that separatists repeatedly reiterated that "the personal and individual liberty, and the principles of equality for those who had the disgrace of being slaves in another era, will never be threatened" (Campillo Pérez 1994, 125–126).

Writing the Constitution

The ideological tensions between Trinitarios and separatists are also evident in the constitution each group designed. Led by a contingent of separatist political leaders, the newly formed Dominican state created a constitutional assembly that designed a new constitution that went into effect on November 6, 1844. This first Dominican constitution signaled that separatists had temporarily triumphed in formalizing and legalizing their conception of the state. Yet Duarte disputed the separatist victory in his famous constitution, a text that embodies his romantic conception of the state. Duarte's document, which remained little more than a few notes in his notebook, reveals definitions of the concepts of "nation," "Dominican," and "sovereignty" that contrast starkly with the separatist constitution of November 6. Analyzing these two different conceptions of basic principles of nationhood further reveals the intellectual fault lines between separatists and Trinitarios.

On September 26, just before separatists drafted the first official Dominican constitution, Bobadilla delivered a passionate speech to the constitutional assembly in the town of San Cristóbal. He underscored the grand moment and task that lay ahead for the legislators charged with writing the fundamental law. For Bobadilla, the formation of the Dominican state under the rubric of a liberal and republican constitution was the island's ultimate achievement. He asserted that although Santo Domingo had undergone many "systems of political organization," the most "glorious" and "grandest" had been reserved for himself and his contemporaries. According to Bobadilla, the achievement of independence on February 27, 1844, was "a new and admirable political transformation." This new transformation was legitimated by the "will of the *pueblos*," who, "upon naming us [political leaders] to write their constitution and fundamental law," granted the constitutional assembly "their special powers without entirely renouncing to their sovereignty." The legitimacy of the new constitution rested in the formal transfer of sovereignty from the local jurisdictions of the *pueblos* to the newly formed larger political community of the state (Rodríguez Demorizi 1938, 20–30).

Although separatists celebrated the formation of a new republican state, they continued to define citizenship according to beliefs and practices that had long been a part of the Hispanic world. The novel aspect was not the concept of citizenship, but rather the transfer of sovereignty. Separatists used an early modern Spanish notion of local citizenship (*vecindad*) to define Dominican citizenship. As Tamar Herzog (2003) argues, rather than being a condition of the *jus soli* (law of birth) and the *jus sanguinis* (law of descent), "belonging to a local community or the community of the kingdom in the early modern period was a process" that was related to the *jus commune* and was determined by an individual's intention to reside and comply with a set of duties in a given community (4). The separatist constitution of November 6 defined Dominican nationality as a process that was not a direct function of birth or culture. (Although birth was a powerful factor, it did not guarantee permanent citizenship.) The constitution stipulated that Dominicans were "all those individuals who at the moment of publication of this constitution enjoy this quality" (Rodríguez Demorizi 1980, 164).

The constitution thus defined citizenship in temporal terms (signaling that it might have been otherwise sometime in the past or that it could be different in the future) and stipulated that citizenship was an earned rather than a given status. Following this notion of citizenship, the separatist constitution defined the essential components of acquiring or maintaining citizenship as love for and loyalty to the community and an intention to maintain residence in the Dominican Republic.[10]

In contrast, Duarte's notes about an alternate constitution defined citizenship as a finality, an ascribed status that was achieved through birth or through legal means. "Dominicans are those who obtained this quality either by birth or by having obtained a nationality warrant as prescribed by the law," Duarte wrote. Duarte argued that being Dominican was a fixed status. Because he assumed the a priori existence of Dominicans, he affirmed that "the Dominican Nation is the reunion of all Dominicans" (quoted in Hernández Flores 2001, 28). Duarte outlined a tautological construction that implied that Dominicans were a natural community that existed prior to the state. In essence, he took as a given the existence of Dominicans and transposed that alleged existent community to the political constituent body of the state. For Duarte, as for many contemporary historians who have uncritically accepted this vision, the Dominican nation existed prior to 1844 despite people's intentions and actions and despite the fact that before 1844 there was no state to legitimize the Dominican nation.

The contending parties also disagreed about the function and purpose of a national constitution. While separatists saw the constitution as an international document meant to facilitate Dominicans' participation in the "civilized world," Trinitarios mainly saw a constitution as a way to make national sovereignty a permanent feature of statecraft. For separatists, the purpose of the constitution was to assure that the Dominican state would become a part of the international community of states, what they called the "civilized world," by instituting a responsible government that would assure the inalienable rights of nature to its citizens and allow Dominicans to form commercial bonds with the rest of the world. The separatists' concern with international recognition differs radically from the romantic nationalist conception of Trinitarios. In his notes for a constitution, Duarte asserted that "given that national independence is the source and guarantee of Patriotic Liberties, the Supreme Law of the Dominican people is and will always be its political existence as a nation free and independent of any foreign domination, protectorate, intervention, and influence" (Hernández Flores 2001, 23). For Duarte, the independent political existence of the Dominican people was both inalienable and the source of patriotic liberties. His constitution established that sovereignty not only "essentially resides in the nation" but is also inalienable from the nation (Hernández Flores 2001, 27). This metaphysical commitment to national independence was quite literally unthinkable among separatists.

This distinction between an international and a nationalist vision for the state explains why separatists were willing to cede parts of national territory for the public good while Trinitarios remained reluctant to alienate any portion of national territory. Separatists espoused that because sovereignty stemmed not from any particular nation that always already existed by virtue of shared cultural traits but from the wills of the *pueblos* and from the recognition of the international community of states, the category of nation was never a stable one. For separatists, the nation was always a contingent collectivity whose shape had to adapt to the demands of the political will of its citizens at any given time. In contrast, because Trinitarios explained sovereignty in terms of a fixed and preexisting nation, ceding any part of national territory constituted a violation of the nation, which existed as an essence and not as a function of political will or of the international community of states.

Both separatists and Trinitarios envisioned a limited citizenship, but in distinctly different ways. While separatists construed a notion of citizenship that distinguished between citizens and citizens with the right to vote, Trinitarios could not conceive of this distinction because they deemed the republic as an egalitarian community of men bound together through comradeship (Anderson 1991). In the November 6, 1844, constitution, separatists outlined property and literacy requirements for suffrage and for the right to run for political office. And yet they still considered people who did not fulfill these requirements but showed their intention to support the national cause to be citizens. For Trinitarios, the distinction was paradoxical because they saw all Dominican citizens as equal before the law. Hence, from a contemporary perspective, we are left with a conundrum. On the one hand, we have a group of separatists who had fluid but hierarchical conceptions of citizenship and, on the other hand, a set of Trinitarios who wanted to expand citizenship to all the inhabitants of the eastern portion of Hispaniola but who systematically excluded foreigners and construed an essentialist Dominican culture.

This presents a unique challenge for those seeking to recover either separatists or Trinitarios as the "good" or more democratic actors of history. The universalism and fluid conception of nation of the separatists did not allow for the construction of essential differences and thus the space for racist attitudes toward Haitians. Trinitarios, in contrast, advocated for equality before the law and fiercely fought colonialism but opened the door for a discourse about the Haitian barbaric "other." This dynamic of the Dominican foundational moment has been ignored principally because it does not offer a usable past, especially to those with nationalist sensibilities. But history does not have to be usable in order to be useful. By extending hermeneutic sympathy to all of the historical actors we study, we can position ourselves to understand in a balanced and rigorous way the key historical events that defined the world we live in today.

Conclusion

In proposing that Dominican independence was a highly contingent and contested process, this chapter has put forward two main suggestions. First, it is not enough to explain independence, as many have, by appealing to the internal development of Dominican national self-consciousness. Dominican independence would not have been possible without the unforeseen political and constitutional crisis that occurred in Haiti in 1842 and 1843 and without the subsequent role France played in encouraging a Dominican revolution. Second, Dominican independence did not have the same meaning for all the political leaders who participated in the revolutionary process. While many scholars of the Latin American national period explicitly or implicitly assume that the concept of "nation" has a univocal history, this chapter builds on work that is critical of Benedict Anderson's (1991) notion of "imagined communities." It shows that the "nation" was a contentious idea whose meaning cannot be reduced to an apodictic formula (Lomnitz 2000, 329–359; Donghi 2003, 33; Adelman 2006, 8–9).

The argument outlined in this chapter has at least two important implications. First, the recurring *antihaitianismo* that currently runs through Dominican political discourse was not present among most of the political leaders of Dominican independence. Second, to many contemporary Dominicans' dismay, it was the Trinitario conception of nation, with its emphasis on ethnic purity, that eventually gave way to anti-Haitian sentiment. The triumph of ethnic nationalism was slow, as Dominicans continued to collaborate with other Caribbean nations, including Haiti, in the battle against imperialism. Nonetheless, the seeds of anti-Haitian sentiment based on the idea of national purity were clearly implied in the Trinitario conception of nation. While it may be impossible (and certainly inadvisable), to re-create the intellectual world of the separatist political leaders at the time of independence, reconsidering how we think about the Dominican foundational moment may allow us to begin to rethink the idea of the supposed naturalness and inevitability of the clash between Haitians and Dominicans. Reimagining the present can and should begin by denaturalizing and historicizing some of our most insidious categories, including the concepts of nation, state, and citizen.

Notes

1. Libro [de Actas de Sesiones] #3144, 130, Ayuntamiento de Santo Domingo, 1843–1844, Depósito 4, Archivo General de la Nación, Santo Domingo, Dominican Republic.

2. Ibid., 131, 134.

3. Historians vacillate between asserting that these men threatened national sovereignty because they were ambitious politicians who placed their interests before those of the nation and affirming that they were experienced politicians who doubted the ability of Dominicans to govern themselves.

4. This interpretation, however, has taken different twists and turns. A group of intellectuals who lived and wrote under the dictatorship of Rafael Leonidas Trujillo (1930–1961) emphasized that the Spanish origins of Dominican culture made cohabitation with a black republic with African roots impossible. These scholars include Emilio Rodríguez Demorizi and Manuel Arturo Peña Batlle. But since the 1970s and 1980s, scholars such as Ciriaco Landolfi have downplayed the Spanish components of Dominican culture. Landolfi argues that the struggle with the frontier together with Spain's neglect and constant depiction of Dominicans as uncivilized peasants fostered a distinct sense of community and cultural belonging among the inhabitants of Santo Domingo (Landolfi 1981).

5. Tamar Herzog (2003) argues that from the early modern period until the nineteenth century, local citizenship (*vecindad*) was a process rather than a condition determined by birth, descent, or legal enactment. A man's intention to reside in any

community was what determined whether he was a citizen or not. Thus, citizenship was always contingent upon men's ability to demonstrate that they intended to remain part of that community and to fulfill certain duties. It seems that separatists transposed this old notion of *vecindad* to the nation-state.

6. Báez became deeply resentful of Bobadilla for precipitating independence before France officially offered its support. Nevertheless, despite their personal disputes, they used similar arguments to justify the creation of the Dominican state, and it is on this basis that I group them together as separatists. For a discussion of this issue, see Moya Pons (1998, 153–184).

7. Juan Daniel Balcácer believes that "the text was sent to Sánchez so that he could modify or amend it." Balcácer (1995, 65).

8. It is interesting to note that the document does not mention that the Haitian constitution of 1843 was produced by a constituent assembly that included a few representatives from the east. These quotes certainly express the view of the manifesto's main author, Bobadilla, who had been ousted from the reform movement and from the 1843 constituent assembly.

9. Although in this letter the Trinitario-led junta asserted that they would not cede Samaná to the French, on July 12, when Pedro Santana took control, the junta communicated to the French government its desire to continue with previous plans for annexation. "Nueva ratificación al gobierno de Francia sobre solicitud de reconocimiento y protección, 12 July 1844," in Campillo Pérez (1994, 119).

10. Interestingly, the constitution of November 6 stipulated that only foreigners who had resided in the territory for ten years or more could be part of the *tribunado*. As Herzog demonstrates, the notion that ten years of residence proved one's intention of becoming a member of a community was widespread among jurists of early modern Spain. This conception was a legacy of the *jus commune*, the only law taught at Spanish peninsular and colonial universities until the eighteenth century, which stipulated that anyone, regardless of place of birth, could belong to a given community if they could prove that they intended to reside in the community and fulfill the duties of membership. In the same fashion, acquisition of property and marriage served as powerful indications of an intention to belong to a community. In sum, much like the Spanish constitution of 1812, the Dominican constitution of November 6 formalized long-held juridical and political beliefs (Herzog 2003, 24–25, 36–41, 145).

Works Cited

Adelman, Jeremy. 2006. *Sovereignty and Revolution in the Iberian Atlantic*. Princeton, NJ: Princeton University Press.

Anderson, Benedict R. 1991. *Imagined Communities: Reflections on the Origin and Spread of Nationalism*. London: Verso.

Avelino, Francisco Antonio. 1995. *Reflexiones sobre algunas cumbres del pasado ideológico dominicano*. Santo Domingo: N.p.

Balcácer, Juan D. 1995. *Pensamiento y acción de los padres de la patria*. Santo Domingo: Editora Taller.

Balcácer, Juan D., and Manuel A. García. 1992. *La independencia dominicana*. Madrid: Editorial MAPFRE.

Campillo Pérez, Julio G. 1994. *Documentos del primer gobierno dominicano. Junta Central Gubernativa, febrero-noviembre 1844*. Santo Domingo: Editora Taller.

Coiscou Henríquez, Máximo. 1973. *Documentos para la historia de Santo Domingo*. Madrid: Imp. Sucs. de Rivadeneyra.

Donghi, Tulio Halperín. 2003. "Argentine Counterpoint: Rise of the Nation, Rise of the State." In *Beyond Imagined Communities: Reading and Writing the Nation in Nineteenth-Century Latin America*, edited by Sara Castro-Klarén and John Charles Chasteen, 33–53. Baltimore, MD: Johns Hopkins University Press.

Hernández Flores, Ismael, ed. 2001. *El proyecto de constitución de Duarte*. Santo Domingo: Fundación para la Educación y el Arte.

Herzog, Tamar. 2003. *Defining Nations: Immigrants and Citizens in Early Modern Spain and Spanish America*. New Haven, CT: Yale University Press.

Landolfi, Ciriaco. 1981. *Evolución cultural dominicana 1844–1899*. Santo Domingo: Universidad Autónoma.

Lomnitz, Claudio. 2000. "Nationalism as a Practical System: Benedict Anderson's Theory of Nationalism from the Vantage Point of Spanish America." In *The Other Mirror: Grand Theory through the Lens of Latin America*, edited by M. A. Centeno and F. López Alves, 329–359. Princeton, NJ: Princeton University Press.

Moya Pons, Frank. 1972. *La dominación haitiana, 1822–1844*. Santo Domingo: Universidad Católica Madre y Maestra.

———. 1998. *The Dominican Republic: A National History*. Princeton, NJ: Markus Wiener Publishers, 1998.

———. 2008. *Manual de historia dominicana*. 14th ed. Santo Domingo: Caribbean Publishers.

Palti, Elias José. 2009. *El momento romántico. Nación, historia y lenguajes políticos en la Argentina de siglo XIX*. Buenos Aires: Eudeba.

Pérez Memén, Fernando. 1992. *El pensamiento dominicano en la primera república*. Santo Domingo: Editora de la Universidad Nacional Pedro Henríquez Ureña.

Rodríguez Demorizi, Emilio, ed. 1938. *Discursos de Bobadilla*. Ciudad Trujillo, Dominican Republic: Imp. J.R. vda. García, sucs.

———, ed. 1957. *Guerra domínico-haitiana: Documentos para su estudio*. Ciudad Trujillo, Dominican Republic: Impresora Dominicana.

———, ed. 1980. *La constitución de San Cristóbal, 1844–1854*. Santo Domingo: Editora del Caribe.

———, ed. 1996. *Correspondencia del cónsul de Francia en Santo Domingo, 1844–1846, Colección sesquicentenario de la independencia nacional*. Vol. 11. Santo Domingo: Gobierno Dominicano.

Rodríguez Demorizi, Emilio, Carlos Larrazábal Blanco, and Vetilio Alfau Durán, eds. 2006. *Apuntes de Rosa Duarte. Archivo y versos de Juan Pablo Duarte*. Santo Domingo: Instituto Duartiano.

San Miguel, Pedro L. 2005. *The Imagined Island: History, Identity, and Utopia in Hispaniola*. Translated by Jane Ramírez. Chapel Hill: University of North Carolina Press.

Serra, José María. 1887. *Apuntes para la historia de los Trinitarios.* Fundadores de la República. Santo Domingo: Imprenta García Hnos.

Torres-Saillant, Silvio. 1999. *Introduction to Dominican Blackness.* New York: City College of New York.

Troncoso Sánchez, Pedro. 1974. *Evolución de la idea nacional.* Santo Domingo: Museo del Hombre Dominicano.

Zabala, Roque. 2005. *La Trinitaria y sus fundadores.* Santo Domingo: Editora el Nuevo Diario.

3

To Cap-Haïtien, with My Family

Dominican Passport Petitions, 1862–1863

ANNE ELLER

This chapter presents documents that tell a lesser-known nineteenth-century story: that of Dominicans' regular commercial and family ties to various towns and communities in Haiti. During and after Separation in 1844 (as independence was often known in the east for several decades), Dominicans maintained close family, commercial, and political ties with different regions and towns in Haiti. Usually, this westward travel left little trace in any archive, as many individuals, families, and other groups traveled without passports in those decades. In fact, Dominican authorities well into the 1890s commented that such unofficial travel was both regular and common. The following documents, which are a rare surviving collection of passport petitions written by Dominican citizens to Spanish authorities when Spain reoccupied Dominican territory in March 1861, offer a unique and brief record of these cross-island connections.[1] During the Spanish reoccupation of the east of the island from 1861 to 1865, the greatly increased resources of the administration—hundreds of thousands of *pesos fuertes* arrived from Cuba each year—provoked significantly more interaction between Dominican citizens and the new occupying power in the east.

These passport petitions passed through numerous hands. For example, one November 1862 petition from Puerto Plata reached authorities in Santiago nearly a month and a half later. From there, it would have been passed on to the capital city before word of approval could return northward again. Despite this new Spanish scrutiny, in all likelihood, many simply traveled without official permission, just as they would have done in past decades. These documents offer a small window into a world that largely existed beyond the reach of the Spanish government.

Beyond the regular commercial and familial ties that these remarkable documents reveal, they also recount interesting political legacies that united would-be citizens all over the island with a common past and a common understanding of political claims. Nearly as many Dominican women as men made these petitions, possibly reflecting an ease of interaction with the state that might have grown during the unification period (1822–1844), when authorities extended civil marriage, divorce, and other aspects of legal stature to women (González Canalda 2013). Other clues also highlight women's claims to belonging and authority. Several of the petitions explicitly refer to the woman petitioner as a *vecina*, a person who would have been understood as an established resident with political rights within her community of residence. Several of the petitioners traveled with servants, offering a glimpse into social stratification in some Dominican towns and perhaps in cattle territories. Family ties across the island, by blood and marriage, emerge as commonplace, as do the care for and deep connection with family members that the petitioners felt. When petitioners asked to travel "to Cap-Haïtien, with my family," it was sometimes a reunification that had been many years, even decades, in the making.

The Spanish passport collection in this chapter is drawn from just four months of travel petitions, but their timing, from late 1862 into the first months of 1863, overlaps with a moment when anti-Spanish resistance was about to explode. Spanish authorities granted passes to almost all of the applicants, even as the Dominican opposition grew, first silently and then in open fighting. President Fabre Nicolas Geffrard, in the neighboring independent Haitian republic, condemned the return of the east to Spanish hands in 1861. Although Spanish threats and warships forced him into silence, unofficial east-west collaborations continued to increase. A market for the independence fighters grew at the center of the island, as foodstuffs and other products went east and tobacco went west. Spanish authorities were infuriated by this collaboration, but they could do little to staunch the lifelines of arms, goods, and strategic rebel exile networks that flourished in the center of the island, in a number of Haitian cities.

Although the passport entreaties to the colonial authorities appear innocent enough, Dominican writers sometimes masked anticolonial organizing in their travel requests. Many petitioners mentioned business interests on the north coast, invoking the deep commercial ties many had with Cap-Haïtien, to north-coast lumber sales, and other interests, as pretext for their voyage. Petitioner Norberto (Norverto) Torres, for example, may have had such business interests in the west, as he suggested in his petition. However, he most certainly had larger plans, since he ushered his whole family to refuge in Haiti. Less than one month after submitting his petition, Torres and others plotted armed resistance against Spain. The liberation fighting was widespread by late summer 1863.

During the rebellion against Spain, Dominicans fostered strong ties with Haitian citizens and politicians alike. Rebels regularly took refuge in Haitian towns across the northern coast, in territories in the center of the island, and in the Haitian capital, in direct defiance to Spanish authorities. A secret envoy of Haitian diplomats traveled overland from Ouanaminthe to meet the rebels' emissaries during the height of the fighting, traveling on to Santiago de los Caballeros to discuss urgent negotiations with the Spanish. President Geffrard, too, lobbied from Port-au-Prince in a diplomatic capacity to negotiate Spain's exit and the return of political prisoners, even as he was greatly restrained by threats from the Spanish military.

The anticolonial fighting was successful; in 1865, La Guerra de la Restauración (the War of Restoration) ended, and the Dominican Republic became independent once more. Reflecting on the collaboration of those years, the authors of one newspaper in Puerto Plata, *La Regeneración*, proposed dual citizenship as the fighting ended. In the devastation of the postwar landscape, however, different interests competed for power. A reestablished administration in the Dominican capital forwarded no such proposals that fall, opposing even the markets that had grown during the occupation. This small governing group sought to control, tax, or eliminate this travel and interchange, and they condemned collaboration with Haiti. Nevertheless, commercial and family ties remained steady as before. Furthermore, rebels continued to collaborate in the face of new annexation threats, this time from the United States, in following years.

Despite official opposition, Dominicans and Haitians regularly continued to benefit from travel, commercial exchanges, and other ties across the island. These connections are often buried, distorted, or minimized in the written archival record of those decades, and they are rarely included in discussions about the history of migration on the island. The passport documents that follow offer a small window into daily life at the intense interconnection that flourished in the 1860s and 1870s as citizens of Haiti and the Dominican Republic eagerly sought to preserve their independence in difficult circumstances.

The Petitions

Santiago 7 November 1862[2]
I have received a request written for Don Nicasio Jimenez, Chief of Police of this City, asking for a passport for his wife who wants to make a trip to Haiti with the object of seeing her mother and sisters who, he writes, have been there since the Separation of this territory from the Haitian Government and during which time they have had to live separated from their family. And in light of the content of this petition, I have decided to direct it to Your Excellency so that you might tell me what you deem convenient in the matter, what the guidelines are about this sort of petition, so I can resolve based on precedent what is just and appropriate.
May God &c.

Puerto Plata 14 November 1862[3]
Most Excellent Sir,
Doña Tereza Esmit widow and resident [becina] of this City with the most profound respect tells Your Excellency: that she must travel to the City of Guarico [Cap-Haïtien], with her three daughters, to take care of family business.
She begs that Your Excellency deign to concede to her permission and a passport with said objective; it is charity she does not doubt given the upright and proven justice of Your Excellency whose life heaven may preserve for many years.
Most Excellent Sir
Tereza Smith

Puerto Plata 15 November 1862[4]
Most Excellent Sir,
Maria Antonia Bautista of this town of Puerto Plata
Very humbly asks that you concede to her a passport to go to Cap Haïtien to see her sick and paralytic mother, where she thinks of staying with her for one year.

She begs that God give you many years of life
On behalf of María Antonio Bautista
José Secundario Mañon

Puerto Plata, 15 November 1862[5]
Most Excellent Sir,
Rosa Buisson, property owner residing in this City of Puerto Plata
Begs very humbly that a passport be accorded to her to go to Cap
Haïtien, with her two girls, Cornelia, and Ramona. She requests it
for family reasons and to bring to this [city] an ailing aunt.
May God give you many years of life
Most Excellent Sir
Rosa Bison

Puerto Plata, 29 November 1862[6]
Most Excellent Sir,
Don John A. Poloney, neighbor [*vecino*] of this city, addresses you
with the due respect, making it known that he is in need of going
to Cap Haïtien with the goal of handling some private matters, he
wants to be conceded a month's license with that end in that capacity.
He submissively begs of Your Excellency the concession of that favor
and does not doubt he will receive it from the magnanimous and
noble sentiments of Your Excellency in favor of his subordinates,
begging to heaven that your important life last many years—
J. A. Poloney

Puerto Plata, 29 November 1862[7]
Most Excellent Sir
Don Miguel Malagón resident [*vecino*] of this City, makes it known
to Your Excellency with due respect that needing to travel to Cap-
Haïtien to take care of some personal matters, he wants to be given
a one-month license to the aforementioned end in that virtue.
He begs submissively that Your Excellency concede said favor that
he does not doubt attaining from the magnanimous and noble senti-
ments of Your Excellency in favor of his subordinates: begging that
heaven make your important life last many years.
Most Excellent Sir
Miguel Malagón

Santiago, 8 December 1862[8]

Most Excellent Sir

Don Francisco Reyes, resident and citizen [*habitante y vecino*] of the
City of Santiago de los Caballeros.

To Your Excellency with the appropriate respect he says: that his
Mother finds herself in Haiti since the Separation, and since the son
in that location who was helping her has died, she wants to return to
this town, as a result the petitioner comes before Your Excellency to
seek that you grant him a passport, so that with a *péon* he can travel
to Guarico [Cap-Haïtien] in the neighboring republic in order to
facilitate the trip of his Señora Mother, given that he does not doubt
the charitable heart of Your Excellency whose life heaven may preserve for many years.

Most Excellent Sir

Fco. Reyes

Puerto Plata, 26 December 1862[9]

Most Excellent Sir

The undersigned, Félix Antonio Limardo, property owner living in
this city, has the honor of addressing Your Excellency with the deep-
est respect:

That he wishes to send his son Rodolfo Ovidio Limardo, a minor of
fourteen years of age, to Cap-Haïtien, so that he can get to know his
maternal relatives and reunite with his Mother at the same time, so
that he can accompany her for her return to this Spanish Province.
He humbly begs Your Excellency grant him the corresponding passport, so that his aforementioned son Rodolfo Ovidio Limardo may
take this trip, taking leave of the country for three months.

It is justice begged and solicited from the great kindness of Your
Excellency

F. A. Limardo

Puerto Plata, 31 December 1862[10]

Most Excellent Sir,

Felicia Muños, Wife of Bernardo Abraham, native of Trinidad,
Province of the Island of Cuba, declares before Your Excellency: that
finding my aforementioned husband in Guarico [Cap-Haïtien] in
Haiti, and having sent for me, and my being a poor mother of two

daughters with no resources and it being indispensable to provide me with the corresponding permission of the Government, I appeal before Your Excellency with the object of seeing if it is possible to afford me one for said destination with my two daughters so that I can reunite with my Husband.
I hope for Justice from your grand benevolence.
Most Excellent Sir
Felicia Muños

Santiago, 2 January 1863[11]
Most Excellent Sir,
The undersigned property owner [and] merchant of this City has the honor to come before Your Excellency to say: that his Wife [*Señora esposa*] Doña Melina Charier de García has to travel to the City of Cap-Haïtien or rather Guarico to take care of matters of inheritance that have been pending for eighteen years because of the war. For this reason she asks Your Excellency accord her the corresponding passport for her family comprised of the following people:
Don Ulises Michel, Doña Melina Charier de García, Doña Doleisca Charier, widow, and Doña Cecilia Angraro and three peons.
May God give Your Excellency many years
Juan Francisco García

San Lorenzo de Guayubín, 14 January 1863[12]
Most Excellent Sir:
Don Juan Grullon, merchant and property owner resident in this town, respectfully addresses Your Excellency: that having received reliable news that that on the coast of Haiti from Mar—-[illegible] and Ballajá [Fort Liberté] there are a large number of pieces of mahogany that the Count of Yaque in his many and frequent shipments would bring west from Manzanillo Bay and from there to the aforementioned Haitian port, pieces which have the marks that he usually made on his lumber, so to buy this lumber he must travel to the neighboring Haitian Republic.
He begs Your Excellency permit him to travel to the aforementioned places with said objective accompanied by his son Don Aquilino, promising to follow religiously the instructions that you might make him in the permission he requests.

He hopes to be worthy of grace from Your Excellency's well-known philanthropy
May God grant Your Excellency many years
Juan Grullón

Puerto Plata, 15 January 1863[13]
Most Excellent Sir,
Ana María Laplace, resident of this City, has the honor of asking Your Excellency to deign to give her a passport for two months to travel to Cap Haïtien accompanied by her sister Victoria Emma Laplace and her child Theophilo Laplace, to take care of family business.
May God grant Your Excellency many years
Anna María Laplace

La Vega, 21 January 1863[14]
Most Excellent Sir,
An appropriate passport for the neighboring Republic of Haiti is solicited from the superior authority of Your Excellency for Gregorio Meyreles, resident of Macorís in this Province, as his wife and three children desire to go to said country with the objective of validating some properties in said territory that they have recently come to inherit from his deceased father.
This individual is worthy of the concession he solicits and is of good antecedents.
May God grant you many years
Most Excellent Sir
The Governor General
José de la Roca

Santiago, 21 January 1863[15]
Most Excellent Sir,
The writer of this letter, an artisan in this City, has the honor of presenting to Your Excellency: that as his wife is of Haitian origin, and her parents and all of her relatives in what was formerly enemy territory, from whom she finds herself having been separated for eighteen years, and informed of the fact that at present it is possible

to travel by land to that part if one has legitimate reason, being so, he begs Your Excellency deign to confer a passport so that the writer may travel to said territory accompanying his aforementioned wife Julliett Colón, with four children who make up the members of their family and a *peón*, proposing to return to this Province with great speed.

He hopes to be worthy of your grace

May God grant to Your Excellency many years

Most Excellent Sir

José del Carmen Rodríguez

Guayubin 30 January 1863[16]

Most Excellent Sir

Don Norverto Torres, native and citizen [*vecino*] of this Jurisdiction addresses you with the due respect: that having to resolve some pending matters of interests he holds in the neighboring republic of Haiti and wanting to put in order his hacienda that has for some time been abandoned due to his absence in that locale,

To Your Excellency he humbly begs you deign to concede to him a license for him, a child, and three women of his family to go to the aforementioned Republic with said objective.

A favor that he hopes to attain from the benignity of Your Excellency whose life God may give many years for the good of his subjects

Most Excellent Sir

On behalf of the interested party[,] who does not know how to write

The Military Commander

Juan F. Garrido

Guayubin, 3 February 1863[17]

Most Excellent Sir

Doña Casimira Rodrigues, native and citizen [*vecina*] of the Jurisdiction of Sabaneta addresses you with the due respect; that having some issues pending and particularly that of going to see her father in the neighboring Republic of Haiti—

To Your Excellency she humbly begs you deign to concede to her a license for her a servant and a girl from her family to go to the aforementioned Republic with said objective.

A favor that he hopes to attain from the benignity of Your Excellency whose life God may give many years for the good of his subjects.
Most Excellent Sir
On behalf of the interested party[,] who does not know how to write [no signature, but the same handwriting as that of Garrido in the previous petition]

Notes

1. Anexión 12, Expediente 56, Archivo General de la Nación, República Dominicana (Dominican Republic).

2. Gob. Militar de Santiago [unsigned] to José Hungria, November 7, 1862, AGN-RD, Anexión 12, Expediente 56, Archivo General de la Nación.

3. Tereza Smith to Cap. Gen. Puerto Plata, November 14, 1862, AGN-RD, Anexión 12, Expediente 56, Archivo General de la Nación. The different spellings of the name are in the original text.

4. José Secundario Mañon to Cap. Gen. Puerto Plata, November 15, 1862, AGN-RD, Anexión 12, Expediente 56, Archivo General de la Nación.

5. Rosa Bison to Cap. Gen. Puerto Plata, November 15, 1862, AGN-RD, Anexión 12, Expediente 56, Archivo General de la Nación. The different spellings of the name are in the original text.

6. J. A. Poloney to Cap. Gen. Puerto Plata, November 29, 1862, AGN-RD, Anexión 12, Expediente 56, Archivo General de la Nación.

7. Miguel Malagón to Cap. Gen. Puerto Plata, November 29, 1862, AGN-RD, Anexión 12, Expediente 56, Archivo General de la Nación.

8. Francisco Reyes to Cap. Gen. Santiago, December 8, 1862, AGN-RD, Anexión 12, Expediente 56, Archivo General de la Nación.

9. Félix Antonio Limardo to Cap. Gen. Puerto Plata, December 26, 1862, AGN-RD Anexión 12, Expediente 56, Archivo General de la Nación.

10. Felicia Muños to Cap. Gen. Puerto Plata, December 31, 1862, AGN-RD, Anexión 12, Expediente 56, Archivo General de la Nación.

11. Juan Francisco Garcia to Cap. Gen. Santiago, January 2, 1863, AGN-RD, Anexión 12, Expediente 56, Archivo General de la Nación.

12. Juan Grullón to Cap. Gen. Guayubín, January 14, 1863, AGN-RD, Anexión 12, Expediente 56, Archivo General de la Nación.

13. Anna María Laplace to Cap. Gen. Puerto Plata, January 15, 1863, AGN-RD, Anexión 12, Expediente 56, Archivo General de la Nación. The scribe recorded her name as "Ana," but she signed with "Anna."

14. José de la Roca to Cap. Gen. La Vega, January 21, 1863, AGN-RD, Anexión 12, Expediente 56, Archivo General de la Nación.

15. José del Carmen Rodríguez to Cap. Gen. Santiago, January 21, 1863, AGN-RD, Anexión 12, Expediente 56, Archivo General de la Nación.

16. Norverto Torres to Cap. Gen. Guayubin. January 30, 1863, AGN-RD, Anexión 12, Expediente 56, Archivo General de la Nación.

17. Casimira Rodrigues to Cap. Gen. Guayubin, February 3, 1863, AGN-RD, Anexión 12, Expediente 56, Archivo General de la Nación.

Works Cited

González Canalda, María Filomena. 2013. *Libertad Igualdad: Protocolos notariales de José Troncoso y Antonio Abad Solano, 1822–1840.* Santo Domingo: Archivo General de la Nación.

2

Representations of Hispaniola

4

"A Border between Geographies of Grief"

River Crossings and Crossroads between Haiti and the Dominican Republic

RÉGINE MICHELLE JEAN-CHARLES

> Tragedy, not geography[,] informs the real border.
>
> Michele Wucker, *Why the Cocks Fight*

> Between Haiti and the Dominican Republic flows a river filled with ghosts. The river is called, aptly enough, the Massacre River and is one of several natural frontiers, dividing what is geographically one island into two independent nations. . . . When I got there, I expected to see a river running with blood. In the shadow of such gruesome history. . . . How could there be anything else?
>
> Edwidge Danticat, "Preface" to *Massacre River*

The following paragraph introduces Roxane Gay's short story "In the Manner of Water or Light" from her collection *Ayiti* (2011):

> My mother was conceived in what would ever after be known as the Massacre River. The sharp smell of blood has followed her since. When she first moved to the United States, she read the dictionary from front to back. Her vocabulary quickly became extensive. Her favorite word is suffuse, to spread over or through in the manner of water or light. When she tries to explain how she is haunted by the smell of blood, she says that her senses are suffused with it. (57)

"In the Manner of Water or Light" is about three generations of women differently marked by the 1937 massacre in the Dominican Republic. The genocide of the borderland community of Haitian-Dominicans began in October 1937, when General Rafael Trujillo ordered the Dominican army to kill all Haitians in the northwestern region of the Dominican Republic. Over 15,000 people died in what was known in Kreyòl as *kout kouto* (stabs of the knife) and in Spanish as *el corte* (the cutting). Relating this history, Richard Turits (2002) explains that

> Haitians were slain even as they attempted to escape to Haiti while crossing the fatefully named Massacre River that divides the two nations. After the first days of the slaughter, the official checkpoint and bridge between Haiti and the Dominican Republic were closed, thus impeding Haitians' escape. In the following weeks, local priests and officials in Haiti recorded testimonies of refugees and compiled a list that ultimately enumerated 12,168 victims. Subsequently, during the first half of 1938, thousands more Haitians were forcibly deported and hundreds killed in the southern frontier region. (590–591)

As an example of ethnic cleansing, this episode, the genocide of Haitian-Dominicans on the border, has become one of the important historic markers of the fraught relationship between Haiti and the Dominican Republic.

Told in the first person with no references to proper names other than the dead and unknown grandfather, "In the Manner of Water or Light" begins with the protagonist describing her mother's origins—a conception tale and origin story that links the mother to the massacre even though she was not yet born when it happened. The opening sentence, "My mother was conceived in what would ever after be known as the Massacre River," compels the reader to imagine conception in the context of death.[1] The mother's parents' encounter and coupling in the river serves multiple functions. The reader is surprised when immediately after this introductory paragraph the protagonist divulges that "my grandmother knew my grandfather for less than a day" (57). As the story continues, we learn that the grandparents meet for the first time and have sex in the river during the massacre. Their union in the water is both literally and figuratively life-giving. Their bodies united as one, the grandparents tell each other stories about their lives as they create a new one, surrounded by dead bodies and the imminent threat of violence. While they are together in this horrific yet fruitful moment, the grandfather asks repeatedly to be remembered, as though he is aware of his imminent death. Together the couple creates a sense of emotional protection that defeats the atmosphere of death that surrounds them. The creation of a future generation will allow the grandfather's legacy to survive even though he dies shortly after the child is conceived in the Massacre River.

On the one hand, this moment can be read as the protagonists' attempt to reclaim the Dajabón River and expand the story of the massacre to include life. Yet at no point does this emphasis on life and creation suggest that healing from the massacre has occurred or will occur. Nor does it posit an idyllic or utopian figuration of the river as a new kind of territory beyond what history and the experience of Haitians—the survivors of the massacre, the disenfranchised victims of *antihaitianismo*, and the recently stateless refugees of today—clearly illustrate. Instead, Gay's story depicts a fleeting moment that occupies the border between enmity and unity. Through two people's act of conception, the Dajabón River becomes a place where an experience other than death can take place, if only briefly, although it does not supplant or deny the tragic loss of life.

In this essay, I focus on such moments of possibility to argue that representations of the Massacre River by three contemporary writers—Roxane Gay, Edwidge Danticat, and Évelyne Trouillot—engage the black feminist dialectics of both-and by positing future possibility without negating the trauma of the past and the oppression of the present. As they wrestle with the deplorable current realities (the Dominican government's disenfranchisement of the Haitian minority in the Dominican Republic, its stripping of Dominicans of Haitian descent of their citizenship, ongoing human rights injustices, work conditions in the *bateyes*) and the bleak history (the massacre of 1937) of the relationship between Haiti and the Dominican Republic, these literary representations of the river foreground the long-standing contradictions that characterize the region. As Ginetta Candelario (2016) does with her rich excavation of the *ciguapa* as a "metaphor [that] navigates the contradictions, tensions, and complex desires surrounding the past/present/future of race, gender, sex, sovereignty, progreso, and regreso in the Dominican Republic and its diaspora," I am interested in mining metaphors that embrace contradiction in the imaginings of the border between Haiti and the Dominican Republic (106). My goal here is to add to the study of representations of Haiti and the Dominican Republic by writers of Haitian descent to show how they negotiate the relationship between the two countries.

Of course, Haiti and the Dominican Republic, located on a single island divided into two nations with a border separating them, offer much material for critical analyses of borders, boundaries, frontiers, and liminality—to name but a few of the keywords in border theory discourse. The social, historical, political, and cultural significance of the border between Haiti and the Dominican Republic cannot be understated. As Michel-Rolph Trouillot puts it, it is "the longest and most significant land boundary in all of the Antilles" (quoted in Fumagalli 2015, 1). The impulse to imagine and to conceive of a truly transnational (and less contentious) Hispaniola is beginning to develop an intellectual history of its own. The scholars of the Transnational Hispaniola Collective, for example, have done important and extensive work in this area, using their academic, activist, and artistic production to move beyond the extant theories and representations of Haiti and the Dominican Republic. By rooting their work in the history of social movements that have collaborated to imagine a truly transnational future, these scholars attempt to move beyond the divisive epistemologies of the past. Similarly, in *From Sugar to Revolution: Women's Visions of Haiti, Cuba, and the Dominican Republic*, Myriam Chancy (2012) argues that

> within the Americas, perhaps no transnational relationship is more vexed than that of Haiti and the Dominican Republic. In the age of transnationalism, when the term "transnational" normally refers to the extensive economic and cultural exchanges between and among nation-states as a result of forced and chosen displacements that produce the increased mobilization of bodies and goods through globalization, the interchange between the two nation-states occupying one geographical body has had a more tumultuous history than any other within the Caribbean basin. (53)

The relationship between Haiti and the Dominican Republic inherently calls into question the usefulness of "transnational" as a conceptual category for charting Caribbean relations.

Yet some scholars have taken this challenge as a point of provocation. The explicit mission of the Transnational Hispaniola Collective is to transform "the dominant paradigms in Dominican and Haitian knowledge production" (Mayes et al. 2013, 26). Explaining their use of the transnational framework, they point out that for them, the concept

> allowed us to view exchanges between Haitians and Dominicans not only in terms of cross-border relations, but also in symbiotic terms, as manifestations of neutral and contested spaces of cultural

and political engagement. . . . By continuing to use transnational, we decided to address more specifically a problem in the scholarship and in the popular imagination that would unite Dominican and Haitian cultures, languages, and traditions under the framework of the Haitian diaspora. (30)

From social scientist Eugenio Matibag's *Haitian Dominican Counterpoint* (2003) to literary scholar Lucia Suarez's *The Tears of Hispaniola* (2006), academics have wrestled with different ways to reconcile and move beyond the antagonisms between the two countries. In another example, historian Robert McCormick (2010) writes,

Seeing the bridged river and patrolled checkpoint at Dajabon, having read *Massacre River*, knowing the dynamics of the crossings, meeting the Haitians working, or not having work, on the *bateyes* in the Dominican Republic made me ask, and I am sure I am not alone, if there weren't a better way to reorganize a space formerly unified and known variously as Ayiti, Quisqueya, Hispaniola. (3)

McCormick's rumination is hopeful, acknowledging the difficult present and asking the reader to simultaneously imagine the future and account for the past. The current moment also demands that scholars and students alike consider the promises and pitfalls of the transnational Hispaniola paradigm.

In this essay, I focus on representations of the border rather than on the conflict, although I look exclusively at works by three women writers of Haitian descent. Gay, Danticat, and Trouillot are of different generations, and one lives in Haiti while the other two live in the United States. What interests me here are representations that do not simply imagine the border as a binary or even an in-between space but rather that allow binary qualities to occupy the same space through the use of symbolic language. Whether it is the use of water imagery in the river or the metonymic use of the color blue, these aesthetic practices are marked by ambiguity.

Taken together, my close readings of scenes that take place in the river, from a novel, *The Farming of Bones* (1998), from a short story, "In the Manner of Water and Light" (2011), and from scenes in the truck from the play *Le bleu de l'île* (2012), by Évelyne Trouillot, help map a more complex relationship to transnationalism, to border crossing, and to the past. Fluidity as a metaphor is central to how I am reading these interpretations of the border. The fluid ecology of the river is a useful point of departure for rethinking these dynamics. As a metaphor, the fluidity of the river and its ecology opens a space for thinking about how the river can operate as a space of contradiction that can bring both life and death. It is important to note that what these examples from Gay, Danticat, and Trouillot show is not a vision of a transnational, borderless Hispaniola in which Haitians and Dominicans peacefully exist. While these writers' representations of the river imagine a different possibility, they also seem to question whether such possibilities are even worth imagining. This kind of reading is especially applicable today, given the Dominican Constitutional Tribunal's 2013 decision, also known as La Sentencia, that has resulted in the statelessness and deportation of tens of thousands of Dominicans of Haitian descent from the Dominican Republic.

This latest humanitarian crisis to affect Haitians living and working in the Dominican Republic has created deportees and refugees out of many men and women who had thought of themselves as Dominican and as Dominican citizens. For the characters in the novel and the short story, the river is a complex space that simultaneously generates death, life, survival, and escape. For the characters in the play, the river is a distant space toward which they are traveling, one they are unsure they will ever see, and one that represents the uncertainty of their predicament. As I argue in the discussion that follows, tracing the descriptions of the river and the sky allows readers to see how natural elements make legible different aspects of life on, across, and through the border.

"In the Manner of Water or Light" by Roxane Gay

For the grandmother in Roxane Gay's story, the river helps her survive.

> My grandmother ended up in the river. She found a shallow place. She tried to hold her breath while she hid from the marauding soldiers on both of the muddy shores straddling the river. There was a moment when she laid on her back and submerged herself until her entire body was covered by water, until her pores were suffused with it. She didn't come up for air until the ringing in her ears became unbearable. (2011, 6)

Survival operates in two ways here. The grandmother must hold her breath and cut short her own oxygen supply in order to survive. In addition, she risks her life to escape death from the "marauding soldiers." The water operates in a dual fashion, seeming to save her even while it further endangers her through the ringing in her ears, signaling the possibility of drowning. The use of the verb "suffuse" also links the experience beneath the water with the blood suffusing the mother's senses as described in the first paragraph of the story. Those familiar with the history of the massacre know that thousands were eventually slaughtered in the river in which the grandmother tries to hide. The name alone, Massacre River (coined during the eighteenth century, when French buccaneers were slaughtered by the Spanish for attempting to cross), imbues the water between the two countries with the imprint of violence and death.

The grandmother's experience in the river and ultimately her entire life is transformed when Jacques Bertrand, the man who would become the protagonist's grandfather, finds her in the river. Although the grandmother and the grandfather worked on the same *batey* as migrant workers from Haiti, they had never encountered one another before. "My grandparents bound their bodies together as their skin gathered in tiny folds, as their bodies shook violently" (60). Their bodies save each other in the Massacre River. Explaining her encounter with the grandfather, the grandmother reveals that "I thought he was an angel who had come to deliver me from that dark and terrible place" (60). Entwined together, their flesh frees their minds from death. The safety secured by their bodies is short lived, compromised on the other side of the river's bank in Ouanaminthe, on Haitian soil, where the grandfather is killed by the soldiers. Although he survives the river and crosses to the other side of the island and reaches his native land, a violent death awaits him. Death, the story seems to suggest, is inevitable in the time of the massacre.

In Gay's story, the mother's suffused senses serve as a reminder that escape is illusory because healing is incomplete and ultimately unattainable. For the mother, the massacre exists only in the fact of the existence of her physical body and the memory of the few stories her own mother told her. These stories in turn shape the protagonist's understanding of her family's history and of their present life in the United States. Although the stories are a part of her life, they are cloaked silences of their own. "Everything I know about my family's history, I know in fragments. We are the keepers of secrets. We are secrets ourselves. We try to protect each other from the geography of so much sorrow. I don't know that we succeed" (57). The fragmented family history the protagonist refers to deliberately avoids the past in order to shield family members in the present. That she describes the people in her family as secrets themselves indicates the extent to which memories, bodies, and minds merge with the secrets that are being kept. It also underscores that the secrets inform and define not only the parents' interactions but also their identities. The family members keep secrets, so much so that they become them.

Part of this fragmented knowledge is the way the protagonist learns about the Massacre River, an integral and intimate part of her familial heritage. Each reference to the Dominican Republic comes with a sense of history and with the violent haunting past of the massacre. For the protagonist's grandmother and the generations that follow her, this haunting is etched in and on her body. Memories arrive in the form of smells, like the smell of sugar, which she simply cannot tolerate even several decades later:

> My grandmother is also haunted by smells. She cannot stand the smell of something sweet. If she smells sweetness in the air, she purses her lips and sucks on her teeth, shaking her head. . . . She can neither stand the sight of the cane fields nor the withered men and women hacking away at stubborn stalks of cane with dull machetes. When she sees the cane fields, a sharp pain radiates across her shoulders and down her back. Her body cannot forget the labors it has known. (58)

The body's inability to forget to forget the past is striking. The grandmother's memory occurs in registers that are olfactory, visual, and physical. As with her ability to continue to feel the pain in her body caused by the work she did in the *bateyes*, the grandmother's ability to still smell, see, and hear the signs of many past events speaks to the enduring and inescapable nature of her pain. "My grandmother still hears the dying screams from that night. She remembers the dull, wet sound of machetes hacking through flesh and bone. The only thing that muted those horrors was a man she knew but did not know who wore bridges of scar on his back" (61). Again, we see that although Jacques Bertrand offered a passing moment of respite from the horror of the massacre, this moment does not replace the impact of the grandmother's physical pain and her enduring trauma. He can only temporarily "mute the horror" by protecting the grandmother and allowing her to hold on to him. In fact, we could read his subsequent death as a confirmation of the impossibility of lasting rest from the massacre's psychic wounds. Compared to the sounds the mother still hears and remembers, the memory of Jacques Bertrand is practically inaccessible. Given how little narrative space he occupies, the fact that Jacques Bertrand is the only named character (the protagonist, her grandmother, and her parents are never given proper names) is another contradictory element of the story. The effect here is that his request to be remembered is honored through the appearance of his name, especially in view of the fact that the other characters remain nameless.

The rhythmic pace of the story continues as Gay describes in even greater detail the day after the grandparents survive. "In the morning, surrounded by the smell of silence and death, my grandparents crawled out of the river that had, overnight, become a watery coffin holding 25,000 bodies. The Massacre River had earned its name" (61). Again, the senses feature prominently here, used to describe abstractions such as "silence and death." This technique further accentuates the power of death and the haunting nature of the scene, both of which are so powerful that the grandmother can smell them. In the same way that the smell of blood suffuses her senses, silence and death become an all-powerful smell that she cannot escape. Although the Massacre River was given its name two centuries prior to the 1937 massacre, Gay's description turns the river into a coffin, an unequivocal locus of death and entrapment.

At the end of the story, the mother returns to Haiti for the first time, having refused to do so for many years. When she finally returns to the site of the massacre on the border between the two countries, the smell of blood still haunts her: "I heard my mother whisper to my father that she could hardly breathe but for the smell of blood" (69). The protagonist's mother experiences the massacre exactly as her own mother described it to her. Although she was only conceived in the river and did not live through the massacre, she can still smell the blood that her mother has lived with daily. The trauma has been passed down from one generation to the next.

Eventually, the mother, daughter, and grandmother make their way back to the Massacre River.

> We walked nearly a mile to the banks of the Massacre River. . . . I heard hundreds of frightened people who looked like me splashing

through the water, searching for safety and then, silence. . . . We stood in a shallow place. . . . I had pictured the river as a wide, yawning and bloody beast, but where we stood, the river flowed weakly. The water did not run deep. It was just *a border between two geographies of grief.* (71, my emphasis)

At this moment, the protagonist, her mother, and her grandmother grieve together the events that took place at Massacre River, remembering the past and feeling the weight of the unspoken stories that surround them. "Again I heard hundreds of frightened people splashing through the water, keening, reaching for something that could never be reached" (72). Like the people the protagonist hears, she, her mother, and her grandmother reach for "something"—healing? resolution? reconciliation?— that is ultimately unreachable. In this way, the story takes the reader on an unfulfilling journey of return to the Massacre River. Instead of captivating the reader with a redemptive story about the power and possibility of healing, the writer ends on a deliberately unresolved note.

I propose that this deliberate lack of resolution mirrors the current situation in the Dominican Republic, where a gross lack of resolution in the face of human rights abuses and disenfranchisement leaves thousands of people dangerously trapped in the liminality of statelessness. Gay's story about life within death challenges the perception of devastation and divide that characterizes how the space between Haiti and the Dominican Republic is often viewed in the United States and in human rights discourse. However, Gay refuses to replace or erase the strife; rather, she prefers to pore over its traumatic legacy. This can be read as a creative choice that highlights the greater complexity of the boundary between the two countries. With its watery properties and archival capacity, the river operates in a way that is similar to how Omise'eke Tinsley (2008) theorizes the ocean in her article "Black Atlantic, Queer Atlantic" "as space that churns with physical remnants, dis(re)membered bodies of the Middle Passage, . . . as opaque space to convey the drowned, disremembered, ebbing and flowing histories of violence and healing in the African diaspora" (194). This border between two geographies of grief snakes through death and life, possession and dispossession, safety and danger.

The Farming of Bones by Edwidge Danticat

Edwidge Danticat's novel *The Farming of Bones* (1998) has been the subject of much critical attention.[2] By focusing exclusively on scenes in the book that take place in the water, my goal is to place Danticat's work in conversation with Gay and Trouillot, to expand existing considerations of the novel. As "In the Manner of Water or Light," *The Farming of Bones* concludes with the return of its protagonist, Amabelle Désir, to the river. The Massacre River is where her parents died and is the site she waded through as she fled death during the massacre. Danticat's characterization of the river as a space of multiplicity is spiritual, physical, historical, and personal. It begins with a paratext in the dedication, which is addressed to Mètres Dlo, the river goddess. The river is first marked as a site of death because it is where Amabelle watches her parents die when she is a child, almost two decades before the massacre. This scene of death foreshadows both the massacre that will appear later in the novel and the treacherous crossing that follows that event. Describing that day, Amabelle recalls the moment after her father takes her across:

> My father reaches into the current and sprinkles his face with water, as if to salute the spirit of the river and request her permission to enter. My mother crosses herself three times and looks up at the sky before she climbs on my father's back. . . . Once he is in the river, he flinches, realizing that he made a grave mistake. (1998, 51)

The parents' entry is telling here: each one performs an act of ritual communication. The father anoints himself with water, greets the spirit of the river, and requests permission to enter. The mother crosses herself. Taken together, the couple's acts reflect the syncretized combination of Vodou (salute the spirit) and Catholicism (the sign of the cross). With each ripple, the river acts as a spiritual beacon.

The moment of reverence and prayer for safekeeping prior to crossing is quickly disturbed by the physical properties of the river. In the following paragraph, the parents' bodies are wrapped tightly around one another in an attempt to grasp at life, in much the same way as the couple in Gay's short story. But here the efforts are futile:

> My mother turns back to look for me, throwing my father off balance. A flow of mud fills the shadows. My father thrusts his hands

in front of him, trying to keep on course. My mother tightens her grip around his neck; her body covers him and weighs him down at the same time. When he tries to push her up by her legs, a cluster of vines whisks past them; my mother reaches for the vines as though they were planks of a raft. . . . The water rises above my father's head. My mother releases his neck, the current carrying her beyond his reach. Separated, they are less of an obstacle for the cresting river. (51)

That the mother's body "covers him and weighs him down at the same time" can be read as an expression of the tension of the border itself. In search of protection, the body becomes a weight, but the body, as in Gay's story, also provides a temporary protection from the danger that surrounds them.

Amabelle crosses the river for a second time during the massacre in 1937. She is with a group fleeing Trujillo's soldiers, who are on a killing rampage. This crossing is even more difficult than the first:

A strong scent of wet grass and manure wafted through the current as we forded farther in. I tried to find footholds in the sand, wedges to anchor my feet. The water was so deep that it was like trying to walk on air. When we were nearly submerged in the current, I yanked my hand from Odette's. I heard her sniffle, perhaps fearful and shocked. But I was only thinking of one thing: If I drowned, I wanted to drown alone, with nobody else's life to be responsible for. (200)

Again, there is an inherent contradiction in the description of the water, which is "so deep that it was like trying to walk on air." Walking on air could, like the colloquial expression, be interpreted as effortless and joyful. But it is the physical property of air that matters here, not the figurative connotation. It is impossible to walk on air, so what Amabelle means is that walking was exceedingly difficult, virtually impossible.

The representation of the river as a source of death is especially clear when Amabelle covers the mouth of Odette, a woman that she meets along the way who is also escaping the massacre and heading to the river so she can cross over into Haiti. Amabelle covers Odette's mouth with her hands, trying to quiet her so she will not be detected by the soldiers. But this action accidentally ends her life. This helping and hurting, preserving and destroying, further illuminates the river's function throughout the novel. As is made explicit in the story by Roxane Gay, the river is a site of multiple meanings, where both life (conception) and death can coexist.

In addition to marking the border, Massacre River is a space of crossing and exchange. As many scholars have noted, the border has historically been a space where Haitians and Dominicans peacefully coexist and even intermingle. In their account of the witnesses affected by *kout kouto*, Lauren Derby and Richard Turits (2006) point out that

> a unified community formed across ethnic difference and even across the national border was characterized by relatively respectful and intimate relations between Haitians and Dominicans. Haitian-Dominican unions were commonplace; bilingualism (Spanish and Kreyòl) was the rule; and Haitian and Dominican families frequently included relatives and properties on both sides of the border. (138)

In this same vein, René Philoctète's *Le peuple des terres mêlées* (*Massacre River*; 1989), the classic novel about the massacre, goes to great lengths to depict how Haitians and Dominicans were coexisting and even intermixing on the border prior to the massacre.³ As Danticat explains in the preface to the English translation of *Massacre River*, "What this extraordinary novel reminds us is that sandwiched between the two borders was a group of people who tried to build a new world, people who were as fluid as the waters themselves, the people of Massacre River" (8). The border Amabelle's parents travel back and forth across also reveals ordinary people who are trying to build a new world as the scenes describing the physical border indicate. For example, upon her return, Amabelle notices that "at first glance, the Massacre appeared like any of the three or four large rivers in the north of Haiti. On a busy market day, it was simply a lively throughway beneath a concrete bridge, where women sat on boulders at the water's edge to pound their clothes clean, and mules and oxen stopped to diminish their thirst" (284).

Amabelle's affinity for the water dates back to her childhood. During a conversation with Señora Valencia, the Dominican woman whose family Amabelle works for as a servant, they discuss her pull toward water. As Señora Valencia tells her, "When we were children, you were always drawn to water, Amabelle, streams, lakes, rivers, waterfalls in all their power" (302). This attraction to the water is no doubt a result of Amabelle's parents' death. However, it must also be read as a spiritual invitation to the function of the river as a space of literal crossing or crossroads. The idea of crossing over is central to the Vodou religious system and to understandings of death in Haitian culture. To cross over to the other side is to leave the physical realm and enter the spiritual realm; but the crossroads, or *kafou*, are the sites where the spirit world and the physical world meet. As LeGrace Benson (2013) writes, much of the artistic and intellectual production on Vodou "highlights the importance of crossroads, presenting them as the transcendent geography of life and death" (296).[4] Following Benson, I posit that understanding the river as a "transcendent geography of life and death" becomes another way to perceive the geographies of grief. Recognizing the river as a crossroads where the physical and spiritual meet becomes another way to interpret the dynamics of Hispaniola.

At the end of the novel, Amabelle returns to the river. "The day my parents drowned," she remembers, "I watched their faces as they bobbed up and down, in and out of the crest of the river. Together they were both trying to signal a message to me, but the force of the water would not let them" (308). By telling her parents' story first, she returns to her origin and the beginning of her life as an orphan in the Dominican Republic. As was the case in Gay's story, the origin of the protagonist is linked to the Massacre River. When she physically returns to the river and enters it, she notices that "the water was warm for October, warm and shallow, so shallow that I could lie on my back in it with my shoulders only half submerged, the current flowing over me in a less than gentle caress, the pebbles in the riverbed scouring my back" (311). It is also important to note that Amabelle returns in October, the month when the 1937 massacre occurred. Describing the physical qualities of the water as gentle and almost loving seems to contradict the identification of the river as the locus of death it is at the beginning of the novel.

The description draws attention to the fact that the havoc the river wreaked on Haitian lives was a product of its use, a product of history, not geography. At the same time, Amabelle's return is clearly without hope. As W. Todd Martin argues elsewhere, "Amabelle . . . having returned to Haiti after escaping from the Dominican Republic, has existed in a 'living death' for the last twenty-four years. Only Amabelle's final act of entering into the water, 'paddling like a newborn in a washbasin' . . . suggests renewal, yet the source of hope remains unclear" (Martin 2007, 248). As is the case in "In the Manner of Water and Light," there is no hopeful ending to the story. This conclusion is consistent with Danticat's position on the situation of Haitians in the Dominican Republic, which she describes in the book's acknowledgments: "And the very last words, last on the page, but always first in my memory, must be offered to those who died in the massacre of 1937, to those who survived to testify, *and to the constant struggle of those who still toil in the cane fields*" (312, my emphasis). This, I argue, is the true ending of the book, the current struggle for those still toiling in the cane fields.

Taken as a leitmotif for the relationship between Haiti and the Dominican Republic, the Massacre River can be seen as a generative site of possibility rather than the binary of division or union. Analyzing the river as a crossroads that is what Benson calls a "transcendent geography" further supports this position; it highlights the fluidity of the river and its spiritual dimensions. A transcendent crossroads creates a space of possibility that accommodates both-and. Reading the river as a fluid body of water rather than as a border opens up new ways to analyze the relationship between the two countries. This framework is far more open-ended than the transnational or fatal-conflict models, especially because it links shared spiritual traditions.

Le bleu de l'île by Évelyne Trouillot

Although the next text I will consider does not include scenes in the Massacre River or on the border itself, I want to take a moment to analyze the geography of the border in Évelyne Trouillot's play *Le bleu de l'île* (2005). This theatrical piece is useful for my analysis because of Trouillot's focus on a lesser-known event in the turbulent history between the two countries. The incident Trouillot bases her story on is not well known, at least not internationally, making her work an important intervention in the creative representation of conflict between Haiti and the Dominican Republic that moves beyond the 1937 massacre (Philoctète 1989; Dalembert 2005; Danticat 1996, 1998).

The play, translated as *The Blue of the Island*, is based on an attack by Dominican soldiers on a truck carrying twelve clandestine passengers en route to the Dominican Republic from the Haitian town of Piment that took place on June 18, 2000 (Trouillot and McCormick 2012). The play features twelve Haitian passengers, five women and seven men. The entire play takes place in the pickup truck, which is operated by a Dominican driver while the Haitians lie packed against one another under a blue tarp.

During the attack, Dominican soldiers killed six of the passengers. The event received very little attention outside Haiti at the time it occurred.

For Stéphanie Bérard (2010), the truck represents

> a timeless nowhere, an intermediary in-between space; [it is] that which follows the departure, and precedes the arrival, that which separates what is no longer and what is not yet. . . . It is a spatial and temporal in-between [like] the frontier space between Haiti and the Dominican Republic, between the past and the future. (61)[5]

Trouillot describes this in-between space as confined and confining. Comparing it to a prison, one character tells another who is seeking a better life, "You [have] lost because now you are a prisoner, trapped in this truck with us" (254). The truck stands for the misery of the past and for hope for the future in a very uncomfortable present. It is a space of uneasy transition, a space of hardship, and yet it is a place of hope in its promise of a better future on the other side of the border, or at least a more hopeful future. Nowhere is this fraught dynamic captured more poignantly than in the reflections of one of the hidden passengers, the protagonist Ronald, on the blue tarp covering him. Describing their current circumstances, he comments to another character about

> staring, for hours on end, at that dirty blue tarp that makes you want to punch holes in it in order to rediscover the true blue of the sky. The people seem different, for sure, the language is unknown, but it's the same blue, the same sky. The blue of the island . . . not that dirty, anemic indigo blue soaked too long in water and bleached in an irregular manner, but the real blue, the one that makes my heart skip. In the morning. Without reason. In a few short hours, it will be over. We will be able to see it. Rub our eyes in the light of day. See the blue of the island again. (252–253)

Here the connection of the tarp to the sea and then the sky glides seamlessly from the place of containment and misery to the place of freedom and beauty. It is a hopeful association, one that allows Ronald to see past his present circumstances to something more promising.

The contemporary reader is disabused of the notion of promise that some of the passengers like Ronald seem to feel. The hope that informs their current thoughts and memories is illusory. Whereas the audience and readers of the play are aware of the likely outcome, the characters appear naïve. Through characters like Violetta, another passenger, we are given a more sobering view. Responding to Ronald at one point, she says, "I couldn't give a damn about the blue of your island. It has never helped me out, never adorned my dreams with light" (255). While a hopeful character like Ronald suggests that an alternative future is available, those who see or read the play are all too aware how untenable such hope really is. In his brief introduction to the translation of the play, Robert McCormick (2012) explains how this tension unfolds:

> During the entire trip, the imprudent driving of La Volenta [the Dominican driver], the bad state of the roads, the constant menace of being discovered by the guards, provoke feelings of anguish in the passengers who are already overcome by feelings of guilt, anxiety, and regret. Hope is a cord that unites them as well, with various degrees of skepticism. (212)

Trouillot treads the line between hope and despair, the dismal conditions of the current reality and the elusive possibility of the future. Her attempt to accommodate these contradictory emotions can be interpreted as a way to capture the paradox of the border.

This constant movement between and beyond these binaries is evident in the longings the characters voice to one another on the journey. The five women and seven men on the truck come from diverse backgrounds, and for most of them the life they seek in the Dominican Republic is only temporary. For some, crossing the border represents the opportunity for a better life, though the improvement is only relative to their current suffering. When Lorette explains her choice to leave on the truck, asking "Why stay here? I'd prefer to take my chances across the border," the fact that she uses the expression "take my chances" reveals that she is not certain that life would be better elsewhere (219). Similarly, when Madeline says, "We have plenty of reasons to cry; otherwise we wouldn't be here," she acknowledges what has brought many of her fellow travelers to this point (223). While on the journey, the members of the group express the different longings (mostly sexual), grief, and sadness they have experienced in their lives. For Man Étienne, it is the loss of her twin daughters; for Lorette, it is the abrupt interruption of her education; for Romaine, it is the death of her son. Through these examples, the speakers associate suffering with their past in the village in Piment, but their suffering is magnified by the discomfort, danger, and ultimately by the death they will experience in the truck.

The color blue is a metonymic device for the relationship between the two countries and for the border itself. Maria Fumagalli (2015) sees

> the blue of the island in Trouillot's play [as] the sky that the migrants are not able to see while in transit: stuck in the truck, they can see only the artificial blue tarpaulin which covers them, and, the play suggests, they have clearly lost sight of the bigger picture, both literally and metaphorically. (287)

While I agree that the tarp comes to symbolize more than its material function, I interpret the use of blue more widely. In the play, blue serves a function similar to that of the river in Gay's short story and Danticat's novel. Blue signifies at least four things: the island, the sea, the sky, and the tarp. As a metonym for the island, the sea, and the sky, it connotes beauty, freedom, and the ease of island life. But because it is also the color of the blue tarpaulin, it stands for the passengers' current confinement. Often these different meanings stand in contradiction to one another. In the field of color psychology, blue has more contradictory meanings than any other color; it can represent peace or sadness, depending on the shade (Elliott, Fairchild, and Franklin 2015). As a contradictory color, blue becomes an especially apt metaphor for the border between Haiti and the Dominican Republic.

The phrase from which *Le bleu de l'île* takes its title is rendered most explicit in the conclusion. The play ends just after Dominican soldiers attack the truck and kill half the passengers. Those who are not killed by the gunshots are rounded up and taken prisoner. Amid this chaos, Ronald has a final conversation with his dying sister. She says, "Promise me you won't forget the blue of the island. Promise me to come back from the other side of the island and take care of my daughter and your son" (263). Ronald responds, "So many things to do. It seems to me that we wanted to find a solution and we forgot that *the blue sky doesn't change crossing the border*" (263, my emphasis). Immediately afterward, Ronald leaves the corpses of his sister and brother-in-law and "heads off towards the West," meaning that he goes back toward Haiti (263). The stage directions further specify: "Gradually, as he advances, the stage becomes blue, more and more blue, an almost unbearable blue. The dead rise and accompany him. Finally, the silhouettes of the children become enormous and invade the back of the stage. They, too, head off towards the West" (263).

In this final passage the color blue signals life, death, and the afterlife. Interpreting the myriad emotions and images the color connotes is essential for understanding the entire play. If blue is the sea's promise, it is also its treachery. If it is the clarity of a beautiful afternoon sky, it is also the fact that this same sky hovers over both sides of the island. Perhaps most important is the reflection that "the blue sky doesn't change crossing the border," which means that life on the two sides of the island is similar in ways that are too easily forgotten. It is this realization that ultimately causes Ronald and all the others to head back west, abandoning their goals to cross the border.

Conclusion

By way of conclusion, I want to reflect on the genesis of this essay, which began with a course I first taught in 2013. The interdisciplinary class, offered in the department of African and African Diasporic Studies, "Haiti and the Dominican Republic: Beyond the Border?" was in some ways my own attempt to explore, address, and reconcile some of my personal, political, and intellectual challenges with "the other side of the island" as a scholar of Haitian descent deeply troubled by the injustice suffered by Haitians, Dominicans of Haitian descent, and dark-skinned Dominicans in the Dominican Republic. The class was small, made up of fourteen students. There were three Haitian-Americans and the rest were Dominican-Americans or of mixed heritage, such as Dominican and Puerto Rican. The class seemed to bridge a chasm, or represent the kind of Hispaniola that I thought could only exist in the imagination. As we read novels about the massacre, compared the colonial histories and the U.S. invasions of these two nations on one island, challenged students' assumptions about what they knew about each place, and grappled with current events such as the Dominican government's revoking of citizenship to people of Haitian descent, it was clear that the work we were doing was intellectual, personal, and political. My Haitian students would refer to the Dominican students as "*hermano*" (bro), while my Dominican students were fond of exclaiming "*sak pase*" (what's up!) as they entered the classroom. These performative utterances of solidarity came from a feeling of a genuine desire to connect and engage with one another. My students' stances suggested that real reconciliatory work could take shape within the walls of my class-room. It was a safe space, a protected area where Haiti and the Dominican Republic coexisted without strife or violence. Together, we were engaged in being mindful of the history and the difficulties of the present, yet be-lieving tenaciously in the possibility of a dynamic beyond conflict. It was a space where students grappled with what April Mayes and Kiran Jayaram call "transnationalism in the Dominico-Haitian context as a long-stand-ing form of dual social consciousness" (introduction, this volume). This dual consciousness allowed them to think critically about Haiti and the Dominican Republic together. It was a space in which students of Haitian and Dominican descent could be "relationally involved [and entangled] with each other" (Glissant quoted in introduction, this volume).

And then, a month after class began, the Dominican Republic's Con-stitutional Tribunal ruled to retroactively strip citizenship from anyone born in the country to undocumented parents dating back to 1929. The ruling, also referred to as La Sentencia, began with the case of Juliana Dequis Pierre, who was born in 1984 to Haitian migrants.

> In 2008, when she attempted to acquire her national identity card, government officials confiscated her birth certificate and informed her that they could not issue her any documents because her last names were Haitian. After a lower court rejected Pierre's appeal for the return of her birth certificate, the case eventually reached the Constitutional Tribunal, which ruled that Pierre was not a Domini-can citizen because her parents were not in the country legally. In addition, the judges gave the electoral commission one year to com-pile a list of people like Pierre to be excluded from citizenship. The ruling applies to anyone born in the Dominican Republic to Haitian migrant workers after 1929 and could potentially impact hundreds of thousands of Dominicans. (Hintzen 2014, 108)

When the government officially revoked the citizenship of thousands of Haitian-Dominicans like Pierre in October 2013, centuries of sanc-tioned enmity between the two nations were confirmed. It was a shatter-ing setback for those working for justice such as Sonia Pierre (1963–2011), who had tirelessly addressed human rights abuses and those, such as the Transnational Hispaniola Collective, seeking to transform the epistemol-ogies of division that have been the precedent for scholarship on Haiti and the Dominican Republic. In the face of the government's denial and stripping of citizenship that rendered an entire generation stateless, the possibility that the class had theorized and imagined looked untenable. It was, to say the least, a teaching moment for both my students and for me.

At that moment, I realized that what was needed, and what I had to offer my students, was not a polarizing conceptualization of Haiti and the Dominican Republic that reduced the problem of Hispaniola to either division or transnational belonging, but rather an approach that rested uncomfortably at the crossroads, taking into account all of the possibilities for death and life together. Not either/or, or even in-between, but uncomfortably, together. Likewise, to conceptualize the Massacre River as a crossroads is to refuse to supplant the traumatic past with a hopeful future (Shemak 2002; Misrahi-Barak 2013). The fictive renderings of Gay, Danticat, and Trouillot remind us that theorizations of border crossings must be specific and historically situated; focusing on the river as *kafou* (a crossroads) can begin to do this work. When she was questioned about the enduring legacy of 1937, Edwidge Danticat replied, "I think of that period as a historical scar, but we can't let that overshadow the moment we're living, which is potentially as tragic" (quoted in Rivero 2015).

When La Sentencia went into effect and stripped thousands of Dominicans of their citizenship, deported thousands more to Haiti, and rendered Dominicans of Haitian descent stateless, the tragic potential of this current moment became abundantly clear, and it continues to unfold. Fiction—whether it is a short story, a novel, or a play—is a space to further parse these paradigmatic limitations. When viewed in relation to the present, the images of the border produced in these texts provide different ways of seeing the conflict, ways that pause to accommodate both-and perspectives. Taken together, these texts evince striking features of life and death, hope and despair, safety and danger. It is in this context that the crossroads is a fitting figure of analysis for Haitian and Dominican epistemologies. Perhaps all these texts can do is help us imagine Hispaniola at the crossroads, if only as a way to wrestle with the history that meets at the border.

Notes

1. Interestingly, though the protagonist states that the river would be known as such "ever after" the massacre, it was given the name long before 1937. The name "Massacre River" originated during a seventeenth-century battle between the French and Spanish colonizers fighting for control of the island. According to the story, as the French

and Spanish fought on the banks of the river, the violence was so intense that the river seemed to run red with blood.

2. Almost three dozen scholarly articles have been devoted to analyzing *The Farming of Bones*. That and René Philoctète's *Le peuple des terres mêlées* (*Massacre River*) might be considered Ur-texts of the massacre.

3. The original French title *Le peuple des terres mêlées* goes much further in emphasizing this point than the English translation.

4. "They took kafou—crossroads—to mean the individual and community position of human beings at the conjunction of earth and sky, the secular mundane and the divine numinous, visible being and invisible existence before birth and after dying: a singularity of space and energy and time" (Benson 2013, 296–300).

5. "*Un nulle part intemporel, un espace-temps intermédiare, celui qui succède au départ et précède l'arrivée, celui qui sépare ce qui n'est plus et ce qui n'est pas encore. . . . C'est [un] entre-deux spatial et temporal, cet espace frontière entre Haiti et la République Dominicaine, entre passé et future.*"

Works Cited

Benson, LeGrace. 2013. "Review of *Haiti at the Crossroads*." *Journal of Haitian Studies* 19 (1): 296–300.

Bérard, Stéphanie. 2010. "Dramaturgie haitienne de l'exil: *Le bleu de l'île* d'Evelyne Trouillot." *Journal of Haitian Studies* 16 (1): 60–69.

Candelario, Ginetta E. B. 2016. "La ciguapa y el ciguapeo: Dominican Myth, Metaphor, and Method." *Small Axe* 20 (3): 100–112.

Chancy, Myriam. 2012. *From Sugar to Revolution: Women's Visions of Haiti, Cuba, and the Dominican Republic*. Waterloo, Ontario: Wilfrid Laurier University Press.

Dalembert, Louis-Philippe. 2005. *L'autre face de la mer*. Paris: La serpent à plumes.

Danticat, Edwidge. 1996. *Krik? Krak!* New York: Vintage.

———. 1998. *Breath, Eyes, Memory*. New York: Vintage.

———. 2008. "Preface." In René Philoctète, *Massacre River*, 7–10. New York: New Directions Press.

Derby, Lauren, and Richard Turits. 2006. "Temwayaj Kout Kouto, 1937. Eyewitnesses to Genocide." In *Revolutionary Freedoms. A History of Survival, Strength, and Imagination in Haiti*, edited by Cécile Accilien, Jessica Adams, and Elmide Méléance, 137–143. Coconut Creek, FL: Caribbean Studies Press.

Elliot, Andrew, Mark D. Fairchild, and Anna Franklin, eds. 2015. *Handbook of Color Psychology*. Cambridge: Oxford University Press.

Fumagalli, Maria Christina. 2015. *On the Edge: Writing the Border between Haiti and the Dominican Republic*. Liverpool: Liverpool University Press.

Gay, Roxane. 2011. *Ayiti*. New York: Artistically Declined Press.

Hintzen, Amelia 2014. "Historical Forgetting and the Dominican Constitutional Tribunal." *Journal of Haitian Studies* 20 (1): 108–116.

Martin, Todd W. 2007. "Looking for the Dawn in Edwidge Danticat's The Farming of Bones." *The Explicator* 65 (4): 248.

Matibag, Eugenio. 2003. *Haitian Dominican Counterpoint: Nation, State, and Race on Hispaniola.* New York: Palgrave.

Mayes, April, Yolanda Martín, Carlos Ulises Decena, Kiran Jayaram, and Yveline Alexis. 2013. "Transnational Hispaniola: Toward New Paradigms in Haitian and Dominican Studies." *Radical History Review* 115 (Winter): 26–32.

McCormick, Robert H. 2010. "Reconceiving Hispaniola: An Introduction." *Journal of Haitian Studies* 16 (1): 2–6.

———. 2012. "An Introduction to *The Blue of the Island* by Evelyne Trouillot." *Journal of Haitian Studies* 18 (2): 210–212.

Misrahi-Barak, Judith. 2013. "Exploring Trauma through the Memory of Text: Edwidge Danticat Listens to Jacques Stephen Alexis, Rita Dove, and René Philoctète." *Journal of Haitian Studies* 19 (1): 163–183.

Philoctète, René. 1989. *Le peuple des terres mêlées.* Port-au-Prince, Henri Deschamps.

Rivero, Daniel. 2015. "Junot Díaz and Edwidge Danticat Jointly Speak Out Against Dominican Republic Refugee Crisis." Splinter, June 25. http://fusion.net/story/156597/junot-diaz-and-edwidge-danticat-jointly-call-for-travel-boycott-of-the-dominican-republic/. Accessed October 15.

Shemak, April. 2002. "Re-Membering Hispaniola: Edwidge Danticat's *The Farming of Bones*." *MFS Modern Fiction Studies* 48 (1): 83–112.

Suarez, Lucia. 2006. *The Tears of Hispaniola: Haitian and Dominican Diaspora Memory.* Gainesville: University Press of Florida.

Tinsley, Omise'eke Natasha. 2008. "Black Atlantic, Queer Atlantic: Queer Imaginings of the Middle Passage." *GLQ: A Journal of Gay and Lesbian Studies* 14 (2–3): 191–215.

Trouillot, Évelyne. 2012. *Le bleu de l'île* (The Blue of the Island). Translated by Robert H. McCormick Jr. *Journal of Haitian Studies* 18 (2): 213–264.

Turits, Richard. 2002. "A World Destroyed, A Nation Imposed: The 1937 Haitian Massacre in the Dominican Republic." *Hispanic American Historical Review* 82 (3): 589–635.

Wucker, Michele. 1999. *Why the Cocks Fight: Dominicans, Haitians, and the Struggle for Hispaniola.* New York: Hill and Wang.

5

"The Tam-Tam of Drums from the West"

Shifting Representations of Haiti in the Later Work of Aída Cartagena Portalatín

ELIZABETH C. RUSS

Aída Cartagena Portalatín (1918–1994),[1] who has been lauded as the most influential Dominican woman writer of the twentieth century, is admired by critics who characterize her later work as defying traditional images of femininity and urgently repudiating social, political, and racial injustice. As Daisy Cocco de Filippis (1988) writes, "In the 1950s, Portalatín . . . begins to redefine the limits of the feminine world. The Dominican woman, until then relegated to the most hidden corners of the home, sets out to travel the world" (28).[2] Cocco de Filippis notes that Cartagena's later works—and their globe-trotting women—grapple with broad questions of political oppression and social justice: she "is among the poets who assume the obligation to be witnesses to the reality that surrounded them, and to defend the rights of those dispossessed by social 'justice'" (29).[3]

Néstor Rodríguez (2007) similarly argues that Cartagena's work from the mid-1950s onward "acquires a markedly iconoclastic tenor with respect to prevailing cultural norms" (107).[4] Beginning with the 1955 publication of her landmark poetry collection, *Una mujer está sola*, and accelerating after the 1961 assassination of Dominican dictator Rafael Trujillo, Cartagena produced a steady stream of politically charged publications that denounced sexism, racism, and imperialism; brought to light abuses of power; and demanded justice for oppressed groups around the world.[5] At the same time, she harnessed her transnational vision of the global fight against inequality and imperialist interventionism to foreground the past, present, and future struggles of her own nation, the Dominican Republic.

Given her commitment to justice, her denunciation of imperialism and racism, and her tendency to employ strategies of transnationalism to better understand her own homeland, it is surprising how infrequently Cartagena's imaginative gaze rests upon Haiti. Despite the geographical proximity and central role of Haiti and its people in both global anti-racist struggles and Dominican history, they would appear to be largely irrelevant to her examinations of racism, injustice, and the Dominican Republic. This is not to say that they are entirely absent. They do make fleeting appearances in works as varied as the experimental novel *Escalera para Electra* (1970), the "documentary poem" *Yania Tierra* (1981), and the essay collection *Culturas africanas: rebeldes con causa* (1986). But their representation fluctuates startlingly and in ways that are unmoored from chronology. For example, although *Yania Tierra* was published more than a decade after *Escalera para Electra*, its portrayal of Haitians relies on antagonistic stereotypes that the earlier text bluntly rejects. Cartagena's uneven depictions of her island neighbors are best understood as emerging from the complex relationship, in the Dominican context, between strategies of transnationalism and nationalist rhetoric.

As April Mayes observes in the introduction to this volume, the social and historical experience of transnationalism, far from being a new phenomenon, has long shaped the Caribbean. This experience has engendered strategic ways of knowing that Martinican poet and theoretician Édouard Glissant has called the Poetics of Relation. Relation seeks to uncover deep links between apparently separate entities in a way that does not collapse two into one but rather respects what is unknowable or opaque in each. In this sense, as Glissant writes, Relation preserves "the possibility for each one at every moment to be both solidary and solitary" (Glissant 1997, 131).

Much of Cartagena's corpus evinces a Poetics of Relation by employing strategies of representation that search for connection while respecting difference. Her wide-ranging explorations of the corroding effect of racism, for example, examine legacies of colonialism that are connected at the same time that they are unique. She writes with cultural and historical specificity about apartheid in South Africa, Jim Crow in the United States, and independence struggles in the Congo (Cartagena 1970; Cartagena 2000; [Cartegena] 1962a, 1962b). Above all, she respects the opacity of Relation—that is, the idea that connection as well as difference can be recognized and respected—by insisting upon her own local reality through a fierce defense of Dominican sovereignty and cultural autonomy that informs almost all of her post-1961 publications. Yet there are times when this defense grows impatient with the delicate and complex entanglements of Relation and instead veers into the harsh exclusionary rhetoric that is so characteristic of nationalist discourses around the world.

As we shall see, this impatience manifests itself most clearly at the moments when her work touches upon Haiti, the nation that since the nineteenth century has been posited as the antithesis of the Dominican Republic in the nationalist discourse promoted by Dominican political and intellectual elites. According to this discourse, Haitians are African-descended, black-skinned, Kreyòl-speaking Vodou practitioners, while Dominicans are European-descended, light-skinned, Spanish-speaking Catholics. As a result, as historian Pedro San Miguel (2005) succinctly states, "The definition of 'Dominican' became 'not Haitian'" (39). Within this rhetoric, Haiti and its people are defined as perpetual threats, whether through military conquest or a slow but steady invasion of migrants fleeing poverty and political instability. This anti-Haitian sentiment has roots in historical events, most notably Haiti's 22-year occupation (1822–1844) of what is now the Dominican Republic. Yet the ruthless dichotomy of Dominican anti-Haitianness simplifies a complex past, exaggerates differences, and suppresses moments of confluence and cooperation.

Silvio Torres-Saillant (1994) affirms that one consequence of "an ideological system that construes the two people sharing the island as insurmountably dichotomous" is the creation of "an equation whereby anti-Haitianism becomes a form of Dominican patriotism" (54–55). Those who suggest links—or, more audaciously, Relation—between Haiti and the Dominican Republic thus run the risk of being accused of disloyalty, if not treason. This might explain why Cartagena, like most other Dominican writers, more often than not averts her writerly gaze from Haiti. It also helps us understand the inconsistencies that appear when she does consider her western neighbor. For example, throughout her oeuvre, one can trace a relationship between a text's register of nationalism and its representation of Haiti and its people. The more a text depends on territorial or "patriotic" notions of the nation—the more it engages the dominant nationalist discourse the Dominican elite cultivate—the more stereotypical and negative the representation. Conversely, the more a text emphasizes the possibilities of transnationalism, whether by urging solidarity against hostile outside forces or by recognizing a shared history, the more nuanced its portrayals of Haiti and Haitians become.

Cartagena's 1970 novel *Escalera para Electra*, for example, is highly critical of both Dominican politicians and U.S. interventionist politics, but is not built upon reflexive patriotic nationalism. Instead it employs a transnational, relational gaze to generate a critical testimony about the Dominican Republic's traumatic past. The novel's narrator, a writer named Helene (who bears a not-coincidental resemblance to Cartagena), realizes that she can carry out her testimonial project only while traveling through Greece:

> [A] la distancia, creo que es mucho más fácil que lo que ha sido visto y registrado pueda salir mejor de su propia objetividad. Debí interca- lar la palabra perspectiva. Además, en Dominicana esas tragedias se esconden, se guardan como un tótem maldito encerrado en silencio. (1970, 6)

> From a distance, I think it is much easier for what has been seen and recorded to manifest itself in an objective light. I should insert the word perspective. Besides, in Dominicana those tragedies are hid- den, stored away like a damned totem buried in silence.

As a traveler, Helene uses a literal transnationality to create geographi- cal and psychological distance from her homeland. In various passages in the novel, she describes the anti-imperialist and anti-racist struggles of other countries, such as Iran and South Africa. She consistently uses these strategies of transnationalism to redirect the conversation to the Domini- can context and break the silence surrounding the "damned totems" of her homeland's traumatic past.

Throughout *Escalera para Electra*, Cartagena confronts a long history of Dominican leaders who exploit their people and people who blindly embrace their leaders or die while attempting to oppose them. She also bluntly decries the constant, corroding influence of the United States (Russ 2009, 2014). Amid this litany of lamentations and condemnations, however, one totem remains almost entirely shrouded in silence. It is not until the novel's twenty-second chapter that the complex history Haiti and the Dominican Republic share emerges, fleetingly and incompletely, in a brief flashback to Helene's childhood.

The scene depicts an encounter between a young Helene and two servants who work for her family, Tila and Agliberto. It begins when Helene overhears Agliberto talking to Tila about the exploited Haitians laboring in nearby *bateyes*, or sugarcane fields. Expressing his amazement at the laborers' ability to save their meager wages, which he claims they bury in the ground, he describes them as *tragones de hombrecitos*, literally "gluttons for" or "guzzlers of" little men. Agliberto continues:

> *Son unos negros que tienen mucha fuerza. Cortan cada día varios cordeles de caña. El tiempo que les queda lo pasan en riñas, averiguaciones, asaderas de batatas y de hombrecitos; casi siempre terminan a medianoche con una fiesta de brujería: un baile vudú.* (1970, 90)

> They are strong black people. Every day they cut several cords of sugar cane. They spend their free time in arguments and interrogations, and in barbequing sweet potatoes and little men (*hombrecitos*); they almost always finish up at midnight with a celebration of witchcraft: a Vodou dance.

Conveying admiration as well as disgust, the old servant's speech subtly incorporates elements of Dominican anti-Haitian rhetoric. For example, he emphasizes the workers' race (they are "strong black people") and religion ("a Vodou dance") and alludes to their linguistic difference by describing their speaking activities (arguments and interrogations). But it is his evocation of cannibalism that most powerfully conjures the Haitians' "otherness" and most violently disturbs the imagination of the child Helene, who pictures elaborate rituals in which primitive savages gorge themselves on tiny men:

> *Son raros esos haitianos. Mi imaginación se dilata aun más: pienso en enanos, también en hombres normales de estatura muy pequeña: tragados: digeridos: defecados por haitianos.* (1970, 90)

> Those Haitians are strange. My imagination goes even wilder: I think of dwarves, as well as of very small normal men: swallowed: digested: defecated by Haitians.

Far from remarkable, the representation of Haitians as cannibals is a common feature of Dominican anti-Haitian imagery, as the well-known Dominican writer Marcio Veloz Maggiolo (1977) notes in "Typology of the Haitian Theme in Dominican Literature," where he writes that among "the world of inventions inherited by Dominicans about Haitians" is the notion that "Haitians 'still' eat people" (105).[6] When the frightened girl voices her horror, Tila hastens to inform her that the *hombrecitos* of which the old man speaks are not little men but rather a local word for herring.

On the one hand, this passage uses macabre humor to filter anti-Haitian stereotypes through the innocence of childhood and the linguistic ambiguity of the word *hombrecitos*. On the other hand, the vivid image of Haitians devouring, digesting, and defecating their human victims remains imprinted in the minds of the narrator and the reader. The intentionality with which Cartagena invokes and critiques culturally ingrained stereotypes of Haitians is reinforced when her narrator proclaims, "*Lo que hacían con los haitianos, se llamaba: explotación del hombre por el hombre*" ("What they did with the Haitians was called: the exploitation of man by man") (1970, 91). Although the sentence lays blame on an imprecise "they"—which could refer to the Dominican government or the U.S. government, to companies or individuals who profited from the sugarcane industry, or to society as a whole—it openly condemns the abuse of Haitian labor in the Dominican Republic. As such, it stands as the novel's most direct criticism of Dominican anti-Haitianism.

A few paragraphs later, the novel underscores this critique when it describes Helene's laughter the following morning at the fear that Agliberto's comments provoked. The youthful version of the narrator muses:

> *Era simpático aquello que llegó a asustarme: lo de las gentes que comían hombrecitos. Era imposible valorar aquello entonces. Eso de ser machetero.* (1970, 91)

> It was funny that that scared me, that thing about the people who ate *hombrecitos*. It was impossible then to give that any credit. That thing about being a *machetero*.

If the earlier passage points to an ill-defined "they," this passage exaggerates the effect by relying on a series of imprecise referents for the word "that" such as *aquello, lo de*, and *eso de*. The final word, *machetero*, simultaneously reinforces and undercuts this imprecision. Often used as a generic term to describe those who cut sugarcane, *machetero*—literally, "machete wielder"—refers, most simply, to the Haitians Agliberto has described who use machetes to cut cane in the *bateyes*. But within the Dominican context, *machetero* is never a simple word. Charged with historical and symbolic meaning, it evokes the violent history of slavery in the Caribbean, where sugar was king. The machete, a ubiquitous tool in the sugar-growing islands of the Caribbean, was also used as a weapon in numerous slave uprisings. In this context, the word *machetero* might also serve as a reminder of the Haitian Revolution. More specifically, it might recall one of the revolution's leaders, Jean-Jacques Dessalines, and his oft-cited war cry, "*Koupe tet, boule kay*" (Cut off the heads, burn the houses). While the brash Dessalines is a hero for Haitians, he is a villain for many Dominicans because he led Haiti's invasion of the eastern half of the island in 1804–1805. Although it was relatively short lived, this incursion resulted in hundreds of deaths and the destruction of many settlements, including Cartagena's hometown of Moca, whose entire population was slaughtered.[7]

The multivalent word *machetero* also gestures obliquely toward the most taboo of the "damned totems" of Dominican-Haitian relations: the 1937 massacre, when Trujillo ordered Dominican soldiers to use machetes instead of firearms to slaughter thousands of Haitians along the northern section of the border. In 1937, Dominicans became the *macheteros* and thousands of Haitian peasants became their victims.[8] The resulting slaughter not only acted as a defining moment in Haitian-Dominican relations, it also helped harden the official discourse of anti-Haitianism during Trujillo's long rule. By using an exaggeratedly imprecise syntax, Cartagena unmoors the word *machetero* from any specific context, which allows her to critique the treatment of Haitian workers in the *bateyes*, decry the lasting legacies of African slavery and European colonization, and obliquely recognize the deep wounds Haiti and the Dominican Republic have inflicted upon each other at different moments in history.

Even though *machetero* generates the possibility (among others) of reading the 1937 massacre into her narrative, Cartagena ultimately bends to Dominican cultural mores that view the shameful event as a taboo topic and does not name it directly (Russ 2009, 134–135). Even so, her willingness in 1970 to broach the topic, however indirectly, can be seen as an act of courage. It is therefore surprising that, eleven years later, she seems to embrace aspects of the anti-Haitianism that she rejects in *Escalera para Electra*. A longform poem, *Yania Tierra*, narrates Dominican history from 1492 to 1981, the year when it was published. While recounting the successive invasions and occupations of Santo Domingo by outside powers, the poem celebrates the heroic deeds of patriotic women who helped defend their embattled pueblo. As Mariana Past (2011) has noted, Cartagena "represents an alternative genealogy of Dominican history; a roll-call of politically-active mothers, grandmothers, daughters and sisters who formed their own revolutionary networks alongside the country's male heroes and leaders." In this sense, *Yania Tierra* can be identified as a counterhegemonic text. Yet within its pages, as Past notes, Cartagena "echoes dominant national discourse with respect to Haiti" that "complicates her position as a strong subaltern voice" (87, 91).

More specifically, *Yania Tierra* describes the Haitian occupations of 1801, 1804–1805, and, especially, 1822–1844, as patriotic struggles for territorial autonomy. Most of the section devoted to these events celebrates the galvanizing activities of female patriots in the period leading to the 1844 declaration of independence from Haiti. The first four stanzas, however, make direct reference to Haiti and the Haitian invaders, beginning with the following:

AÑOS de Boyer / Hera[r]d / Borgellá y Carri[é]
Deshechos de deshechos
Horizonte negado a la esperanza
Tam-tam tambores de Occidente (1981, 37)

YEARS of Boyer / Herard / Borgellá and Carrié
Scum of the scum
A horizon without hope
The tam-tam of drums from the West (1995, 85)

This section opens in the style of an epic with a catalog of the presidents and governors who ruled over the unified island from 1822 to 1844. By concluding with the ominous line, "The tam-tam of drums from the West," which emphasizes the beat of the drums so crucial to Haitian ritual and history, Cartagena represents the "West"—that is, the western part of the island—as a threatening Other. Toward the end of *Yania Tierra*, the drum acquires a positive value when it is linked to the patriotism of the Mirabal sisters, anti-Trujillo activists who were murdered by the dictator's henchmen in November 1960:

Las tres amaban la Patria
el tambor / la libertad (1981, 73)

The three loved their Nation
the drum / freedom (1995, 155)

Five years later, in *Culturas africanas: rebeldes con causa*, Cartagena again asserts her admiration for the drum when she praises the dramatic effect of the drum's beat in the writings of the Senegalese poet and politician Léopold Sédar Senghor:

> *Por eso los conjuros del "tam-tam escondido" y del "tam-tam lejano"*
> *se repiten con insistentes modulaciones y pueblan de mágicas resonan-*
> *cias la atmósfera de sus cantos.* (1986, 31)

Thus the incantations of the "hidden tam-tam" and the "faraway tam-tam" are repeated with insistent modulations and fill the atmosphere of his songs with magical reverberations.

Here, the tam-tam of the drum soulfully expresses the humanity of Senegal and its people. In *Yania Tierra*, in contrast, it serves as a menacing image of the violation of national autonomy inflicted on a proto–Dominican Republic agonizing "*al caótico golpe de Occidente*" (1981, 45), or "under the chaotic blow from the West" (1995, 101).

The second and third stanzas of this section configure Haiti's acts of violation in real, not just symbolic, terms:

Sube el llanto de Dominga de los
Núñez de Cáceres
De Francisca Hurtado / inmolada
La misma suerte imponen a Gregoria
                Ceferina y
                Felipa las hijas de
                Medina

EN Galindo
        Agueda
        Anita y
        Marcelina Andújar

Vírgenes profanadas
Violadas por la insania
Asesinadas
Oh / repudio total (1981, 37–38)

The [weeping] rise[s] from Dominga de los
Núñez de Cáceres
From Francisca Hurtado / slaughtered
They order the same fate for Gregoria
                              Ceferina and
                              Felipa daughters of
                              Medina

IN Galindo
        Agueda
        Anita and
        Marcelina Andújar
        [Profaned] virgins
        Raped by madness
        Murdered
        Oh / total [repudiation] (1995, 85, 87)

As words like "weeping," "slaughtered," "profaned," "raped," and "murdered" suggest, these lines commemorate Dominican women victimized by violent Haitian oppressors. Although Cartagena reveals only their names and a few descriptive words, they are all real women associated in historical and literary texts with offenses committed by or attributed to Haitian men. The first, Dominga Núñez,[9] was allegedly present in Santo Domingo's Plaza de Armas on January 26, 1801, when the great leader of the Haitian Revolution, Toussaint Louverture, began his brief occupation of the Spanish capital by declaring the abolition of slavery. In 1899, the Dominican poet Gastón F. Deligne published "La intervención, 1801," to commemorate the events of that day. The poem culminates in a confrontation between the "brave Dominga Núñez" and "Toussaint, the invader." When the latter dares to touch the former with his cane—to violate her with his symbolic phallus—she responds: "Insolent man! For Spanish women, learn other manners!" (Deligne 1963, 166).[10] According to Deligne's poem, the fair protagonist eludes the "mad fury" (*furia loca*) of the Haitian thanks to a miraculous intercession by the Virgen de las Mercedes.

The Dominican intellectual Ramón Marrero Aristy tells a similar story, minus the miracle, in his history of the "oldest Christian nation of the Americas": "the usurper went along inconsiderately touching each lady with the tip of his cane, asking them in poor Spanish if they were French or Spanish. Confronted with such behavior, Doña Dominga Núñez—a young lady from the capital's best society—rebelled, protesting against such brusque manners" (Marrero Aristy 1957, 202).[11] By naming Dominga Núnez, Cartagena invokes the tradition Deligne and Marrero Aristy had established. Somewhat startlingly, however, she reduces Núñez's act of rebellion to the sound of weeping (*"Sube el llanto de Dominga de los Núñez de Cáceres"*). In a poem full of praise for brave female patriots, this is a strange move. Instead of highlighting the well-bred young woman's foolhardy bravery, she underscores her helplessness. In doing so, she ties Núñez's fate to those of the other victims named in these stanzas. Francisca Hurtado and the three daughters of Medina (Gregoria, Ceferina, and Felipa), for example, died in the notorious massacre and conflagration of the village of Moca, which occurred as Haitian troops withdrew in 1805 from the eastern portion of the island following their brief occupation.[12] Seventeen years later, the Andújar sisters (Agueda, Anita, and Marcelina) were murdered, raped, and dismembered during the first weeks of the 1822 Haitian invasion, supposedly by Haitian soldiers.

In her important study *Modernity Disavowed*, Sibylle Fischer argues that nineteenth-century Dominican literary representations of the Haitian occupations of 1801, 1804–1805, and 1822–1844 become progressively more lurid: "As the century unfolds, anti-Haitian writings seem to be driven by increasingly bizarre fantasies about the unfathomable perversity of the Haitian project. By the end of the nineteenth century . . . Haitian desire has become identified with deviant sexuality, the desecration of everything holy, and superstitious dreams of absolute control" (Fischer 2004, 171). By invoking women who were threatened, raped, and killed by Haitian men, Cartagena embroils her poem in this tradition, especially since the story of the Andújar sisters, the so-called virgins of Galindo, is one of the most enduring narratives to emerge from it. The sisters are the protagonists of Félix María Del Monte's 1860 poem "The Virgins of Galindo."[13] Later they were immortalized in the national canon as the doomed heroines of the culminating tale in César Nicolás Penson's perennial best seller, *Cosas añejas*. Although Del Monte's and Penson's versions of the story differ in significant ways, like Cartagena, both authors attribute the brutal murders and post-mortem rapes of the Galindo sisters to soldiers from the occupying Haitian army. The historical archive, however, indicates that the culprits were actually Dominicans.[14] Nevertheless, in popular memory, as in *Yania Tierra*, this lurid crime symbolizes "the unfathomable perversity of the Haitian project."

As we have seen, Cartagena commences the portion of *Yania Tierra* under examination by announcing the "years of Boyer / Herard / Borgellá and Carrié"—that is to say, the years of the Haitian occupation of 1822–1844. Yet only the murder of the Andújar sisters took place during those years, and only in the early days. The other events—Louverture's fleeting occupation of Santo Domingo and the massacre at Moca—occurred during the 1801 and 1804–1805 occupations, respectively. Such chronological imprecision underscores Cartagena's intention of calling to mind emblematic moments that capture the traumatic nature of the Haitian occupations. Participating in a nationalist discourse that represents Haiti as an existential threat, she omits detailed descriptions of the acts of violence inflicted upon the women she names because such detail is unnecessary. The mere evocation of Toussaint's arrival to Santo Domingo, the obliteration of an entire village in the Moca massacre, or the virgins of Galindo would inevitably awaken the indignation of the prototypical Dominican reader. By making use of a historical and literary tradition that represents Haiti as a place of murderous madness, Cartagena draws on an anti-Haitian discourse that requires the "total repudiation" of the neighbor to the west in order to ensure the survival of the homeland. It is not surprising, then, that the women Cartagena identifies in the Haiti passages of *Yania Tierra* are passive victims rather than active patriots. Indeed, with the exception of the weeping Dominga Núñez, they are mutilated, desecrated bodies.

How, then, do we interpret the fact that Cartagena condemns anti-Haitianism in *Escalera para Electra* but uses it in *Yania Tierra*? It is worth emphasizing that both works share the ethical and political framework associated with the author's post-1961 production: they celebrate strong, active women (except for the victims of the Haitian invaders); condemn imperialist power; and denounce institutionalized racism. Moreover,

Cartagena's commitment to anti-racist discourse remains unwavering in *Yania Tierra*. The poem's final words explicitly unite Dominican women of all races in the project of peaceful nation building:

> *INDIAS / NEGRAS / BLANCAS / MESTIZAS/*
> *MULATAS / . . .*
> > *¡Soltad los pájaros de la esperanza!*
> > ¡Ea! ¡Mujeres!
> > ¡Soltad palomas! (1981, 82)

> INDIAN WOMEN / BLACK WOMEN / WHITE WOMEN /
> MESTIZA WOMEN / MULATTA WOMEN . . .
> > Release the birds of hope!
> > Come on! Women!
> > Release the doves! (1995, 173)

Moreover, despite its reliance on aspects of anti-Haitian thought, the poem never links Haitian aggression to blackness. On the contrary, it likens Haitians, with their imperialistic hubris, to their counterparts in Spain, France, and the United States. For example, the phrase "scum of the scum," used to describe the "years of Boyer / Herard / Borgellá y Carrié," first appears three stanzas earlier to denounce both the Spanish conquistadors for their annihilation of Hispaniola's indigenous population and Napoleon for his attempts to take control of the island (Cartagena 1981, 35; Cartagena 1995, 80). In this sense, *Yania Tierra* suggests that Haiti is just another imperialist power, another incarnation of the "West."

Cartagena's conflation of Haiti with (other) Western powers emphasizes one aspect of Haitian history (its military and political encroachments on proto-Dominican territory) over many others (its revolutionary struggle against French imperialism; its commitment to racial equality, including its proclamation of the abolition of slavery in the Dominican Republic; its economic suffering at the hands of European and American powers). Such flattening out of Haitian history is the result of a key difference between *Yania Tierra* and *Escalera para Electra*: their respective strategies for approaching the Dominican nation. Helene, who narrates *Escalera para Electra* while traveling through Greece, takes advantage of her geographical and psychological distance from home to develop a perspective deeply embedded in transnational notions of Relation. As a result, her narration acquires an ironic and critical tone that permits her to exhume, at least partially, the "damned totem" of anti-Haitianism. *Yania Tierra* also reflects upon tragic historical episodes. Its primary goal, however, is to celebrate women who participated in the struggle for national autonomy. It is, simply put, a patriotic poem, and as we have seen, the Manichean nature of Dominican nationalist discourse generates "an equation whereby anti-Haitianism becomes a form of Dominican patriotism" (Torres-Saillant 1994, 54–55). Furthermore, in contrast to *Escalera para Electra*, in *Yania Tierra* there is no geographical or intellectual distance between the narration and the nation. On the contrary, the poem's titular character, Yania, is literally an incarnation of the island of Hispaniola. To confuse matters further, she embodies not just the island but also the Dominican nation (Past 2011; Morris 2006). Thus the poem fuses (or confuses) the protagonist with the island and the island with the territory of the Dominican Republic. By erasing the distance between narration and nation, *Yania Tierra* reduces Haiti to the role of an imperialist invader who has no "natural right" to the land.

In contrast, in *Culturas africanas: rebeldes con causa* (1986), Haiti emerges as an autonomous nation worthy of respect and even emulation. *Culturas africanas* is a collection of loosely connected essays that mix personal memories and literary history with commentaries about a variety of cultural actors from Africa and the African diaspora. Among its twenty or so chapters, three are dedicated to Haiti and Haitian cultural production. These praise the high quality of Haitian literature and underscore Haiti's role in the development of important literary movements, including négritude and the "boom" in Latin American literature. They also hold up as exemplary Haiti's long tradition of honoring its African roots. While effusive and sincere, Cartagena's musings in these chapters hardly break new ground. In some cases, she offers basic information on writers such as Jacques Roumain, René Depestre, Jean Price-Mars, and Stephen Alexis (Cartagena 1986, 70–87); in others, she simply (in both senses of the word) repeats worn ideas about the region's "magical" or "mythical" nature (93–95).[15] Nevertheless, she strongly affirms Haiti's historical integrity and national autonomy:

> *Después de la Revolución Haitiana de 1804, le corresponde al negro de ese país buscar la raíz de su identidad por el hecho de una toma de conciencia de la situación histórica en que vive. Libre, explora la verdad de su identidad.* (Cartagena 1986, 75, my emphasis)

After the Haitian Revolution of 1804, it fell to the black man of that country *to search for the root of his identity* as a result of his becoming aware of the historical situation in which he lived. Free, *he explored the truth of his identity.*

This affirmation rejects the negation of Haiti inscribed in *Yania Tierra*, but it is complicated by the final sections of *Culturas africanas*, in which Cartagena looks once more upon her own homeland, momentarily retreating to old stereotypes even as she explores the shared history of Hispaniola's sister nations.

The penultimate chapter of *Culturas africanas* does not directly reference this shared history. Instead, it embraces Glissant's Poetics of Relation by arguing that all the nations of the Americas should throw off the yoke of imperialism and embrace their multifarious origins in order to better understand not only their cultural roots but also their common suffering. It does this through a layering of narratives anchored by the story of Teodora and Micaela Ginés, sisters born into slavery in sixteenth-century Spanish Hispaniola who won their freedom and moved to Cuba, where they became recognized musicians.[16] Reclaiming these black women and freed slaves as Dominican compatriots, Cartagena uses their life stories and musical accomplishments to generate links between her homeland and a pan-Caribbean Africanist tradition. The first paragraphs of the chapter connect this New World tradition directly to the twentieth-century African continent and, I would argue, indirectly to nineteenth-century Haiti:

Ya son muchos los pueblos liberados en África, pueblos racialmente discriminados y explotados en el corazón de sus propias riquezas. Pero aquellos pueblos ofrecen lecciones a los de América. Se han superado porque están conscientes de su identidad, *de su capacidad y de la explotación de que han sido víctimas.*
Busquemos nuestras raíces. *Los pueblos de las ínsulas extrañas somos pueblos mestizos y mulatos.* Busquemos nuestras raíces. *No hay color sino hombres sobre la tierra. Por ello, siempre que puedo, recuerdo a las dos negras esclavas y libertas dominicanas. . . . Y se nos ocurre algo exacto: las Ginés de Santiago de los Caballeros, esclavas y músicas, también rompieron barreras.* (Cartagena 1986, 124, my emphasis)

There are already many liberated peoples in Africa, peoples who have been racially discriminated against and exploited in the heart of their own riches. But these peoples offer lessons to those of America. *They have overcome because they are conscious of their identity*, of their capacity, and of the exploitation of which they have been victims.

Let us search for our roots. We, the peoples of the strange isles, are mestizos and mulattos. *Let us search for our roots*. The earth is not populated by color, but by men. For this reason, whenever I can, I remember those two black women, slaves and free Dominicans. . . . And something precise occurs to us: the Ginés sisters of Santiago de los Caballeros, slaves and musicians, also broke barriers.

The first paragraph of this passage focuses on twentieth-century African independence movements but uses phrases almost identical to those that, in the earlier essay cited above, describe Haitians just after their nineteenth-century revolution: Haitians, upon "becoming aware of the historical situation in which [they] lived . . . explored the truth of [their] identity"; Africans "have overcome because they are conscious of their identity." While this replication of language links Haiti to Africa, the next paragraph connects both of these places to all "the peoples of the strange isles"—including Dominicans—whom Cartagena exhorts to seek freedom through self-knowledge, which comes through embracing their mestizo and mulatto roots. The resonances of this essay with the earlier one on Haiti are deeply suggestive of Cartagena's desire to generate what we might call a pan-American and pan-African Poetics of Relation. At the same time, with its insistence on the groundbreaking nature of "those two black women, slaves and free Dominicans," this piece also serves as a fine (and feminist) contribution to what Raj Chetty, in his chapter in this volume, calls "an alternative, Dominican-centric genealogy of black-affirming literary art and criticism."

The final essay in *Culturas africanas* turns to an episode of shared Hispaniola history, recounting the time when free black men and women from the United States moved to the Samaná peninsula on the northeastern coast of the island at the invitation of the Haitian government during its 1822–1844 occupation.[17] Embedded in this history is an unspoken acknowledgement that people of African descent from across the

Americas—including the United States—could be free in the Dominican Republic because Haiti had abolished slavery on the island. Yet rather than highlight this historical fact, Cartagena emphasizes that the new immigrants quickly distanced themselves from Haitian culture in order to draw closer "*a los españoles, a las costumbres superiores, integrándose a la vida nacional*" ("to the Spaniards, to the superior customs, integrating themselves with the national life") (1986, 140). Here, Cartagena seems to endorse the nationalist notion that the Dominican Republic represents a "Spanish" civilization that is inherently superior to the African-influenced Haitian culture. Two pages later, however, she explains Haiti's apparent inferiority in economic and political terms:

> *Estaban los gobernantes occidentales comprometidos con potencias europeas para servirles, en grandes cantidades, cacao, café, maíz, algodón, etc.* (1986, 142)

> The occidental [i.e., Haitian] rulers were compromised by their involvement with European powers, whom they supplied with great quantities of cocoa, coffee, corn, cotton, etc.

In this account, Haiti's deficiencies derived not from any natural cultural inferiority but rather from an unnatural economic dependence on Europe. In *Yania Tierra*, then, Cartagena equates the Haitian invasions of Spanish Hispaniola with the imperialism of Spain, France, and the United States. In *Culturas africanas*, she suggests that the Haitian leaders failed their people by capitulating to the imperialist agendas of other, more powerful, nations. In both cases, her critiques of Haiti are not racist. They are anti-imperialist.

The vision of the nation Cartagena promoted in *Culturas africanas* differs from that in both *Escalera para Electra* and *Yania Tierra*. *Escalera para Electra* presents imperialism as a problem nations around the world share. Over the course of the novel, however, its narrator favors the history of the Dominican Republic above all others. *Yania Tierra* focuses exclusively on the Dominican Republic, which it conflates with the island of Hispaniola and represents as a territory violated by external powers and defended by patriotic men and women. *Culturas africanas* strives to engage the nation writ large in terms of transnationalism and Relation. Cartagena does not diminish the importance of the nation-state in *Culturas africanas*; on the contrary, she speaks with great emotion about African, Haitian,

and Dominican struggles for political autonomy. However, she no longer insistently privileges her homeland. Although she concludes with two
essays dedicated to her country, she also narrates the histories of black
people from Haiti, the United States, Cuba, South Africa, and Senegal,
among other nations. What is more, she insists on the importance of both
transnational solidarity and of the multiple "roots" that nourish the mulatto and mestizo peoples of "the strange isles." By defining culture and
identity in terms of multiplicity, entanglement, and Relation, Cartagena
rejects the false patriotism of anti-Haitianism and presents a more complex vision, both of her own people and of her neighbors to the west.

Given the potential for violence that lurks behind the mandate to be
Dominican by not being Haitian, it is unsurprising that at least until quite
recently, Dominican writers tended either to embrace the anti-Haitian
narrative or, as in the case of Cartagena, to avoid the topic of Haiti as
much as possible. Such avoidance has resulted in a vast and unknowable
loss, since a writer such as Cartagena could have contributed to a rich debate about Dominican-Haitian relations had she engaged the topic with a
depth and vigor that is absent from the oblique allusions I have analyzed
in these pages. Yet despite their insufficiency, her references to Haiti reveal how an artist and intellectual who rejects racist ideology and affirms
Dominican blackness might engage the "damned totem" of Dominican
anti-Haitianism in order to assert a counterdiscourse rooted in complexity, contradiction, and Relation.

Notes

1. A different version of this article was published in *Revista Estudios Sociales* (Santo
Domingo), 41, no. 151 (2009) under the title "La representación cambiante de Haití en
tres obras tardías de Aída Cartagena Portalatín." In the present version, except in the
case of *Yania Tierra*, where I have used an existing translation, all translations from the
Spanish to the English are mine.

2. "*En la década de los cincuenta, Portalatín . . . comienza a redefinir los límites del
mundo femenino. La mujer dominicana hasta entonces relegada a los más recónditos
rincones del hogar, emprende el camino y recorre el mundo.*"

3. "*Cartagena Portalatín se coloca . . . entre los poetas que asumen la obligación de ser
testigos de la realidad que los circunda y de defender los derechos de los desheredados por
la 'justicia' social.*"

4. "*adquiere un marcado cariz iconoclasta con respecto a la norma cultural vigente.*"

5. Focusing on Cartagena's literary writings, Cocco de Filippis (1988) identifies *La
tierra escrita* (1967) as the beginning of this overtly political phase. Taking her publishing

activities into account, I would suggest an earlier date, starting immediately after the assassination of Trujillo. From December 1961 to March 1963, Cartagena published *Brigadas Dominicanas*, a journal of testimonial and politically oriented literature. During that time, she also created Colección Baluarte, an apparently self-published series of books, under the imprint Ediciones Brigadas Dominicanas, that featured political poetry and prose. *La tierra escrita* was published as part of this series. Earlier titles included the first Dominican-produced edition of Pedro Mir's *There Is a Country in the World* [*Hay un país en el mundo*] and Hilma Contreras's *Stories from the Underground* (*Cuentos de la Clandestinidad*). For an analysis of the legacy of *Brigadas Dominicanas*, see Russ (2016).

6. The title in Spanish is "Tipología del Tema Dominicano en la Literatura Dominicana." "*Los haitianos 'todavía' comen gente*" is the first of six notions the author described as constituting "*todo el mundo de invenciones que acerca del haitiano hereda el dominicano*." The notion of Haitians as cannibals can also be linked to the historically documented frenzy surrounding the figure of the *comegente*, or people-eater, a serial killer who was said to have operated in the Dominican countryside in the late eighteenth century. For a careful analysis of these events, see González (2004).

7. Spain had ceded its half of Hispaniola to French control at this time. Frank Moya Pons (1998) observes that "the Haitian invasion was a direct response to [the French governor] Ferrand's proclamation on January 6, 1805[,] that authorized armed incursions into Haiti for the purpose of hunting black children less than 14 years old to be sold as slaves in the colony and abroad" (111).

8. As Richard Turits (2002) notes, machetes were used instead of guns for strategic purposes: "Trujillo sought to simulate a popular conflict, or at least to maintain some measure of plausible deniability of the state's perpetration of this genocide. The lack of gunfire was consistent with civilian rather than military violence. It also reduced noise that would have alerted more Haitians and propelled them to flee" (615).

9. More than once, the names Cartagena invokes seem to be corruptions of those found in historical documents. For example, "Dominga de los Núñez de Cáceres" appears in Marrero Aristy and Deligne as "Dominga Núñez." Similarly, "Gregoria," "Ceferina," and "Felipa" appear as "Gregoria," "Zeferina," and "Florentina," in chapter fifteen of Gaspar de Arredondo y Pichardo, "Historia de mi salida de la isla de Santo Domingo el 28 de Abril de 1805" (reprinted in Rodríguez Demorizi 1955).

10. "—*Insolente!, / . . .—para españolas, / otros modales aprende . . . !*"

11. "*el usurpador iba tocando desconsideradamente a cada señora con la punta de su bastón, preguntándoles en mal español, si eran francesas o españolas, ante lo cual se rebeló doña Dominga Núñez, señorita de la mejor sociedad de la capital, protestando contra tan bruscos modales.*"

12. They are named in the only eyewitness account of the events in Moca, written in 1814 by Gaspar de Arredondo y Pichardo, one of the massacre's few survivors. See chapter 15.

13. The full title of the poem in Spanish is "Las vírgenes de Galindo, o la Invasión de los haitianos sobre la parte española de la isla de Santo Domingo el 9 de febrero de 1822."

14. Archival documents that record the court cases and the convictions of Dominicans are found among the "Sentencias penales de la época de la dominación haitiana,"

published in the following issues of the *Boletín del Archivo General de la Nación*: 79 (October–December 1953): 329–353; 80 (January–March 1954): 24–46; 81 (April–June 1954): 219–230; 82 (July–September 1954): 327–337; 83 (October–December 1954): 400–408; 84 (January–March 1955): 66–79; 85 (April–June 1955): 157–165; 86 (July–September 1955): 275–292; 87 (October–December 1955): 388–399. Many thanks to Quisqueya Lora for providing me with these citations.

15. Although Cartagena writes about Haiti's magical qualities in positive tones, as Veloz Maggiolo points out, the association of Haiti with magic is part of "the world of inventions" Dominicans inherited about Haitians, which includes beliefs about Haitians having supernatural powers (1977, 105–106). For a nuanced study of Dominican views on Haitians and magic, see Derby (1994).

16. Teodora Ginés composed the "Son de la Ma' Teodora," an early example of the Cuban son. Cartagena briefly recounts the story of the Ginés sisters in *Yania Tierra* (Cartagena 1981, 30–31; Cartagena 1995, 70, 72).

17. In this essay, Cartagena quotes extensively from investigations done in the 1980s by ethnomusicologist Martha Ellen Davis.

Works Cited

Arredondo y Pichardo, Gaspar de. 1955. "Historia de mi salida de la isla de Santo Domingo el 28 de abril de 1805." In *Invasiones haitianas de 1801, 1805 y 1822*, edited by Emilio Rodríguez Demorizi, 121–160. Ciudad Trujillo: Editora del Caribe.

[Cartagena Portalatín, Aída]. 1962a. "Huéspedes de Brigada." *Brigadas Dominícanas* 9 (October/November/December): 9–11.

———. 1962b. "Ventana al exterior." *Brigadas Dominícanas* 9 (October/November/December): 31–32.

Cartagena Portalatín, Aída. 1970. *Escalera para Electra*. Santo Domingo: Brigadas Universitarias.

———. 1981. *Yania Tierra: poema documento*. Santo Domingo: Colección Montesinos.

———. 1986. *Culturas africanas: rebeldes con causa*. Santo Domingo: Ediciones de la Biblioteca Nacional.

———. 1995. *Yania Tierra: A Documentary Poem*. Translated by M. J. Fenwick and Rosabelle White. Washington, DC: Azul Editions.

———. 2000. *Obra poética completa (1944–1984)*. Santo Domingo: Colección de la Biblioteca Nacional.

Cocco de Filippis, Daisy. 1988. *Sin otro profeta que su canto: antología de poesía escrita por dominicanas*. Santo Domingo: Biblioteca Taller.

Deligne, Gastón F. 1963. "La intervención, 1801." In *Galaripsos*, 163–167. Santo Domingo: Editorial Librería Dominicana.

Del Monte, Félix María. 1885. *Las vírgenes de Galindo, o la Invasión de los haitianos sobre la parte española de la isla de Santo Domingo el 9 de febrero de 1822*. Santo Domingo: Imprenta de García Hermanos.

Derby, Lauren. 1994. "Haitians, Magic and Money: Raza and Society in the Haitian-

Dominican Borderlands, 1900 to 1937." *Comparative Studies in Society and History* 36 (3): 488–526.

Fischer, Sibylle. 2004. *Modernity Disavowed: Haiti and the Cultures of Slavery in the Age of Revolution*. Durham, NC: Duke University Press.

Glissant, Édouard. 1997. *Poetics of Relation*. Translated by Betsy Wing. Ann Arbor: University of Michigan Press.

González, Raymundo. 2004. "El Comegente, una rebelión campesina al final del período colonial." In *Homenaje a Emilio Cordero Michel*, 175–224. Santo Domingo: Académica Dominicana de la Historia.

Marrero Aristy, Ramón. 1957. *República Dominicana: origen y destino del pueblo cristiano más antiguo de la América*. Ciudad Trujillo: Editora del Caribe.

Morris, Andrea E. 2006. "*Yania Tierra*: enterrando el cuerpo de la madre patria." *Letras Femeninas* 32 (2): 181–196.

Moya Pons, Frank. 1998. *The Dominican Republic: A National History*. Princeton, NJ: Markus Weiner Publishers.

Past, Mariana. 2011. "Problematic Cartographies: Hispaniola as Truncated Island in Aída Cartagena Portalatín's *Yania Tierra*." *Afro-Hispanic Review* 30 (2): 85–100.

Rodríguez, Néstor. 2007. *Escrituras de desencuentro en la República Dominicana*. Santo Domingo: Editora Nacional.

Rodríguez Demorizi, Emilio, ed. 1955. *Invasiones haitianas de 1801, 1805 y 1822*. Ciudad Trujillo: Editora del Caribe.

Russ, Elizabeth Christine. 2009. *The Plantation in the Postslavery Imagination*. New York: Oxford University Press, 2009.

———. 2014. "Walking in the Ciudad Trujillista: Remapping Dominican Identity in *Escalera para Electra* and *La estrategia de Chochueca*." In *Escritoras dominicanas a la deriva: marginación, dolor y resistencia*, edited by Sintia Molina, 115–136. Madrid: Verbum.

———. 2016. "Between the Unthinkable and the Unsayable: The Legacy of *Brigadas Dominicanas* (December 1961–March 1963)." *Hispanic Review* 84 (4): 381–403.

San Miguel, Pedro L. 2005. *The Imagined Island: History, Identity, and Utopia in Hispaniola*. Translated by Jane Ramírez. Chapel Hill: University of North Carolina Press.

Torres-Saillant, Silvio. 1994. "Dominican Literature and Its Criticism: Anatomy of a Troubled Identity." In *A History of Literature in the Caribbean: Hispanic and Francophone Regions*, edited by Albert James Arnold, Julio Rodríguez-Luis, and J. Michael Dash, 49–64. Amsterdam: John Benjamins.

Turits, Richard Lee. 2002. "A World Destroyed, A Nation Imposed: The 1937 Haitian Massacre in the Dominican Republic." *Hispanic American Historical Review* 82 (3): 589–635.

Veloz Maggiolo, Marcio. 1977. "Tipología del Tema Dominicano en la Literatura Dominicana." In *Sobre cultura dominicana . . . y otras culturas*, 93–119. Santo Domingo: Alfa y Omega.

6

Archives of Afro-Affirmation

Post-Trujillo Journals and Dominican Literary Blackness

RAJ CHETTY

In U.S. popular culture, the Dominican Republic is an unending source of baseball talent, not "the cradle of blackness in the Americas" (Torres-Saillant 2000, 1107). In a strangely similar way, the U.S. academy fails to recognize the fact that the entire island of Hispaniola—the colonial precursor to today's Dominican Republic and Haiti—gave birth to and nurtured blackness in the "New World" as the site of the first slave plantation, the first slave revolt, and the first maroon community. Instead, a cross-disciplinary chorus chants the refrain of Dominican self-hatred, negrophobia, and *antihaitianismo*, a refrain echoed for a broader audience in the 2011 PBS series *Black in Latin America*, which features as one of its hour-long episodes a discussion of Haiti and the Dominican Republic (Chetty 2013, 15). This story of racial relations in the Dominican Republic emphasizes the Afro-negating or Afro-obscuring practices and policies that are dominant in elite and official discourse and are dispersed throughout the nation.

So far, little has been done to underscore the anti-racist counternarratives, counterpoetics, and countermovements that have existed throughout Dominican history (Eller 2016; Reyes-Santos 2015; Chetty and Rodríguez 2015). Often located at a remove from elite positions, these projects to counter racism and *antihaitianismo* challenge the image of the Dominican Republic as the racial pariah of the Caribbean, a self-hating nation bent on occluding or erasing black identities. A properly transnational approach would attend to island-based projects aimed at opposing both *antihaitianismo* and negrophobia.

Instead, the sort of transnational approach that is currently in vogue emphasizes—sometimes explicitly, more often implicitly—that Dominicans' self-consciousness as blacks emerged after large-scale migration to the United States created what is now called *la diáspora*. This narrative presents a history of affirmation of Afro or black identity that is indebted to contact with the racial dynamics of the United States. But there is much more to the emergence of black- and Afro-affirmative politics than what Juan Flores (2009) describes as "the [cultural] remittance of Afro-Dominican, Afro-Puerto Rican, and Afro-Cuban identities . . . after a veritable apprenticeship in black consciousness acquired in working-class diaspora 'hoods' in the United States" (47–48). While Flores does well to undermine island-based resistance to seeing Africa and blackness as constitutive of the Dominican Republic (and Puerto Rico and Cuba), his point may unwittingly contribute to a vulgar transnationalism in which "a lesson in blackness" (47) or in black struggle is learned in the United States and subsequently transmitted transnationally to advance racial struggles abroad (see also Moya Pons 1981, 32–33; Torres-Saillant 2000, 1109). To be sure, a fruitful cross-fertilization occurs when Dominicans, including artists, writers, and scholars, engage with counterparts while they are in the United States, in the broader Caribbean, in Africa, and in Europe. Nevertheless, this decidedly one-sided transnationalism runs the risk of ignoring how such cross-fertilization works within the Dominican Republic.

Thus, while many Dominicans develop a certain kind of black consciousness in the United States, by my reading it is not that they "discover" their blackness but instead that they discover a discourse of blackness distinct from what is available in the Dominican Republic, a discourse in which blackness is valorized in a particular way because of a distinct historical trajectory (in the United States) (García-Peña 2015, 17–18). Herein lies the limit of a transnational perspective that moves unidirectionally from the United States to the Dominican Republic. The discourses about blackness that are available in the Dominican Republic are not recognizable to those in the United States who are looking for echoes of a particular discourse and practice of blackness, ones that look like the expressions that flowered during the Harlem Renaissance and the Black Power and Black Arts movements in the United States, or at least like the *négritude* and *negrismo* literary movements that flourished in places as close as the French- and Spanish-speaking Caribbean. Perhaps this explains why so many U.S. commentators on Dominican racial relations begin with a question rooted in disbelief: "How can black people deny their own blackness?"[1]

An analysis of the immediate post-Trujillato period (from General Rafael Trujillo's assassination in 1961 through the end of that decade) reveals a struggle over national identity that addressed not just race, blackness, and Africanness but also intersecting inequalities structured by class. This struggle stemmed from conflict between those who espoused a logic of white supremacy and those who argued for a racial identity founded on a mulatto mixture that included African ancestry and an affirmative connection to enslaved forebears. Publications that disseminated the latter view emerged in the late 1960s and early 1970s. The most forceful expressions of this view emanated from Marxist historians. Their publications are the culmination of important work begun by social scientists, historians, and literary figures in the early 1960s that sought not just to reincorporate enslaved blacks into recorded history, and thus into Dominican identity, but to put their contributions in the center of the formation of Dominican politics and culture (Larrazábal Blanco 1967; Cordero Michel 1968; Franco Pichardo 1969; Tolentino Dipp 1974; Mayes and Austerlitz this volume).

Along with these Marxist historians, a number of literary groups that formed during the 1960s, some even in the last years of Trujillo's dictatorship, sought to redefine Dominican political and cultural landscapes through the literary and expressive arts. These short-lived literary and arts groups and the literary/arts journals they contributed to emerged in a Dominican atmosphere wracked by the end of *el Trujillato* in 1961 and the 1965 Revolución de Abril (the April Revolution), a movement that aimed to restore leftist leader Juan Bosch and the constitutional government. The four short years between these events were momentous. As elections loomed in the wake of Trujillo's death, the U.S. government overtly and covertly worked to undermine Bosch's base of support, citing the threat of a Cuba-like revolution. Bosch, who had won a popular election with a wide majority, was deposed by a military coup in 1963 after only seven months in office. Even though U.S. president Lyndon Johnson poured financial aid into the military provisional government, opposition continued apace. U.S. intervention surged again in late April 1965, on the heels of the Revolución de Abril.

Because of the wide-ranging impact of the Revolución de Abril and the second U.S. occupation, it is appropriate to use 1965 as a landmark moment that decisively altered the nation's literary and cultural production. Pre-1965 journals such as *Brigadas Dominicanas* (1961–1963) and *Testimonio* (1964–1967) and groups such as El Frente Cultural and Arte y Liberación catalyzed the post-1965 emergence of such literary groups as El Puño, La Isla, and La Antorcha. In addition to working in these literary groups and publishing literary art and criticism in these journals, many writers published in the weekly cultural supplements of major newspapers, gaining a wider audience for their socially engaged art and criticism. Though most of these literary groups and journals were short-lived, they register an important tradition of counterhegemonic discourse that challenged political, literary, and social traditions and promoted anti-racist and Afro-embracing ideologies. The post-Trujillo literary currents that are evident in journals, groups, and the weekly cultural supplements of major newspapers indicate an alternative, Dominican-centric genealogy of black-affirming literary art and criticism. However, I do not want to suggest that Dominican engagements with blackness and Africanness burst onto the scene simultaneously with the bullets fired by Trujillo's assassins. This literary beginning had important precedents during the *Trujillato* but did not emerge in the Dominican Republic in an explicit and organized way until after Trujillo's death.[2] This tradition offers an alternative story to the sense that Dominicans did not, do not, and cannot imagine answers to white supremacy and anti-black racism except through migration to the United States.

Post-Trujillo Afro-Diasporic *Testimonio*

The literary journal *Testimonio: Revista de Letras y Arte*, published from 1964 to 1968, is a key early instance of incipient Afro-Diasporic consciousness and demonstrates the important cultural and racial work that began immediately after Trujillo's death. However, the journal is not reducible to what Torres-Saillant (2006) has dubbed the "good" and "bad" stories of Dominican racial relations (182). Instead, *Testimonio* is important because it is possible to extract from it another story about Dominican racial relations, one that was fraught with tension but was nonetheless indicative of the sort of grappling with both black and African affirmation that was characteristic of black cultural movements across the globe during this time. The pages of *Testimonio* offer a range of literary engagements with Africa and blackness.

In May 1964, in the fourth issue, renowned Dominican novelist Marcio Veloz Maggiolo published an article introducing Léopold Sédar Senghor's *négritude* poetry. Veloz Maggiolo's article came some three decades after Senghor participated in the formation of the *négritude* movement with Aimé and Suzanne Césaire, Léon Gontran Damas, Paulette and Jane Nardal, Suzanne Lacascade, and others, so the piece was not novel in global terms. However, it was novel in a Dominican context that was (and continues to be) not thought to be very conducive to *négritude*, especially as a movement from black anticolonial writers of the French-speaking world, both black Africans and black Antilleans.[3] The move by a Dominican writer to embrace Senghor's black-affirming political poetry is what makes this article so important.

Veloz Maggiolo appears to have been most compelled by one facet of Senghor's poetry: "Senghor's poetry overcomes . . . the myth of the supremacy of the white race" (1964, 255).[4] His article, however, does not express the full embrace of *négritude* that would imply its complete relevance for Dominicans. While Veloz Maggiolo opposed the myth of white supremacy, he did not exactly embrace an Afrocentric movement for Dominican society. This is most evident in his analysis of why French surrealism exerted such an influence on Senghor and other *négritude* poets:

> So much has come out of that strange and subtle alchemy, an intellectual alchemy ineluctable for a race naturally inclined to the most bizarre analogy and to fantastic things, to the point that Breton's famous "psychic automatism" and the rupture of logical-grammatical forms coincide amazingly with the pre-logical state of primitive African languages. In other words, it is possible that the process of semantic barbarization inaugurated by surrealism opens the channels of the cry of the spirit of the literature indigenous to each African country. (Veloz Maggiolo 1964, 256)[5]

Veloz Maggiolo was no fan of French surrealism, but more disconcerting is his depiction of African languages, and by extension Africans, as monolithically primitive.

Veloz Maggiolo's closing paragraph is even more strange. It connects Senghor with "*otros poetas de Africa francesa*" (other poets of French Africa), including in that list Senegalese poet David Diop and Jacques Roumain and Léon Damas (1964, 256). Identifying the French Guyanese Damas and the Haitian Roumain as part of "*Africa francesa*" aligns with views that see Haiti as essentially African and the Dominican Republic as characteristically not. Even if Veloz Maggiolo used Senghor to register an implicit critique of white supremacy in the Dominican Republic, at this point he could not see the Dominican Republic as African. In the pages of *Testimonio*, Veloz Maggiolo both extolled Senghor's *négritude* poetry in order to oppose white supremacy and maintained an anti-African discourse.

Ramón Emilio Reyes's two-part essay in issues 5 and 6 (April and May 1964) is a similar introduction to black-centered poetics, this time via Nicolás Guillén's poetry. Reyes asserted that "Guillén . . . principally writes black poetry," but then added an interesting qualification: "Nonetheless, his message is not essentially racist [or racialist]. The question of the Negro, one aspect of the social problems in our world, in most instances functions for Guillén as a way to express his ideas regarding social protest and his preaching on human character" (1964, 356).[6] This argument that black opposition is fundamentally rooted in social oppression reveals more about Reyes's attitudes as a Dominican writer and thinker in the Dominican political context of the 1960s than it does about the politics of Guillén's poetry. Whatever the accuracy of his assessment of Guillén, it is no stretch to think that Reyes viewed "the question of the Negro" in the Dominican Republic in a way that was similar to how he interpreted Guillén's poetry, namely, as less about anti-black racism and more about broader social struggle.

Perhaps even more pertinent to the Dominican context, Reyes speculated about why Guillén and other poets of "*poesía negra*" turn to irony as a literary technique: "Perhaps . . . because of necessity the language of the Negro has been ironic, given his status as a social outcast, condemned to hide his feelings of justice, which he releases, fearful, amidst a language that does not have permission to be direct" (1964, 356).[7] Even though Reyes did not invoke Dominican literary practice or a specifically Dominican *poesía negra*, his comment is quite revelatory. Applied to Dominican literature during the *Trujillato* and in its immediate aftermath, his comment suggests that seeking out blackness in Dominican cultural and literary practices must be attentive to forms of expression that are ironic, evasive, indirect, or otherwise unrecognizable to those seeking clearly affirmative embraces of blackness or *négritude*.

Veloz Maggiolo's and Reyes's articles are complex examples of early post-Trujillo engagements with international black poetics. They offer indirect commentary on race relations in the Dominican Republic and challenge the dominant perception that Dominicans are negrophobic. But in the case of *antihaitianismo*, *Testimonio* offers an even more direct response to the dominant narrative: the inclusion of the Haitian-Dominican poet Jacques Viau Renaud. Viau's presence in the journal is obvious evidence of an alternative to *antihaitianismo*. The biographical blurb accompanying his poem indicates that he was born in Port-au-Prince in 1941[8] and lived in Santo Domingo from 1948 onward; it offers no suggestion that because Viau was Haitian he could not be Dominican. The fact that *Testimonio* included his Spanish-language poetry in the mid-1960s is significant. This history counters the arguments of Dominicans who promote *antihaitianismo* discourse today and the U.S. academics who see nothing but *antihaitianismo* in the Dominican Republic.[9]

Viau's first poem in *Testimonio*, "El Nuevo Torreón," was published in the second issue, in March 1964. A second poem, "Canción de Gesta," was published in issue 8, in September of the same year. "El Nuevo Torreón" contains no direct engagement with race or blackness, but the poem's use of nature imagery beautifully imagines "the unbroken unity of all comrades" (Viau-Renaud 1964a, 138).[10] The poem's combination of earthy, vegetal, life-giving equality pulled into the Dominican present of 1964 the writings of the Césaires in *Tropiques*, their journal of the early 1940s, and Jacques Roumain's 1944 novel, *Gouvernours de la rosée*. "Canción de Gesta" did explicitly address race, but only briefly, and again only in terms of a future, universal, post-race human unity: "All shall die: the Negro / the white / the Mongol / and the *mestizo*; man shall be born" (Viau-Renaud 1964b, 90).[11] Viau's political alignment with the oppressed, which he made explicit various times in both poems, and his vision of a future "*de todos para todos*" took precedence over an explicitly black-centered poetics or political project.[12]

These three contributors to *Testimonio* are an important early index of an embryonic attempt to come to terms with both the Dominican Republic's African past and its black and mulatto present through an emphasis on socioeconomic struggle. The writings *Testimonio* published suggest that in addition to turning to black struggles abroad, Dominican activists, writers, and intellectuals today can draw upon island-based racial discourses and racial projects—a usable past—as they work to forge more progressive racial agendas.

"Listen: American Negro"

Veloz Maggiolo and Reyes turned to the Afro- and black-affirmative poetics of Senghor, a continental African, and Guillén, a diasporic African,
both of whom have been recognized worldwide for their poetic defiance
of global anti-black racism. A U.S.-centric focus on Dominicans' experiences with progressive race politics misses these much more global engagements with black cultures, an internationalism that demands critical
attention from scholars and activists. This is especially important in the
face of the ideas that Dominicans need U.S. experiences in order to overcome their own racial confusion or that Dominicans with such experiences will function like a Du Boisian racial vanguard for their country
of origin. To put a finer point on these critical stakes, I turn to a letter
Antonio Thomem wrote to black U.S. soldiers serving as part of the U.S.
occupation of 1965 that cut short Viau's life.

Thomem gave his letter to Lt. Col. Montez Arache of the Dominican
revolutionary forces, who then delivered it to Laurence Henry to publish
in his "Report from the Dominican Republic," one of the cover articles
for the June 1965 issue of the monthly satirical magazine *The Realist*.
Henry, an African-American reporter, introduced his report with a star-
tling observation: "More than 40% of the approximately 20,000 American
troops occupying that tropical island are Negroes, a proportion which
must be regarded as a calculated piece of strategy by the Pentagon which
sent them there" (1965, 1). In addition to his own observations, Henry
included a powerful interview with Montez Arache that compared U.S.
and Dominican race relations and ended with two letters: one from an
African American soldier to his wife in which he expresses racial solidarity with the Dominican struggle and the rhetorical salvo Thomem lobbed
at African American soldiers. Its bold title was "Listen: American Negro
Soldier."[13]

Thomem's letter troubles the hierarchy of racial politics that imagines
Dominicans in the United States as eagerly absorbing struggles for racial
equality there, then returning to ameliorate racial problems back home.
Thomem's opening line placed the Dominican civil war on a par with the
U.S. civil rights movement: "We Dominicans are fighting for our free-
dom from social injustice, from racial discrimination. We are giving our
lives so that our sons will have what we have never had: WORK, FOOD.
EDUCATION, SECURITY" (quoted in Henry 1965, 30). While Thomem's

invocation of "social injustice" aligns with post-Trujillo Dominican leftist and Marxist and Third World struggles of the 1960s, his explicit reference to racial discrimination is relatively unique in Dominican politics of the period. It reveals a criticism of anti-black racism within the Dominican Republic that most present-day commentators ignore or push to a later date, after Dominicans have "awakened" to their blackness.

Thomem appealed to the black U.S. soldier in decidedly pan-African terms: "American Negro Soldier: We are your brothers. We have the same color" (quoted in Henry 1965, 30). However, while Thomem's call to the "American Negro Soldier"—the phrase appears six times in an eight-paragraph piece—creates a clear racial link between Dominicans and U.S. blacks, not U.S. whites, it is more instructive to see such a call for unity as both strategy and performance. This rhetorical performance of transnational black unity foregrounds the tension between the fact that U.S. blacks were struggling for political and economic justice at home while U.S. black soldiers were spreading U.S. imperialism by serving in its military. In other words, the call to racial unity must be read as part of a wider *constitucionalista* campaign to rid the Dominican Republic of U.S. interference, not as a call for racial unity for its own sake.[14]

Rhetorically attentive to the racial politics of both nations, Thomem asserted a brotherhood based on color, but he never labeled Dominicans "black" or referred to them as "Dominican Negroes." In contrast, his call to the soldier refuses to disarticulate "American" from "Negro," insisting on the culturally bounded nature of the soldier's blackness and the distinction of U.S. blacks from African-descended Dominicans. He seemed to be saying that even though these two groups shared African ancestry, this common origin did not translate into cultural unity, a way of emphasizing the Americanness of their blackness, while recognizing how white supremacy linked Americans and Dominicans of the same color. Thus, "Listen: American Negro Soldier" was about asking African American soldiers to recognize Dominicans as their brothers, united by the political and material consequences of being black in countries dominated by "white masters": "Open your eyes, American Negro Soldier. Back in Missouri, in Alabama, in Little Rock, in Selma, your brothers, sisters and parents are being killed by the same white men who are sending you to die in this Island" (quoted in Henry 1965, 30).

The injunction "Open your eyes" also directly challenges the sense that Dominicans required experiences with the racist and anti-racist strands of U.S. racial politics to discover their own blackness. The article implicitly encouraged African American soldiers to recognize themselves as blacks by admonishing them not to forget virulent racism in the U.S. South. The message was clear: U.S. blacks should attend to racial discrimination at home instead of fighting Dominicans on behalf of "white masters." Thomem boldly closed his article with this admonishment: "So lay off, American Negro Soldier. Point your gun at your own white oppressor. Don't shoot at your Dominican brother" (quoted in Henry 1965, 30).

Thomem's piece opens a window onto how Dominican blackness was performed in the 1960s in relation to U.S. senses of blackness and in relation to its own racial politics. The article is shot through with imperatives—the "listen" of the title, the implicit call to remember, the "lay off" at the close—that demand that U.S. audiences see Dominican society in another way. Thomem knew how to perform blackness in a way that would resonate with his black brother in the United States, all the while maintaining cultural distance: Dominicans might be the "same color" as the "American Negro," but that did not necessarily mean ontological sameness. This performance of blackness reinforces the idea that scholars must be attentive to the fact that Dominican articulations and performances of blackness are often indirect, masked, and strategic for both historical and politico-aesthetic reasons.

Attention to this unexplored literary archive from the immediate post-Trujillo period reveals something quite different from the dominant narratives about Dominican race relations. The writings in the journals have deep implications for how conceptualizations of the black diaspora articulate and disarticulate with Dominican literary and political culture. To put a finer point on it: U.S.-centric, transnational studies of Dominican race relations overlook the important, black-affirming contributions in the literary archive represented by *Testimonio* and Thomem's letter in *The Realist*. Such myopia runs the risk of turning the concept of the black diaspora or the goal of international black solidarity into an imperialist endeavor. Under such a conceptualization of the black diaspora, both scholars and the broader U.S. public will continue to misrecognize Dominican articulations of blackness or fail to recognize them altogether. Perhaps this is the very problem: Those who define membership in the black diaspora according to a regime that privileges certain recognizable practices of blackness often fail to recognize the way Dominicans perform their blackness. A truly transnational concept would emphasize the plurality of black and African diasporas. This concept would be flexible enough to accommodate Dominican (and other) performances of blackness that are indirect, evasive, and hidden—ones that might not announce their blackness and thus might not be recognizably black.

Notes

1. For example, see "Black in the Dominican Republic: Denying Blackness," the June 10, 2014, panel Marc Lamont Hill hosted on HuffPost Live. This panel was directly influenced by Henry Louis Gates's *Black in Latin America* in its assumption of Dominicans' denial of their blackness. Fortunately, the panel discussion renders Dominican blackness more complicated than mere denial.

2. This post-Trujillo beginning also must be seen in conjunction with the important intellectual contributions of popular cultural practices that were undeniably connected to Africa and that predated the *Trujillato* and persisted during that period. In fact, Dominican writers in the 1960s and 1970s explicitly and consciously turned to Dominican popular practices when formulating their artistic and intellectual reorientations toward a broader conception of Dominican identity.

3. Even in the Dominican context, however, *négritude* arrived much earlier, if not openly, via André Bréton's interactions with surrealist poets on the island in 1944. More to the point, he gave Aída Cartagena Portalatín the final issue of Suzanne and Aimé Césaire's journal *Tropiques*. See Cartagena Portalatín (1986) and Morrison (2012). For more on Cartagena Portalatín's writings, in particular her treatment of Haiti, see Russ's contribution to this volume.

4. "*La poesía de Senghor supera . . . el mito de la supremacía de la raza blanca.*" All translations from the Spanish are my own.

5. "*Cuánto ha salido de aquella alquimia extraña y sutil, alquimia intelectual indescontable para una raza naturalmente inclinada a la analogía más bizarra y a las cosas fantásticas, al punto que el famoso 'automatismo-síquico' de Breton y la ruptura de las formas lógico-gramaticales coinciden maravillosamente con el estado pre-lógico de los lenguajes primitivos africanos. En otros términos, es posible que el proceso de barbarización semántica inaugurado por el surrealismo abriera los cauces del grito del espíritu a la literatura indígena de cada país africano.*"

6. "*Guillén . . . escribe principalmente poesía negra*"; "*Sin embargo, su mensaje no es racista esencialmente. El tema negro que es uno de los aspectos del problema social en nuestro mundo, sirve la mayoría de las veces a Guillén para expresar sus ideas de protesta social y su prédica de carácter humano.*"

7. "*Tal vez . . . porque el lenguaje del negro ha sido por necesidad irónico dada su condición de apartado social; condenado a esconder sus sentimientos de justicia, que deja escapar, temeroso, en medio de un lenguaje que no tiene permiso para ser claro.*"

8. The journal erred in listing his year of birth as 1942; Viau Renaud was born in 1941.

9. Viau Renaud, who died in 1965 at age 23 while engaged in the uprising against the U.S. occupation, remains important to Dominicans of Haitian descent and their

struggles today. See, for example, the online activist network La Red de Encuentro Do-minicano-Haitiano Jacques Viau: https://www.facebook.com/RedJacquesViau/.

10. "*la unidad sin roturas de todos los camaradas.*" In addition to signifying a break or fracture, *roturas* also carries a sense of something plowed, as in broken earth, fitting with the larger earthy sense of the poem.

11. "*Morirá el negro, / el blanco / el mongol / y el mestizo, nacerá el hombre.*"

12. For a strained attempt to read Viau's poetry as black-centered, based on the false assumption that Viau was a "black Haitian," see Stinchcomb (2004, 81).

13. Thomem's letter was reprinted at least two times, once in the August 9, 1965, issue of the Socialist Workers Party's *The Militant* in an article titled, "Dominican Freedom Fighters Address Appeal to Negro GIs," and a second time, accompanied by its original title, in the September 18, 1965, issue of the Dominican weekly *Ahora!*. In this chapter, I cite the letter as it first appeared, as a component of Laurence Henry's "Report from the Dominican Republic" in the June 1965 issue of *The Realist*.

14. The Constitucionalistas were a revolutionary group that attempted to restore the constitution that had been promulgated under deposed president Juan Bosch. They also fought against the U.S. military invasion.

Works Cited

Cartagena Portalatín, Aída. 1986. *Culturas africanas: Rebeldes con causa*. Santo Domin-go: Ediciones de la Biblioteca Nacional.

Chetty, Raj. 2013. "'La Calle es Libre': Race, Recognition, and Dominican Street Theater." *Afro-Hispanic Review* 32 (2): 15–30.

Chetty, Raj, and Amaury Rodríguez. 2015. "Introduction: The Challenge and Promise of Dominican Black Studies." *The Black Scholar: Journal of Black Studies and Research* 45 (2): 1–9.

Cordero Michel, Emilio. 1968. *La revolución haitiana y Santo Domingo*. Santo Domingo: Editora Nacional.

Eller, Anne. 2016. *We Dream Together: Dominican Independence, Haiti, and the Fight for Caribbean Freedom*. Durham, NC: Duke University Press.

Flores, Juan. 2009. *The Diaspora Strikes Back: Caribeño Tales of Learning and Turning*. New York: Routledge.

Franco Pichardo, Franklin. 1969. *Los negros, los mulatos y la nación dominicana*. Santo Domingo: Editora Nacional.

García-Peña, Lorgia. 2015. "Translating Blackness: Dominicans Negotiating Race and Blackness." *The Black Scholar: Journal of Black Studies and Research* 45 (2): 10–20.

Henry, Laurence. 1965. "Report from the Dominican Republic." *The Realist* (June): 1, 18–21. http://www.ep.tc/realist/60/. Accessed October 20, 2017.

Larrazábal Blanco, Carlos. 1967. *Los negros y la esclavitud en Santo Domingo*. Santo Do-mingo: Julio D. Postigo e hijos.

Morrison, Mateo. 2012. "Aimé Césaire y la relación del movimiento de la negritud con la literatura dominicana." In *Presencia de África en el Caribe, las Antillas y Estados Unidos,* edited by Natasha Despotovic, 143–154. Santo Domingo: FUNGLODE/GFDD.

Moya Pons, Frank. 1981. "Dominican National Identity and Return Migration." Occasional Papers No. 1, Center for Latin American Studies, University of Florida, Gainesville.

Reyes, Ramón Emilio. 1964. "La Ironia y otros temas en Nicolás Guillen." *Testimonio: Revista de Artes y Letras* 5: 355–370.

Reyes-Santos, Alaí. 2015. *Our Caribbean Kin: Race and Nation in the Neoliberal Antilles.* New Brunswick, NJ: Rutgers University Press.

Stinchcomb, Dawn. 2004. *The Development of Literary Blackness in the Dominican Republic.* Gainesville: University Press of Florida.

Tolentino Dipp, Hugo. 1974. *Raza e historia en Santo Domingo: los orígenes del prejuicio racial en América.* Santo Domingo: Editora de la Universidad Autónoma de Santo Domingo.

Torres-Saillant, Silvio. 2000. "The Tribulations of Blackness: Stages in Dominican Racial Identity." *Callaloo* 23 (3): 1086–1111.

———. 2006. "Blackness and Meaning in Studying Hispaniola: A Review Essay." *Small Axe* 19 (1): 180–188.

Veloz Maggiolo, Marcio. 1964. "Sedar Senghor: El Gran Poeta de Africa: La Poesía de Sedar Senghor." *Testimonio: Revista de Artes y Letras* 4: 254–256.

Viau-Renaud, Jacques. 1964a. "El Nuevo Torreón." *Testimonio: Revista de Artes y Letras* 2: 138–139.

———. 1964b. "Canción de Gesta." *Testimonio: Revista de Artes y Letras* 8: 87–92.

7

Transnational Romances and Sex Tourism in *Chochueca's Strategy*, by Rita Indiana Hernández; "Emoticons," by Aurora Arias; and "Heading South," by Dany Laferrière

ELENA VALDEZ

Caribbean literature has a long tradition of using transracial intimacy to reveal tensions among classes and races. One striking example is Cirilo Villaverde's 1839 novel, *Cecilia Valdés,* in which Cecilia, a lower-class, light-skinned Cuban mulatta, unknowingly commits incest with her white half-brother, the son of a land magnate and slave trader (Villaverde 2005). In the twentieth century, while anti-colonial Caribbean male authors wrote about the redemption of black manhood and political power through the conquest of the white female body, their female counterparts rethought heterosexual love as an "anti-romance" in order to challenge patriarchal colonial hierarchies of sex and race and to recover female subjectivities (Francis 2010). By the 2000s, Dominican and Haitian literature had begun to reinsert transracial romance in the context of sex tourism in narratives in which black sex workers conquered financially well-off white female tourists from other countries. The novel *Chochueca's Strategy* (*La estrategia de Chochueca*) (2000), by Rita Indiana Hernández, and two short stories, Aurora Arias's "Emoticons" (2007) and Dany Laferrière's "Heading South" (2009), are examples of recent literary works that explore sex work and the desirability of transnational relationships.

Transracial romances are especially important for fictional works in the Spanish-speaking Caribbean. In her seminal study *Foundational Fictions*, Doris Sommer (1991) coins the term *national romances* to refer to a genre of nineteenth-century Latin American fiction in which romantic couplings between two characters with different and presumably insurmountable class and racial backgrounds end in marriage. According to Sommer, these heterosexual unions symbolized national reconciliation in an era defined by internecine conflicts and wide-scale warfare. Therefore, a novelized romance prescribed a way to consolidate the concept of *nation* at a time when Latin American republics faltered under the weight of political turmoil. One of the first novels in this genre, *Enriquillo*, romanticized the sixteenth-century story of Mencía, a woman of Spanish-indigenous origins, and Enriquillo, a Taíno-born cacique who is educated by Franciscan friars, was written by the Dominican Manuel de Jesús Galván. In Jesús Galván's hands, christianized and assimilated Enriquillo becomes a metaphor for the modern Dominican nation that he argued was ethnically indigenous but culturally Hispanic and Catholic (de Jesús Galván [1882] 2010). With his colonial-period romance, Jesús Galván established the indo-Hispanic as representative of a coherent, Dominican national identity that emerged during the colonial period.

Recent works by Hernández, Arias, and Laferrière have redefined the national romance to include heterosexual interactions that are transnational and emerge through sex tourism. These authors are highly critical of tourism-derived romances. Although the sex workers, or beach boys, in these stories repeatedly enact romantic passion, these transnational—and transactional—romances are doomed to failure. The authors examined in this chapter refuse to narrate these romances as symbolic representations of the nation. I argue that in this body of work by Hernández, Arias, and Laferrière, transnational and transactional romances are sites of conflict over norms governing sexuality, masculinity, and gender relations within the Dominican Republic and Haiti. Tourism-derived relationships simultaneously undermine the whole notion that romance can provide the means to imagine national unity or to reproduce the nation symbolically. Moreover, as contrived and problematic as these relationships are, I suggest that these authors see within them the potential for resisting neocolonialism. While *Chochueca's Strategy* manifests the first signs of criticism of and disillusionment with sex tourism, "Emoticons" and "Heading South" show a much stronger resistance to both sexual exploitation and the inclusion of the Dominican Republic and Haiti in a transnational pleasure industry.

Hispaniola became a tourist destination when the Haitian and Dominican governments moved toward a neoliberal agenda in the late twentieth century and made a major shift to recreational tourism in the 1990s and

the 2000s. During that time period, both countries also became important destinations for tourists seeking corporeal and sexual pleasure. As
Denise Brennan writes, Hispaniola became "a transnational sexual meeting ground" (2010, 308–310) as a result of tourist-oriented development.

Chochueca's Strategy, "Emoticons," and "Heading South" center on
white female tourists' sexual desires for black men. Hispaniola forms part
of a "sexscape" for European tourists who imagine Hispaniola as a site
for exploring sexual pleasure. In all three stories, though, the sexscape,
once limited to hotels and beach resorts, extends beyond the beach/tour-
ist area into the national capitals of Port-au-Prince and Santo Domingo.
In Laferrière's "Heading South," middle-aged North American women invade Port-au-Prince seeking to gratify their sexual appetites; one of them
calls Haiti "one big sex park" (125). Similarly, two Haitian characters, the
seventeen-year-old sex worker Legba and an older maître d'hôtel, Albert,
migrate to Port-au-Prince from the northern parts of the country, Legba
from the small village of Ouanaminthe and Albert from the city of Cap-
Haïtien. Heading south, for tourists and for Haitians alike, creates opportunities for financial gain.[1] Complementing Elizabeth Manley's chapter
in the volume, this essay examines how the sexual economy that emerges
from this dialectic of female tourist mobility and male sex worker immobility challenges the status quo of masculinity and gender norms in
Dominican and Haitian societies.

The transnational Hispaniola paradigm foregrounds the entire island
as a place of convergence of what Mimi Sheller (2003) has termed "binding mobilities," a term that refers both to those who move and those who
stay. As these stories illustrate, these binding mobilities transform Haitian and Dominican cities into transnational meeting points. I argue that
when read together, the stories discussed here present male sex workers as protagonists who do not embody any particular national type of
manhood yet perform a particular vision of denationalized masculinity
that has become common in Hispaniola and the broader Caribbean. In
"Heading South" Legba is a Haitian beach boy, and Octaviano and Salim,
characters in Hernández's novel, and Pepe, a character in Arias's story,
embody *sanky-pankies*, the Dominican variation. This name for Dominican beach boys is a dominicanization of the English term "hanky-panky."
Their physical appearance draws upon cultural and racial stereotypes
that clients already have about Caribbean men: *sanky-pankies* are usually

young, dark-skinned, in good shape, and wear dreadlocks. These young male sex workers have hustled foreign females in tourist-oriented beach areas since the late 1970s and early 1980s. They often initiate what Amalia Cabezas (2004) calls "the performance of love" (999). *Sankies* aim to create a pseudo-relationship that can be continued through letters, phone calls, faxes, and emails after the guest returns home. They then ask for money to be sent to them by wire transfer, often claiming that they need to care for sick relatives.

A *sanky-panky*'s ultimate goal, though, is to obtain a marriage visa to the tourist's home country. Affection and intimacy become a commodity sex workers exchange in order to accumulate capital, to ascend the socioeconomic ladder, and to emigrate. The "performance of love" becomes an important element of what Cabezas (2009) calls tactical sex and what Brennan (2004) calls an advancement strategy. To be sure, *sankies* and Haitian beach boys exploit desire as a commodity, but in so doing, they perpetuate racist and sexist stereotypes of Caribbean people. Thus, the success of romances in this transnational, transactional landscape, as these authors make clear, remains both elusive and problematic as a symbol of the nation and even as a site of resistance against the economic imperatives that have made tourism and sex tourism in particular necessary to national development (Medina-Vilariño 2012, 297–316).

In Hernández's *Chochueca's Strategy*, sex tourism is present mainly as a cultural backdrop, described briefly through allusions to the topic and through the comments characters make. The novel depicts Silvia's attempts to return a stolen stereo while accompanied by her friends Tony, Franco, Salim, Octaviano, and Amanda. One of the indirect references to the sex tourism phenomenon appears when Silvia observes "Italians looking for black women who would make their lives impossible" as Silvia and her friends walk through Santo Domingo (2000, 48).[2] In another allusion to sex tourism, Octaviano, one of Silvia's friends, picks up a blue-eyed girl in Sosúa, a small town on the northern coast of the Dominican Republic that is famous for its sex tourism resorts.[3] This reference to Sosúa suggests that Octaviano is in Sosúa because he is a *sanky-panky*.

Chochueca's Strategy refers several times to another of Silvia's friends, Salim, as a sex worker. He is involved with a group of Scandinavian tourists and caters only to women who have enough money to spend on him after their week-long vacations. Even though Hernández depicts Salim as a secondary character, she clearly wants to grapple with the consequences of his sex work, as is evidenced in a scene when Silvia berates him as they walk through Santo Domingo. Silvia points out that Salim acts like a *sanky* when he gets involved with his clients. She reproaches him with this evidence:

> One day I went with you to pick up a parcel, one of many sent to you by girls you deceived from around the world. When we arrived at the post office, which was filled with those types, friends of yours, who, thanks to high levels of melanin and twerking, were receiving gifts and letters from their girlfriends all over the world, I just waited around for you. (22)[4]

Salim is clearly a *sanky* who maintains long-distance relationships with various foreign women. He has multiple "Western Union Mommas."[5] He is also dark-skinned, as suggested by the fact that he has "high levels of melanin," as do his counterparts. Indeed, dark skin seems to be particularly appealing to foreign women and is a feature that Dominican sex workers market. But this image is somewhat troubled in the text, because Salim is clearly an Arabic name that may suggest a connection with so-called Árabes, immigrants from present-day Palestine, Lebanon, and Syria who settled in the Dominican Republic in the early twentieth century. Using his Middle Eastern look to blacken himself, Salim appears to market erotic exoticism and his masculine body as an export commodity in which local and global values coincide.

In another allusion to Salim's status as a *sanky*, Silvia says to him, "Knowing how you used to tell one of your women that she was the one and coming on to the other one with yet another recital of arrows and little hearts was disgusting to me" (21).[6] On the one hand, the statement confirms that the performance of affection is an important part of sexual conquest within the sex-tourism context. On the other hand, the fact that Salim has multiple women and makes false promises to them provokes Silvia's anger. Behind her denigrating remarks lies a reproach of the difficult economic conditions that push Dominican men to enter the sex trade, a field traditionally seen as the domain of women.

At the same time, the fact that Hernández's and Arias's texts name the activities of *sanky-pankies* or mention them indirectly indicates that they have become an important part of everyday life. In Arias's "Emoticons,"

Pepe does not identify himself as a *sanky*, but he follows a *sanky* script: "James Gatto . . . drove them to the city, to the door of Kika's house, who, besides being Pepe's cousin, was his eternal accomplice, to whom he entrusted everything, all his long-distance love stories with their corresponding goodbyes" (69).[7] Centering one's attention on financial gain instead of seduction transforms the *sanky* into a sex worker (Cabezas 2004, 999). Similarly, "Heading South" opens with the investigation into Legba's mysterious death. Readers become familiar with Legba only through the testimonies of white women; Legba remains silent, just as Pepe and Salim are about their participation in sex work. Yet the silences of these sex workers are conspicuous by their inclusion in the texts. As a result, they register as submerged histories that deserve recognition and recovery and become sites for articulations of "citizenship from below" (Sheller 2012, 3). To claim their freedom and citizenship, sex workers assert themselves as raced, gendered, sexual subjects as a result of their encounters with white female clients. By doing so, they repeat a scenario of a romantic passion so recognizable across Hispaniola, that it becomes unnecessary to name it.

Moreover, *Chochueca's Strategy* brings attention to *sanky-pankynismo*, the extension of *sanky-pankies'* modus operandi beyond beaches and white, female tourists. Similar to the ways in which female tourists make assumptions about the sexuality of all local men, including presumptions about their sexual availability, *sanky-pankies* have broadened their range of action to include ordinary relationships, rendering all potential and actual romances transactional.[8] Thus, Salim does not abandon his pursuit of intimate relationships with women in good financial standing even when the women are Dominican. For example, he courts Lorena whom Silvia describes as "a very cool girl . . . [She] had money because her mother had died from cancer when she was young and had left her a little treasure."[9] The references to the inheritance and the word *cool* reveal that Lorena is middle or upper-middle class, which suggests that Salim's relationship with her is part of his socioeconomic advancement strategy. In her analysis of Silvia's friends in the novel, Maja Horn observes: "The apparent absence of any such demands [familial, communal and economic] put on them reveals that these characters are ultimately not as unmoored from certain social and class privileges as the narrative would like to suggest" (Horn 2014, 115). Such is the case of Salim. The character is not a *sanky* by necessity; rather, he performs the script of a *sanky* to secure social and class mobility through his transactional relationships with all women, foreign and domestic alike.

Hernández's novel suggests that any relationship between a darker-skinned male and a lighter-skinned woman might be a case of *sanky-pankynismo*, even though they take place in the political and cultural heartlands of capital cities. Silvia's preoccupation with public perceptions of her relationship with Salim reveals these realities: "While we walked the streets, the foolish and insensitive people were always probably thinking, 'look, that poor little American girl fell into that sanky's hands'" (21).[10] Silvia, a young white Dominican woman, subverts this image explosively: "That's why when we were cutting through the commotion on the sidewalks and people were turning to look at the white woman and the black man, I would raise my voice like a fire truck, with a capital-city accent that left any thug from Villa Agricola terrified" (21).[11] The Santo Domingo district of Villa Agricola is infamous for high delinquency because of gang and drug wars as well as the lack of police control. When loudly projecting her "capital-city accent," Silvia makes very clear that she is a Dominican girl "from da hood" and, perhaps, not as upper-class as her whiteness implies. Although she uses her race privilege by raising the voice, she defends herself against the perception that she might be the victim of a *sanky*. By performing incompatibility with Salim, Silvia repudiates the silence that has allowed Salim's body, and those of others like him, to occupy the center of a commercialized fantasy that sustains whitening ideology. Even though for male sex workers, dark skin is essential to desirability, for them, whitening ideology no longer stands for the desire to have a lighter skin. Rather, it signifies improvement of their socioeconomic circumstances through sex tourism and transactional relationships with white female tourists. In this sense, Silvia also criticizes the silent consensus that has allowed *sanky-pankynismo* to be identified with *dominicanidad* (Dominicanness) and to define heterosexual masculinity by its relationship to transactional sex to obtain socioeconomic mobility.

Thus, both Hernández's and, as I will show later, Arias's works are thoroughly infused with a type of romance that prioritizes sexual pleasure with a racialized other and the *sankies'* economic advancement. Yet in both texts, sex workers fail to consummate relationships with female tourists despite all the rituals of flirtation. This failure points to the authors' attempts to demystify sex tourism and to emphasize the barrenness of neocolonial relationships. If *Chochueca's Strategy* can be understood as one of the first manifestations of this failure, "Emoticons" fervently denounces the local effects of sex tourism's reach beyond the beach.[12]

In Arias's "Emoticons," Julieta, a Spanish tourist, arrives in the Dominican Republic to meet Pepe, a Dominican man whom she married on the Internet. While in Santo Domingo, she spends time with Pepe's female cousin, Kika, and suspicious characters who invade Pepe's house and thereby prevent Pepe and Julieta from consummating their romance. As in Hernández's novel, this short story exceeds simple representation of transnational romances between sex worker and tourist.

"Emoticons" comes from Arias's collection of short stories by the same name. Fernando Valerio-Holguín suggests that the characters in the collection lack real emotional expression, emitting instead, "icons or ideas of emotions" from available scripts and emotional clichés found in movies and soap operas (Valerio-Holguín 2009, 3). To this end, Julieta and Pepe enact a scenario of romantic passion. While Pepe performs the role of a *sanky-panky*, Julieta, the Spanish tourist, acts the role of a foreign woman in love with one. Julieta's email address, julietakieroser@hotmail.com, for example, reveals her desire to be like the famous lover in Shakespeare's *Romeo and Juliet*. "Julietakieroser," or *Julieta quiero ser*, literally means "I want to be Julieta." The desire to occupy that role becomes even clearer when Julieta confesses that "she had lied to Pepe about two things that she did not consider important: she was not thirty-five but fifty; nor was her name really Julieta, but Dolores" (72).[13] Interestingly, they also represent a romantic union of two disabled characters: Julieta is unaware of Pepe's having a stutter because she is deaf. They compensate for the absence of auditory communication by deploying the scripts available to them—their emoticon is the sex-tourist relationship.

"Emoticons" describes the expansion of *sanky-pankynismo* into virtual reality. In this way, the story exemplifies how the Dominican Republic maintains transnational ties with the Caribbean and global community via the Internet. The fact that people meet and interact intimately in cyberspace undermines the fantasy that sex tourism takes place in a "tropical paradise." In Arias's story, moreover, *sanky-pankynismo* even manages to enter the private sphere. Because Pepe and Julieta have married, albeit virtually, Pepe brings her to his house, which fills with strangers: Julieta, a Spanish tourist; James Gatto, a foreigner of unknown origins; and Agent Lali, a Dominican anti-drug ex-policeman with a suspicious reputation.

This household represents a Dominican society invaded by foreign tourists. Also, the home never becomes the ideal domestic space symbolic of the patriarchal social order: Pepe is not the strong, masculine head of household and Julieta is not his helpful, submissive wife.

Although Pepe and Julieta spend most of their time at home, Julieta's behavior contradicts traditional gender roles for women within the nuclear family. She does not perform as a spouse or as a woman who subordinates herself to a man. Instead, Julieta inverts this passive relationship by committing adultery online with Lali, whom she meets over the Internet and even invites to Pepe's house. This way, Julieta subverts several stereotypes about female sex tourists. Rosamond King (2014) notes that "just as white people hold stereotypes of nonwhites, nonwhite people also hold stereotypes of whites" (166). On the one hand, according to King, one such stereotype concerns white women's supposed hypersexuality and their uncontrollable sexual drive. Apparently, this is precisely what Pepe expects from Julieta, and he expresses concern that they are not intimate: "Several days later, Pepe, who due to stress or apathy, didn't succeed in having sex with her, looks at Julieta anxious, ill-tempered, uneasy (70).[14] Then, a month after Julieta's arrival to the Dominican Republic, Pepe complains again: "Does she refuse to have sex because she has already spent a month in this tropical heat and I have not yet seen Julieta swim?" (73).[15] Despite his flirting and pleas for intimacy, his courtship of her fails and they do not have sex. He concludes: "I definitely think that you don't want to fuck me" (73).[16] At the same time, Julieta fails to represent a typical female tourist, a white passive victim who, according to Jacqueline Sánchez Taylor, "cannot be sexually predatory but only preyed upon" (Taylor 2001, 758–759). Put differently, she can be perceived as exploited only if she gives a *sanky-panky* access to her body. That is why, at some point she states: "But my body is mine and I do with it whatever I want" (73).[17] That Julieta refuses to have sex with Pepe undermines his masculinity and emphasizes his subordinate status in the relationship. If that were not enough, Julieta also challenges Pepe's ability to *sankipankiar*, or to act out the role of a *sanky-panky*, by trying to legally marry him. When she asks, "What if we really get married properly, Pepi?" (74), he fervently refuses.[18] While this may be because her proposal lacks the additional promise to take him to Spain, his refusal to accept the ultimate goal of all *sankies* seems counterintuitive. In this refusal, I propose, Arias's

story offers a critical response to the economic, racial, and sexual subjugation articulated through transracial intimacies in the Caribbean.

Pepe accepts his fate instead of negotiating the marriage proposal as
an exit strategy like other *sankies* would have done. According to Jack
Halberstam, failure serves as an alternative that questions conventional
understandings of success and progress in heteronormative society: "Under certain circumstances, failing, losing, forgetting, unmaking, undoing,
unbecoming, not knowing may in fact offer more creative, more cooperative, more surprising ways of being in the world" (Halberstam 2011,
2). Building on this insight, I argue that Pepe's resignation becomes an
act of resistance against *sanky-pankynismo*. While Hernández's novel
uncovers how transactional sex has become important for heterosexual
men's socioeconomic mobility, "Emoticons" targets *sanky-pankynismo*'s
detrimental effects on Dominican masculinity. One of the episodes from
the story shows how transactional sex and maleness tightly intertwine:
"[Pepe] was a professional; unemployed, but professional, and besides, he
had left an island more than once. He did not consider himself a *sanky*,
but for the same reason he didn't have the necessary *tigueraje* to face a
possible mishap" (68).[19]

As Pepe himself confesses, he does not possess the necessary qualities to embody a "traditional" Dominican masculinity, coded in terms
of *tigueraje* or the tíguere. The *tíguere* (the Dominican pronunciation of
the Spanish word *tigre*) that emerged as a reaction against the Trujillo
regime refers to a streetwise hustler, a cunning and intelligent trickster,
and a womanizer (Collado 2002; Derby 2009; Krohn-Hansen 2016). Pepe
is no *tíguere*: he fails to seduce Julieta, he cannot provide for her, and he is
not astute enough to solve his problems. Although his complaints about
unemployment and financial difficulties are similar to the stories invented
by *sanky-pankies* to swindle money from their clients, he increasingly becomes embittered because his failed performance as a *sanky* means that he
is unable to translate sexual prowess into economic mobility or masculine
power within the household.

Moreover, Pepe's maleness becomes a site for neocolonial power games
that sex tourism in the Dominican Republic intensify. Writing about Dominican hegemonic masculinity, Antonio de Moya observes that the
norm of men's dominating practices is established by those who control
power. While not all Dominican men necessarily embody that norm, it

still functions as a "measure against which all men will compare themselves" (de Moya 2004, 99). In "Emoticons," Pepe is measured unfavorably against Agent Lali and James Gatto. On the one hand, as Agent Lali competes against Pepe to win Julieta, he constantly begs her to marry him and repeats that he is in love and even "ready for anything" (75).[20] His military background complements his voracious sexuality, attracting Julieta's attention: "Another man [Lali], an urban warrior in a greenish grey helmet, leaves quickly to keep getting around, riding his scooter, 'so gorgeous like a nazi soldier,' the Spaniard whispers in a joke" (71).[21] Lali's masculine play references the self-styling of the General Rafael Trujillo, a dictator who maintained power from 1930 until his assassination in 1961. According to Maja Horn, Trujillo projected a personal image grounded in a militarized masculinity that emerged from his service in the armed forces during U.S. occupation of 1916–1924 (Horn 2014, 27). In the love triangle of Pepe-Julieta-Lali, Lali symbolizes Trujillo's legacy in Dominican daily life, which Pepe fails to confront as he does not have "the necessary *tigueraje*," as he says.

James Gatto is superior to Pepe because he is foreign, has money, and enjoys sexual prowess. For example, Gatto helps Pepe and Julieta by paying for their meal at a restaurant when Pepe's wallet is stolen. His self-reliance makes Pepe suspect him of being a CIA informant (73). Gatto's presentation is important here: "The timely arrival of that tall white guy [James Gatto] with light-colored eyes, with a face of a good bandit, made [Pepe] feel unexpectedly calm. Anywhere, and more so in Boca Chica, it is convenient to be accompanied by someone like him" (68).[22] Gatto's supposed involvement with the CIA and his physical demeanor suggests that he embodies white imperial masculinity in the postcolonial domain. Again, Maja Horn's analysis is useful here. Imperialism and U.S. intervention profoundly shaped Dominican racial formations and brought to crisis Dominican masculinity (Horn 2014, 27). In contrast with Gatto, Pepe's racialized maleness is subordinated. His romantic failures with Julieta differ from Gatto's sexual conquests, especially when Gatto successfully flirts with another female character, Pepe's cousin Kika. Thus, his white imperial masculinity undermines Pepe's sexual performance as a *sanky-panky*.

That is why, during one of his many reproaches, Pepe mentions Guacanagarix's complex, which originated in the colonial period. Guacanagarix was one of the five Taíno chiefs in La Española who met Christopher Columbus during his first journey. He refused to cooperate with other

Indian chiefs when they attempted to expel the Spaniards. Consequently, this concept refers to Dominicans who curry favor with foreigners at the expense of their compatriots. Pepe sees himself as Guacanagarix, pursuing the foreigner regardless of its social penalty which, in this case, includes Pepe's undermined masculinity, as symbolized by his failure to properly court Julieta, and his tolerance of Gatto's presence. In this sense, the transnational romance between Julieta and Pepe recreates the encounter between two worlds that initiated centuries of colonial subjugation and economic dependency. "Emoticons" implicates the whole country in another sexual conquest of the Old World by the New (and vice versa). Yet, the story points out that in this new age, mutual disillusion, rather than national consolidation through romance, is the end result.

"Heading South" comes from Dany Laferrière's collection by the same name and consists of several vignettes depicting Duvalier-era Haiti.[23] The story is set up as a series of responses by three foreign women, Brenda, Ellen, and Sue, and a Haitian maître d'hôtel, Albert, during their interrogation by the Department of Criminal Investigation Services. They all recount their recollections of the events that preceded the mysterious death of Legba, a seventeen-year-old beach boy. In contrast to Hernández's and Arias's texts that either mention female clients or depict only one of them, "Heading South" paints a richer picture of foreign women's interior lives, their social backgrounds, and class status and explicitly draws attention to the racial tensions within the pleasure industry. The story exposes the depravity of female tourists as sexual predators at the same time as it portrays them as subjects who claim their erotic agency.

In "Heading South," each female character represents a different type of sex tourist: Sue is a first-timer, or neophyte, who works at a factory; 55-year-old Brenda from Savannah, Georgia, is a returnee who visits specifically to be with Legba; and the veteran Ellen, a 55-year-old Vassar professor who lives in Boston, is in Haiti for the fifth time and has had sex with multiple partners.[24] Despite their different backgrounds, the women's pursuit of sex abroad is triggered by their sexual undesirability in the United States. For example, Sue acknowledges the impact of her weight on her unattractiveness: "They [men] never look at a woman like me. If you want to get an American white male to notice you, you have to weigh less than a hundred and twenty pounds, and I weigh twice that" (127). Ellen accuses white American men of ageism and elitism: "I've been in every bar in that snobbish whore of a town a hundred times, and believe me there is nothing in the North for women over forty" (129–130). Although married twenty-five years, Brenda confesses that she has had sex with her husband only eight times: "I don't think anyone who isn't called Brenda Lee, and who didn't come from a tiny little town north of Savannah, and who hasn't lived for twenty-five years with a man named Bill who hasn't touched her more than a grand total of eight times in all those years, could ever understand what I went through" (125). While the indifference and rejection by white men in the United States bring out the failures of the Western concept of romantic love, a sex adventure in the Caribbean becomes a liberating experience. This is because the women demand equal attention and satisfaction in terms of sexual gratification. For example, Ellen confesses: "I love love so much—love or sex, I don't know which anymore—that I've always told myself that when I'm old I'll pay to get it" (138–139). As a consequence, the story acknowledges white women's desire for black men, which contrasts to an older notion of transracial intimacy that elevated white men's desire of women of color.[25] Laferrière's story voices a female desire that was previously limited by the colonial constraints of respectability coded in class, racial, and gendered terms. Despite the fact that the three women's public display of sexual desire is considered beyond the bounds of respectability in Caribbean societies, their transnational romances can also be read as manifestations of erotic autonomy and sexual transgression. Nevertheless, this interpretation does not eradicate racialized and gendered power relationships.

Although their sexual and racial transgressions challenge homoracial heteropatriarchy, Sue, Ellen, and Brenda follow a racist logic in their romances with Haitian sex workers. In this context, the case of Sue is exemplary. For example, she explains her preferences for a Haitian sex worker named Neptune: "And I've never set foot in Harlem. I never go anywhere where there's more than ten blacks. It's not that I'm afraid of blacks, it's just that black men aren't my thing. . . . I'm really crazy about Neptune, and Neptune is as black as the ace of spades. But Neptune is Haitian. To me, when I say black, I mean American black" (126–127). Sue's trip to Haiti and her romance with Neptune is part of a symbolic process. As McKercher and Bauer explain, after leaving a place of origin a tourist arrives at a liminal site that suspends racial, gender, and sexual norms, thereby allowing previously unthinkable behavior (10–12). While Sue harbors racist attitudes toward black males in the United States, in Haiti she can pursue Neptune because as a Haitian he is exotic and erotic before he is black.

Thus, her sexual transgression, as well as Brenda's and Ellen's, depends on claiming access to Haitian men whose bodies they can commodify and objectify as they live out their sexualized fantasies. Similar acts of transgression are rendered impossible for them in the United States.

These women's desire for Legba sustains the myth of the exotic and luscious Other. Without knowing, or at least acknowledging Legba's etymology in Haitian Vodou as the *loa* (god/spirit) of the crossroads, sometimes viewed as young and virile, Ellen refers to him as "beautiful as a god" (129) and "looking like a young god" (135). Having an intimate relationship with him becomes a mystical experience for Ellen as demonstrated in her asking: "How could she [Sue] not get down on her knees before such a black sun?" (136). For Ellen, "getting on her knees" has a double meaning—spiritual catharsis and fellatio. Despite her apparent tourist bravado in the sexual conquest of Legba that initially placed her in a more powerful role, "getting on her knees" emphasizes the submissiveness of woman vis-à-vis man in a dominant position. In this context, the phrase "heading south" also acquires a sexual meaning, in addition to its geographical reference. Just as the north-south is associated with another binary of up-down, the action of "heading south" refers to geographic movements of tourists from the north to the global south and to the lower regions of the body, thereby signifying a search for erotic pleasure. However, easy access to male bodies sets a series of traps for these women, who literally head south.

Even when they are outside the United States and despite the power they wield in their relationships with Legba, Brenda and Ellen remain attached to a Western idea of romantic love as they each try to win over Legba. In one episode, the maître d'hôtel Albert sees Ellen "hanging on his [Legba's] neck and complaining that he was driving her crazy" and "crying like a teenager who'd just lost her first love" (136). The women's dreams of male courtship and affection, however, crash into the frigidity and unreachability of Legba, who acts out a beach boy role. Their love triangle breaks into pieces when Legba finds a potentially more suitable partner for himself. After replacing Ellen with Brenda, he conquers a female German tourist who gives him a gold chain: "How a woman like Brenda, who is so serious, such a devout Christian, could fall in love with a little gigolo like him was beyond me. He acted like a prince because this German woman had given him a gold chain that he wore around his neck like a leash" (137).

In both "Emoticons" and "Heading South," the female tourists live out their racialized and sexualized fantasies without dismantling their racial privilege. In Arias's story, Julieta remains ignorant of Pepe's economic struggles, and in Laferrière's text, the Haitian sexscape stands for the sexual permissiveness of female tourists and feeds the stereotype of their hypersexuality. This is particularly evident in Brenda's story. Her experience in Haiti begins when she is on a vacation there with her husband, Bill, with whom she befriends Legba, who is then fifteen years old. According to Brenda, Bill initiated the first interaction with Legba, although it was her lingering gaze over Legba's body that constituted their first intimate encounter: "Legba's body fascinated me: long, supple, delicately muscled. His skin glowed. I could hardly take my eyes off him. I drank him in, trying not to be too obvious about it. It didn't take long for my husband to notice the state I was in, and when Legba got up to walk lankily down towards the water, my husband gave me a wink that I took as a kind of permission" (130). Brenda's husband witnessed her sexual fulfillment: "I clutched at his chest . . . like a woman possessed, and jammed myself one last time on his cock, as deep as I could get it in, and held it there for a long time. He opened his eyes. He was as exhausted as I was. His eyes were red and timid and a bit frightened. Moved by a wave of gratitude, I threw myself on him, kissed him everywhere and cried like a baby. It was my first orgasm. I was fifty-five years old" (133). Brenda does not recall manipulating his, or her, body when Legba was lying immobile on the beach. He does not express surprise or scandal in response to her overtures, which suggests that he had already been initiated into sex work. Brenda's achievement of her first orgasm with Legba at the age of fifty-five overshadows the fact that she has committed what we might now call the statutory rape of a minor.

In this instance, while transnational romances are an occasion for claiming sexual fantasies and erotic transgressions, they also sustain inequalities of power that enable child abuse in Caribbean sexscapes (Kempadoo and Ghuma 1999, 297). Likewise, Brenda's behavior makes her an accomplice in perpetuating violent exploitation of the sexualized Other. At the end of the story, she reveals her predatory plan of heading to other Caribbean islands to pursue sexual adventures: "I don't want to have anything more to do with northern men. I'd like to spend time on other Caribbean islands. Cuba, Guadeloupe, Martinique, Dominica, Jamaica,

Trinidad, the Bahamas . . . They all have such pretty names. I want to know them all" (141).

Albert, the maître d'hôtel, is the only character in "Heading South" who openly voices his discontent with transactional romances, as he has absorbed anti-establishment traits from Cap-Haïtien, a cradle of the Haitian Revolution and the Haitian capital under Henri Christophe until 1820. His family history reveals his true feelings: "I came to work in Port-au-Prince when I was twenty-two, after my father died, and got a job in this hotel right away. If my grandfather knew that his grandson was serving Americans he would die of shame. This new army of occupation isn't armed, but it has packed its suitcase with a scourge much worse than cannons: drugs. The Queen of Crimes, and she always comes with her two sidekicks: easy money and sex" (133–134). Albert's family history alludes to the abusive exploitation of bodies that took place during the U.S. military occupation of 1915–1934 and during sex tourism in the second half of the twentieth century. The impact of imperialist domination on gender dynamics in the Dominican Republic that Horn explores in her book can be extended to Haiti, as Hispaniola shares a history of U.S. invasion and occupation throughout the twentieth century.[26] This is particularly important to Albert, whose entire family fought against the United States Marines during the 1915 occupation. As Albert explains, his father had never shaken a white man's hand. Moreover, his grandfather compared white people with animals: "As far as [my grandfather] was concerned, a white man was an animal, pure and simple" (133). Albert's relatives feel empowered by their resistance, which, in turn, validates a sense of Haitianness that is attached to resistance against foreign incursion. While Albert is troubled by the reality that he serves foreign tourists in a restaurant, he finds Legba's work problematic but also potentially revolutionary because as "the master of desire" (134), Legba transforms white women into "lost women, animals lusting after blood and sperm" (134).

Thus, when Albert finds Legba dying on the beach, "Heading South" leaves the mystery of Legba's death unsolved and opens the possibility of same-sex intimacy: "As I got closer I could see it was Legba, He looked like a sleeping angel. . . . I lay down beside him and took him in my arms. . . . I kissed Legba. It was the first time I'd ever kissed a man" (139–140). Instead of suggesting only that Legba's death is a crime of passion committed by Ellen or Brenda, Laferrière suggests that Albert is somehow involved. If

Albert killed or facilitated Legba's death, he did so to refuse his own and his country's subjugation to tourists. In "Heading South," then, the death of this sex worker highlights the impossibility of validating black masculinity within a preconceived Western ideal of transracial intimacy.

By revealing the presence of Dominican and Haitian men in the sex trade, *Chochueca's Strategy*, "Emoticons," and "Heading South" present transnational romances as phenomena that reinforce an image of the two countries as dependent on global capital through sex and romance. The representations of sex tourism and transactional romance across texts from both countries demonstrate how the roles and scripts associated with sex and romance tourism have moved beyond beach areas to create a sexscape out of the entire Hispaniola region. This movement has profound implications for contemporary gender relations, social mobility, and national identity. Finally, though, a broader Hispaniola framework allows scholars to see how the failure of transactional romances can comprise strategies of resistance against neocolonial practices.

Notes

1. Ouanaminthe is located next to the Dominican-Haitian border and the Dominican town of Dajabón, known for the Trujillo-orchestrated massacre of Haitians in 1937 and for present-day bilateral border crossings.

2. "*Italianos buscando morenitas que les hagan la vida imposible.*" Unless otherwise noted, all translations are my own.

3. In a study of sex tourism, Denise Brennan writes that many Dominican women emigrate to Sosúa from other parts of the country. For these women, sex work is an "advancement strategy," because they work directly with clients and keep their profits (Brennan 2003).

4. "*Un día te acompañé a recoger un paquete, uno de tantos que te mandaban las niñas engañadas del mundo entero. Al llegar a la oficina de correos, que estaba llena de tipos de esos amigos tuyos que gracias a un mayor grado de melanina y culipandeo recibían regalos y cartas de mujeres de todas partes del mundo, me quedé a esperarte en él.*"

5. I am playing on the notion of "Western Union Daddies" (Padilla 2007). Writing about the flow of international remittance via Western Union from foreign tourists to their Dominican girlfriends, Mark Padilla alludes to a slang term of sugar daddy that refers to a rich old man who offers financial support to his younger female companion often in return for sexual favors.

6. "*Saber cómo le contabas a una de tus mujeres que era la única y caerle a otra con otro recital de flechas y corazoncitos me parecía asqueroso.*"

7. "*James Gatto . . . transportó hasta la ciudad, hasta la puerta misma de la casa de*

Kika, además de prima, eterna cómplice a la que Pepe le confiaba todo, todas sus historias de amores a distancia con sus correspondientes adioses."

8. Aparicio and Chávez Silverman define *tropicalization* as follows: "To tropicalize . . . means to imbue a particular space, geography, group, or nation with a set of traits, images and values" (Aparicio and Chávez Silverman 1997, 8). I use this term to address the American way of exotifying the Latin American other—similar to Said's theory of orientalism.

9. "*Una jevita muy cool que había conocido por Salim tenía dinero porque su mamá había muerto de cáncer cuando ella era pequeña y le había dejado un tesorito.*"

10. "*Cuando andábamos las calles a pie, la gente siempre tan necia y poco delicada, probablemente pensaba, 'mira esa pobre gringuita cayó en las manos de ese sanki.*'"

11. "*Por eso cuando cruzábamos cortando tumultos en las aceras y a gente se volteaba a mirar a la blanquita y al negro, yo subía la voz como un carro de bomberos, con un acento capitaleño que dejaba flaco al de cualquier tigre de Villas Agrícola.*"

12. José Enrique Pintor's movie *Sanky Panky* (2007) also documents the first signs of a love failure. In "Geographies of Transit," Medina-Vilariño analyzes the representation of the main character Genaro as an antithesis of the *sanky-panky* because he resists selling his national ideals. He stays in the country and becomes a national hero who forms a couple with a female sex worker. According to Medina-Vilariño, the movie filmed by a Spaniard contains a double coloniality, since it imperceptibly advertises Bávaro-Barceló, a chain of hotels infamous for the availability of sexual services (Medina-Vilariño 2012, 57–58). As a result, the double moral makes one question Genaro's heroism, and his Dominican cinematographic foundation romance, as Patricia Tomé calls it, no longer looks like an acceptable solution for a sex-tourist romance (Tomé 2000, 386–403). However, Pintor's *Sanky Panky 2* (2013), which deserves more detailed analysis, takes it even further by showing that Genaro's relationship with his real fiancée cannot coexist with an affair with an American ex-girlfriend: he gets married only after he rejects the foreigner.

13. "*Había mentido a Pepe acerca de dos cosas que no consideró importantes: no tenía treinta y cinco años de edad sino cincuenta; ni tampoco se llamaba en realidad Julieta, sino Dolores.*"

14. "*Y Pepe, que varios días después, ya sea por tensión o por desidia, no ha logrado tener sexo con ella, la mira ansioso, malhumorado, inquieto.*"

15. "*¿No será que se niega a tener sexo porque lleva casi un mes aquí en este calor tropical, y todavía no he visto a Julieta bañarse?*"

16. "*Creo que definitivamente no quieres follar conmigo.*"

17. "*Pero si mi cuerpo es mío y yo hago con él lo que me venga en ganas.*"

18. "*¿Qué tal si nos casamos de verdad, con todas las de la ley, Pepi?*"

19. "*Él era un profesional; desempleado, pero profesional, y además, había salido una que otra vez fuera de la isla. No se consideraba un sankipanqui, pero por lo mismo no tenía el tiguereaje preciso para enfrentarse a un posible percance.*"

20. "*Dispuesto a lo que sea.*"

21. "*El otro, guerrero urbano de casco gris verdoso, parte raudo a seguir buscándosela por el mundo montado en su passola, 'parece un soldado nazi de tan majo', susurra en son de broma la española.*"

22. *"La oportuna llegada de aquel tipo [James Gatto] alto, blanco, ojos claros, con cara de buen bandido, le [a Pepe] hizo sentir una inesperada calma. En cualquier lugar, y más aún, en Boca Chica, resulta oportuno hacerse acompañar a alguien así."*

23. The Duvalier Era was the rule of François Duvalier, also known as Papa Doc, who was the president of Haiti from 1957 to 1971. He was succeeded by his son Jean-Claude Duvalier, or Baby Doc, who governed the country from 1971 until 1986. The contemporary tourist scene differs drastically from that of the Duvalier era. Among foreigners, primarily embassies and NGOs workers were present in Port-au-Prince after the 2010 earthquake, a disaster that triggered sex violence and the rape of women and girls. Many of those who migrated to the Dominican Republic had to enter sex work.

24. For more information on different types of female sex tourists, see Albuquerque (1999).

25. Shirley Tate explains that, although existent, white women's desire was erased from colonial memory, "leading to the conclusion that white desire for black bodies was male, which was in the interest of empire in constructing colonial citizens" (Tate 2011, 48–49).

26. The U.S. occupation lasted from 1916 to 1924 in the Dominican Republic and from 1915 to 1934 in Haiti.

Works Cited

Albuquerque, Klaus de. 1999. "Sex, Beach Boys and Female Tourists in the Caribbean." In *Sex Work and Sex Workers*, edited by Barry M. Dank and Roberto Refinetti, 87–112. New Brunswick, NJ: Transaction Publishers.

Aparicio, Frances, and Susana Chávez Silverman. 1997. *Tropicalizations: Transcultural Representations of Latinidad*. Hanover, NH: Dartmouth/University Press of New England.

Arias, Aurora. 2007. "Emoticons." In *Emoticons*. San Juan: Terranova Editores.

Brennan, Denise. 2003. "Selling Sex for Visas: Sex Tourism as Stepping Stone to International Migration for Dominican Women." In *Global Woman: Nannies, Maids, and Sex Workers in the New Economy*, edited by Barbara Ehrenreich and Arlie Russell Hochschild, 154–168. New York: Metropolitan Books.

———. 2004. *What's Love Got to Do with It? Transnational Desires and Sex Tourism in the Dominican Republic*. Durham NC: Duke University Press.

———. 2010. "Sex Tourism and Sex Workers' Aspirations." In *Sex for Sale: Prostitution, Pornography, and the Sex Industry*, edited by Ronald Weitzer, 307–324. New York: Routledge.

Cabezas, Amalia L. 1999. "Women's Work Is Never Done: Sex Tourism in Sosúa, the Dominican Republic." In *Sun, Sex, and Gold: Tourism and Sex Work in the Caribbean*, edited by Kamala Kempadoo, 93–123. Lanham, MD: Rowman & Littlefield Publishers.

———. 2004. "Between Love and Money: Sex, Tourism, and Citizenship in Cuba and the Dominican Republic." *Signs* 29 (4): 987–1015.

———. 2009. *Economies of Desire: Sex and Tourism in Cuba and the Dominican Republic.* Philadelphia: Temple University Press.

Collado, Lipe. 2002. *El tíguere dominicano: hacia una aproximación de cómo son los dominicanos.* Santo Domingo: Editora Collado.

Derby, Lauren H. 2009. *The Dictator's Seduction: Politics and the Popular Imagination in the Era of Trujillo.* Durham, NC: Duke University Press.

Francis, Donette. 2010. *Fictions of Feminine Citizenship: Sexuality and the Nation in Contemporary Caribbean Literature.* New York: Palgrave Macmillan.

Halberstam, Jack. 2011. *The Queer Art of Failure.* Durham, NC: Duke University Press.

Hernández, Rita Indiana. 2000. *La estrategia de Chochueca.* Santo Domingo: Riann Editorial.

Horn, Maja. 2014. *Masculinity After Trujillo: The Politics of Gender in Dominican Literature.* Gainesville: University Press of Florida.

Jesus Galván, Manuel de. (1882) 2010. *Enriquillo: Leyenda histórica Dominica (1503–1533).* Charleston: Nabu Press.

Kempadoo, Kamala, and Ranya Ghuma. 1999. "For the Children: International Policies and Law on Sex Tourism." In *Sun, Sex, and Gold: Tourism and Sex Work in the Caribbean,* edited by Kamala Kempadoo, 291–308. Lanham, MD: Rowman & Littlefield Publishers.

King, Rosamond S. 2014. *Island Bodies: Transgressive Sexualities in the Caribbean Imagination.* Gainesville: University Press of Florida.

Krohn-Hansen, Christian. 2016. *Political Authoritarianism in the Dominican Republic.* New York: Palgrave Macmillan.

Laferrière, Dany. 2009. "Heading South." In *Heading South.* Translated by Wayne Grady. Vancouver: Douglas & McIntyre.

Mbembe, Achille. 2003. "Necropolitics." *Public Culture* 15(1): 11–40.

McKercher, Bob, and Thomas G. Bauer. 2003. "Conceptual Framework of the Nexus Between Tourism, Romance, and Sex." In *Sex and Tourism: Journeys of Romance, Love, and Lust,* edited by Bob McKercher and Thomas G. Bauer, 3–18. Binghamton, NY: The Haworth Hospitality Press.

Medina-Vilariño, Kristina. 2012. "Geographies of Transit: Representations of the Dominican Body in Contemporary Film and Literature." PhD diss., University of Illinois at Urbana-Champaign.

Moya, Antonio de. 2004. "Power Games and Totalitarian Masculinity in the Dominican Republic." In *Interrogating Caribbean Masculinities: Theoretical and Empirical Analyses,* edited by Rhoda Reddock, 68–102. Kingston: University of the West Indies Press.

Padilla, Mark. 2007. *Caribbean Pleasure Industry: Tourism, Sexuality, and AIDS in the Dominican Republic.* Chicago and London: University of Chicago Press.

Sheller, Mimi. 2003. *Consuming the Caribbean: From Arawaks to Zombies.* London: Routledge.

———. 2012. *Citizenship from Below: Erotic Agency and Caribbean Freedom.* Durham, NC: Duke University Press.

Sommer, Doris. 1991. *Foundational Fictions: The National Romances of Latin America.* Berkeley: University of California Press.

Tate, Shirley. 2011. "*Heading South*: Love/Sex, Necropolitics, and Decolonial Romance." *Small Axe* 15 (2): 43–58.

Taylor, Jacqueline Sánchez. 2001. "Dollars Are a Girl's Best Friend? Female Tourists' Sexual Behaviour in the Caribbean." *Sociology* 35 (3): 749–764.

Tomé, Patricia. 2010. "De amores y fundaciones transnacionales: La dominicanidad cinematográfica desde Punta Cana hasta *Nueba Yol*." In *Cinema paraíso: Representaciones e imágenes audiovisuales en el Caribe hispano*, edited by Rosana Díaz-Zambrana and Patricia Tomé, 386–403. San Juan: Isla Negra.

Valerio-Holguín, Fernando. 2009. "*Emoticons* de Aurora Arias: Condición post-dominicana, identidades trashumantes e iconos de emociones." *Confluencia* 24 (2): 2–6.

Villaverde, Cirilo. 2005. *Cecilia Valdéz or El Angel Hill: A Novel of 19th-Century Cuba*. Translated by Helen Lane. New York: Oxford University Press.

3

The State, the Market, Bodies, and Commodities of Hispaniola

8

Developing an Economy of Sex

Intersecting Histories of Tourism, Beach Boys, and Masculinity in Hispaniola

ELIZABETH S. MANLEY

In Laurent Cantet's film *Heading South*, three women travel to Haiti in the 1970s and end up competing for the attention of "the virile Legba," a young and handsome local man.[1] Many other fit and attractive men surround these European and North American women throughout their stay, providing companionship and—it is implied—much more. Legba is portrayed as suave and knowledgeable about the foreign tourist women, and other Haitian men seek him out for advice. However, Albert, a restaurant waiter, looks down upon Legba while at the same time despising his own position of serving the "Americans" that his family fought against during the occupation.

Based on a short story by Haitian-Canadian Dany Laferrière and set during the Duvalier period, the film depicts the women dismissively discussing the rampant political corruption of the regime even as they fail to recognize their role in exploitative relationships as tourists (Laferrière 2009). Ellen, one of the three female protagonists, proclaims that "Legba belongs to everyone. He makes the decisions." Yet it is clear to the viewer that his decisions are highly restricted. His eventual death affirms the warnings of those who saw exchanges of sex, companionship, and money between local men and foreign women as part of a larger cycle of moral decay. As the detective who investigates Legba's death says, "Boys like him often end up that way." "Boys" like Legba are at the center of a set of issues that tie Haiti and the Dominican Republic together historically and contemporarily. Sex tourism, particularly the reliance of female sex tourism on certain models of neoliberal economic development, location exoticization, and a denationalized hypermasculinity, presents scholars with an opportunity to reexamine the intertwined histories of the island with a truly transnational lens.

Sex tourism generally refers to the "varieties of leisure travel that have as part of their purpose the purchase of sexual services" (Wonders and Michalowski 2001, 545). Caribbean scholar Kemala Kempadoo (1999) argues that sex work not only "stands as an integral part of the local and global economy" but is also intimately connected to the region's history of colonialism because it "continues the ambiguities and contradictions that were evident under slavery" (27). Visitors view sex-tourism providers across the region as exotic figures who are available for consumption. For their part, sex workers provide experiences for purchase to global North clients even as they attempt to create their own agency in an industry known for its precarious link to development.

The social and economic history of travel to the region reaching back to the colonial era is central to the present-day practice of sex work and, as Kempadoo argues, helps explain how "the [tourism] industry hinges on the exploitation of a number of the region's resources," particularly the black and brown bodies that are consumed as the exotified other (Kempadoo 1999, 20). While this type of travel generally invokes images of white, heterosexual U.S. or European men traveling to the Caribbean and other parts of the world to engage with local female sex workers (Brennan 2004), women and gay men are also clients in the exchanges Erica Williams (2013) refers to as "ambiguous entanglements."

Female sex tourism, or "romance tourism," as some label it, has existed in the Caribbean since the early twentieth century, when, according to scholar Klaus de Albuquerque, "older white women . . . arrived with steamer trunks, took up residence in large quarters, and tapped young black males to service them discreetly for the duration of their stay" (de Albuquerque 1998, 50).[2] The practice grew up alongside more traditional tourist endeavors as black and brown men, who dominated the formal and informal sectors of the tourist economy, transitioned into the roles of tour guides, companions, and, in some cases, boyfriends. For a significant number of these men, becoming a tour guide entailed providing sexual services in exchange for dinners, shopping, drinks, and, frequently, cash for "expenses."

Embedded within this imagined tableau of a tropical island paradise and affluent female travelers, what scholar Denise Brennan refers to as a "sexscape," is a complicated and overly generalized image of the Caribbean tour guide-turned-companion (Brennan 2004, 15). "Rent-a-dreads," "sankies," and "beach boys," as they are variously called by foreigners and locals, enact a particular and consistent form of Caribbean masculinity. They generally speak in Jamaican-inflected English, demonstrate fluency in reggae lyrics, and are physically fit, dark skinned, and often dreadlocked. Even though these guides-turned-companions have a laid-back image, foreign observers often depict them as potentially dangerous hustlers who threaten innocent female travelers. These contradictions— between exotic and approachable, casual and hustler, national and pan-Caribbean—construct the lived realities of male practitioners across the region and are embedded in a larger history of foreign imaginings of the tropics.

Since the earliest accounts of the island, travelers to Hispaniola have described it to foreign audiences as a place of exotic beauty, forbidden pleasure, and virile men. These descriptions have fueled tourist imaginaries in multiple ways. While the image is a far from adequate description of a multifaceted island, it has remained central to the tourism marketing of both the Dominican Republic and Haiti into the twenty-first century and is a key element in the growth of female sex tourism. When tourism became a central cog in the island's economic machinery, a number of scholars sought to shed light on the role of sex tourism within the industry and its image-making. While several studies have underscored the importance of integrating such analyses into larger understandings of development and globalization, little work has connected the "pleasure industry" with the economic and social history of tourism in Hispaniola as a single imagined community and as a community that outsiders imagine as exotic, fecund, and consummately consumable. Moreover, while scholarship has addressed the impact of tourism on the Caribbean's female sex workers, research is only beginning to uncover the realities of the region's male providers who, somewhat surprisingly, embody strikingly similar characteristics despite the varied tourism histories of their distinct nations (Hernández 2005; Pruitt and LaFont 1995; Sánchez Taylor 2001).

The trope of the hypermasculinized "beach boy" of Quisqueya, available for the needs of visiting Western women, has begun to enter academic studies and cultural readings of sex tourism in the last two decades. Focusing in on this figure and its historical antecedents helps render the entire island visible through a single analytical lens. As Elena Valdez points out in this volume, significant literary attention has been paid to the phenomenon of sankies and beach boys, and the archetype of the male sex worker serves as a pervasive symbol of neocolonial influence. It is crucial that scholars begin interrogating the ways sex tourism contributes to the othering of Caribbean male subjects. This chapter argues that two considerations should be incorporated into the scholarly analysis of tourism in Hispaniola. The first is that we should look to a history of tourism that both integrates analyses of gender, sexuality, and the political economy of the sex trade and considers both sides of the island together. The second is that more research should seek to understand the intimate and personal impacts of this broader history on the construction of identity and masculinity among the tourism industry's marginalized male sex workers.   As Mark Padilla (2008) argues, "Much of the research in the Caribbean region has failed to develop empirically grounded analyses of the mechanisms through which political-economic changes resulting from tourism are transforming sexuality and sexual behavior" (784). Integrating the history of female sex tourism with the development of tourism in the economies of Hispaniola provides a way to link their pasts. In the immediate present, these interconnected histories would help shed light on sexuality and sexual behavior and on changing ideas about masculinity and masculine honor in the context of exchanges between global North tourists and global South service providers. For the longer historical narrative, such links would bring the more marginalized individuals back toward the center of an island-wide and evolving struggle for sovereignty and economic development.

By intersecting the intertwined histories of tourism and sex travel with an analysis of the fit, dark-skinned male bodies that inhabit Hispaniola's "sexscapes," this chapter begins the process of reimagining the history of the island beyond national boundaries as one single, albeit complicated, narrative and responds to scholarly calls to shift the paradigm of analysis away from a status quo that reifies damaging tropes of otherness. As Kiran Jayaram and April Mayes point out in the introduction to this volume, engaging with transnationalism—in this case across the island and beyond to the bases tourists depart from—not only reveals the dangers of a naturalized vision of nationalism but also highlights the ways such rigid concepts of the nation-state promote the idea of an exotified and othered citizenry. In linking the economic and developmentalist visions of tourism with the more personal impacts of the sex tourism trade across the island, this project seeks to use the transnational frame to contextualize the ways service providers have become objects of local and international mocking and disdain despite their entrenchment in an industry that has long been touted as a miracle cure.

The growth of female sex tourism across the region demonstrates the continuation of the colonial legacies of dependency, highlights the importance of creating research that considers the island across national boundaries, and points to the perpetuation of a contradictory masculinity that has impacts far beyond the region's coastal communities. The local men who frequent beach areas and resort towns to offer their companionship and services as tour guides to visiting women are both part of and marginalized from the national development projects their governments have promoted as a "cure" for economic problems. While their participation in the industry is crucial to the informal economy of tourism, it is generally understood as somehow distinct or disconnected from structural development issues.

Situating the growth of Hispaniola's sex tourism industry in the context of networks of island exotification and global development strategies highlights the roots of a hypermasculinized, denationalized and often alienating gender identity that has developed across the island among its male sex workers. In an effort to encourage this type of intersectional inquiry, this chapter connects the earliest foreign visions of the island to twentieth-century histories of tourism and the development of a robust sex trade as part of that industry. It begins with an overview of early outsider depictions of the island, provides a brief discussion of the development of tourism in Haiti and the Dominican Republic, and concludes with some implications of the practice of female sex tourism for and masculinity and national identity across Hispaniola.

Visions of Paradise

Since the early accounts of Columbus, Hispaniola has been marketed to and consumed by foreign audiences as an exotic and fecund place of otherness in the tropics. This image has remained central to the tourism marketing of the Dominican Republic and Haiti into the twenty-first century. Upon first landing on the north coast of the island, Columbus declared it to be "a marvel":

Its hills and mountains, fine plains and open country, are rich and fertile for planting and for pasturage, and for building towns and villages. The seaports there are incredibly fine, as also the magnificent rivers, most of which bear gold.

He went on to describe the island's men in contradictory terms that continue into the present, proclaiming that "although they are well-made men of commanding stature, they appear extraordinarily timid."[3] From the very beginning, the island was valued for its "fertile" land and exploitable population. As Mimi Sheller notes, early writings such as this example from Columbus were "informed by an imagery of tropical fecundity and excessive fruitfulness," adding that such descriptions not only narrated the new space but actually brought it into being (Sheller 2003, 25, 42).

Starting in the eighteenth century, foreign visitors set up the Caribbean as a place of diametrically opposed realities (Pattullo 2005; Sheller 2003). One the one hand, they depicted the region as lush, tropical, and fertile. They also described it as enticing and unique. Yet amid all this fecundity, observers also saw danger, incivility, and the opportunity to consume and literally be consumed. Initially, exploration narratives discussed the land and the people and their riches. Sheller (2003) argues that the eighteenth century was marked by scientific collection, the desire for the knowledge that could be extracted from the region, and the possibilities the land offered for cultivation. In the late nineteenth century, travel writing exhibited a marked turn in which observers noted the beauty, but also the "African barbarism" (58) of the Caribbean. This attitude persisted into the twentieth century. For example, in 1906, Teddy Roosevelt referred to the "great, beautiful, venomous, tropical islands" (quoted in Meehan 2009, 254). Finally, although the later twentieth-century imaginings of the Caribbean demonstrate a desire to "fairly" represent the region through ethnography and area studies, these studies embed the concept of the duality of beauty and decay. This "heaven on earth" is possible, according to Polly Pattullo, precisely because the images of lush landscaping coexist with a "mythology of blackness," which, in its association with hedonism and abandon, "reinforces this focus on play and partying" (Pattullo 2005, 142).

Visual renderings of the region have also followed this trend of exoticization, as Krista Thompson (2006) documents in *An Eye for the Tropics*. She refers to this process as "tropicalization," which she defines as "the complex visual systems through which the islands were imaged for tourist consumption and the social and political implications of these representations on actual physical space on the islands and their inhabitants" (5). While tropicalization is a "continually negotiated process" between tourism marketers, consumers, and the consumed, it is one that directly impacts the island's people and places that are in the uncomfortable position of fulfilling (or not) an ideal that is often created externally. Scholars are quick to point out that this external ideal of tropicality and its negotiation is in line with the region's past. Starting with Frantz Fanon, anthropologists have pointed to the intertwined realities of the colonizer—the gaze—and the colonized—the view. Sheller reframes this idea by discussing regimes of mobility and immobility (Sheller 2003).

The ability of the westerner to render the Caribbean as a tropical paradise is directly linked to the islanders' economic, political, and social dependence on the Western world. Tourism on both sides of the island is situated within this binary: the tourist body is mobile while the Caribbean body is fixed, forced into low-paying jobs that service the visitors on which their economies depend. Hispaniola, as the center of the imaginary of the Americas, has been "brought into being" at the nexus of a number of contradictions—fertile and welcoming versus dangerous, beautiful versus barbarous, and foreign and exotic versus accessible. These dualities are the bases on which the modern tourism industry was built.

"Created by God for Tourism"

The development of the tourism industry in Hispaniola in the twentieth century has had profound effects on all aspects of life on the island, from national economies to individual lives. In multiple phases, governments and tourism boards on each side of the island have sought to package their nation for Western observers and potential visitors in ways that matched the expectations of their target audience, mirroring the duality of the historical tropicalization of Hispaniola as both exotic and foreign and approachable and consumable. Marketing efforts that targeted investors and travelers that were intertwined with domestic expectations of progress and development shaped not only the island's external image but also an understanding of itself as a marketable good. As tourism grew into a dominant economic force in the region, both Haiti and the Dominican Republic faced the realities of its varied forms of consumption, ranging from the usurpation of the most pristine beaches for resort enclaves to the expense of human labor, including sex for sale.

Tourism, or travel for leisure, began with the organization of the modern-day tour. This arguably began with Thomas Cook's British travel excursions in the 1840s and 1850s and eventually led to European travel to the Caribbean in the late nineteenth century (Gmelch 2003, 2). By the 1880s, freight carriers such as United Fruit had begun offering tickets to passengers, facilitating European and U.S. travel to the region. The "Great White Fleet" of the fruit company allowed individuals to disembark at a variety of Caribbean ports (Duval 2004, 155). Initially, wealthy travelers were attracted by the climate and the air, frequenting cities but not necessarily beachfront resorts. By the early twentieth century, however, the sun had become "the new icon," and seaside beach travel became desirable, further opening up the Caribbean (Pattullo 2005, 9; Gmelch 2003, 5). The advent of jet travel significantly increased tourism traffic globally and the mantra of "sun, sea, and sand" quickly became the primary reason for traveling to the region. Between the world wars, travel was limited to the very wealthy, but in the 1940s and 1950s, a growing middle class in the West created a much wider demographic that could vacation in the Caribbean.

In the 1950s, Caribbean governments began to actively promote tourism as the new solution to economic woes. The World Trade Organization encouraged tourism development across the region because, it argued, the industry could be developed with minimal capital investment and would require little outlay from either national governments or from international lending agencies.[4] Tourism continued to grow over the next decade and major organizations, both domestic and foreign, began praising its transformative potential. In the late 1970s and 1980s, many organizations and individuals argued that tourism could be a vehicle for positive change globally by promoting universal human understanding, solidarity, and even peace. The Organization of American States argued that tourism would raise the standard of living, while Pope Paul VI contended that world tourism was a "passport to peace" (Gmelch 2003, 7). Members of private industry saw opportunities to enrich their shareholders. Ministries of tourism were created across the region to aggressively promote infrastructure development and building projects. By the 1980s, mass tourism was entrenched in the Caribbean and depictions of it as a tropical paradise—promoted by national governments and industry participants—were ubiquitous.[5]

While Hispaniola followed the general trajectory of tourism development in the Caribbean, it was also unique because periods of authoritarianism there encouraged the industry in distinct ways. Tourism in Haiti began with passengers arriving on shipping boats in the 1930s and 1940s and increased gradually through the 1980s. Industry growth was briefly halted by the upheaval that followed the ouster of Jean-Claude Duvalier, but it continued to grow significantly until the 2010 earthquake. Entering the tourist game early, Haiti developed a National Tourist Office in 1939, shortly after the U.S. military occupation of the island ended (Plummer 1992, 2). Both occupations, in Haiti from 1915 to 1934 and in the Dominican Republic from 1916 to 1924, championed a "progressive imperialism" that promoted and implemented an array of programs and initiatives in health care, education, public works, fiscal management, civil and military service, and infrastructure development at the cost of national sovereignty.[6] As it transitioned out of the occupation years, Haiti looked to the $33 million tourists were spending in Central America and the West Indies as a potential path to economic and political development. The remaining U.S. officials agreed heartily (Plummer 1992, 3). Sidney de la Rue, the U.S. fiscal advisor to Haiti, even suggested the creation of a foreign corporation intended to promote tourism in "all the American Republics," although such an entity was never created (Plummer 1992, 5).

Plans stalled during World War II because of political instability in the country and a lack of interest on the part of U.S. investors. However, a subtle change in Haiti's image due in large part to research social scientists conducted in the 1930s and 1940s facilitated significant growth in tourism. Despite imagery of Haiti from the time of the U.S. occupation as barbarous and uncivilized, scholars and others began to view the nation as a "legitimate research field" and as a potential place for travel—albeit a still highly exotic one (Plummer 1992, 8). Concurrently, a growing educated and urban class of Haitians began embracing indigenous culture, culminating in the election of Léon Dumarsais Estimé as president. His administration and its more middle-class constituency took an interest in the island's possibilities as a vacation destination.

Under Estimé, the Haitian state began reviving tourism plans, for example by staging the National Exposition in 1949 to highlight art and culture. By the early 1950s, Haiti, particularly Port-au-Prince, had become an exotic getaway (Plummer 1992, 7). Brenda Plummer describes the years from 1949 to 1956 as the "golden age" of Haitian tourism. Katherine

Dunham, Maya Deren, Langston Hughes, Zora Neale Hurston, Edna Taft, and others all drew attention, in one way or another, to the opportunities available to travelers on the western side of the island. While the U.S. occupiers represented Haiti as a nation in need of protection and civilization in order to legitimate their military intervention, U.S. marines and playwrights who wrote about Haiti during and after the occupation presented Haiti as an "exotic object of desire" (Renda 2001, 19). Even writers such as African Americans Dunham, Hurston, and Hughes, who sought to redeem the nation from its public shaming by the United States, saw two sides of Haiti. Despite their efforts to describe its complexity, they too envisioned a place that was incredible but also mysterious and "othered." Taft, an elite white woman from a line of New England slave traders, argued that the place was in her blood. Her account, like those of many others, "laid claim to an exotic Haiti figured largely in terms of race and sexuality" (Renda 2001, 231).

Tourism in Haiti withered after François Duvalier was elected in 1961, despite a \$2.8 million U.S. loan to rebuild the Port-au-Prince airport in exchange for Haiti's vote to dismiss Cuba from the Organization of American States, but it revived in the 1970s (Plummer 1992, 12). This revival, which continued through the mid-1980s, gave rise to the phenomenon of sex tourism and was a portent of things to come in the post-earthquake period of redevelopment.[7] As an anthropologist living in Haiti in the late 1970s has argued, the decisions tourists made to visit Haiti were based largely on ideas that it was exotic that had developed in the previous decades (Goldberg 1981). Now fueled by post-disaster philanthropic tourism initiatives, travelers continue to imagine a place that is both desperately in need and "othered" and exotic.

Similarly, the Dominican Republic experienced uneven progress toward the purported miracle industry of tourism. Despite the infrastructure developments U.S. occupiers made on the Dominican side, the iron-fisted rule of dictator General Rafael Trujillo (1930–1961) forestalled the tourism heyday of the postwar period that took place in Haiti. Trujillo made an effort in the 1950s to replicate Haiti's success by building luxury hotels and hosting a lavish world's fair and attempting to attract visitors to Ciudad Trujillo, as Santo Domingo was known during most of his tenure. As Evan Ward notes in *Packaged Vacations* (2008), Trujillo's efforts "created a splash for a couple of years, and then tourism would begin to ebb" (155). Several geographers contended in the early 1990s that Trujillo's initiatives "served more to showcase the modernity of the country than stimulate tourism" (Meyer-Arendt, Sambrook, and Kermath 1992, 220). The modernity showcased to the tourist during that brief window was decidedly unmodern and steeped in fascist dictatorship. The turmoil and political instability surrounding Trujillo's final years and the return of the U.S. Marines in 1965 kept potential tourists away. Moreover, as interests had begun to turn to "sun, sea, and sand," the efforts of the *Trujillato* that focused on urban and mountain resorts failed to create an increase in tourism to the Dominican Republic (Meyer-Arendt, Sambrook, and Kermath 1992, 220).

In the late 1960s, Trujillo's successor, Joaquín Balaguer, began massive investment in the tourism industry, a strategy that had proven successful elsewhere in the Caribbean. He commissioned a study of the viability of tourism, as did UNESCO and the Organization of American States. The government-commissioned report came up with a list of recommendations for encouraging international tourism, while the UNESCO study pinpointed particular places on the island that were ripe for tourist development, particularly Boca Chica (south coast), San Pedro de Macorís (southeast coast), and Playa Dorado (north coast). The Balaguer regime supported the industry around these "touristic poles" by providing tax incentives and attractive low-interest loans, particularly in the development of Casa de Campo and Punta Cana, in the southeastern part of the country removed from San Pedro de Macorís.

Growth continued through the 1970s and 1980s at a rapid pace, including the development of a number of all-inclusive resorts that provided food, lodging, and entertainment in a single vacation package. As Angel Miolán, the director of Dominican Tourism, noted, the country was "created by God for tourism, I have dared say sometimes, excited by the beauty of its potential" (quoted in Gregory 2014, 11). Under Balaguer, the nation consolidated its tourism agenda and followed many of the recommendations of the reports, which included establishing a national agency for tourism, a tourism police force, and *zonas turísticas* (tourism zones or poles). By 1994, the Dominican Republic was the most popular Caribbean destination for tourists.[8]

Across Haiti and the Dominican Republic, the somewhat parallel development of viable tourism industries has been intimately connected by several factors that include the foreign occupations of the two nations, the challenges of authoritarian leadership, and the developmentalist push to create a "paradise fantasy" for foreign visitors. Through the expansion of tourism in the mid-twentieth century and its embedded idea of tropicalization, tourism promoters on both sides of the island created opportunities for Western travelers to figuratively and literally consume the exotified island. Such tourism development efforts implicitly enabled a particular vision of imperialized masculinity for the male tourist that was embedded in historical depictions of the island beginning with Columbus. Marketing materials encouraged Western male tourists to explore the Caribbean and even conquer, if they desired, and many had the financial means to do so. However, in the 1970s and 1980s, as North American and European women began making more money and choosing to vacation independently, female travelers began coming for an experience that was sold to them as safe yet foreign and titillating. Such travel was a confirmation of women travelers' advantaged social, racial, and economic status. Unlike male tourists, however, female travelers could find a level of social hierarchy in the Caribbean that was likely unavailable to them at home (Gregory 2014, 155).[9]

For both male and female tourists, Caribbean service workers came to represent a dually embodied consumption. Consumption is always already a physical act for the consumer. However, tourism in the tropics also exemplifies a practice in which the exotic island experience becomes embodied by the individuals the tourist engages. In all the effort expended to make the island enticing for foreign travelers, underlying assumptions and contradictions remain. For consumers, travel to the tropics can occur without any understanding of or guilt about the unequal relationships of power between themselves and those they encounter precisely because of the ways the islands are sold as an experience or a fantasy rather than as a simple purchase. The intertwined historical outsider renderings of the island and modern tourism campaigns together created a space for the figurative consumption of local inhabitants.

Female Sex Tourism: The Role of the Male Worker

As many scholars have noted, the integration of prostitution into the equation of tourism globally is not surprising given the "erosion of boundaries between the formal and informal sectors of the economy" (Cabezas 2004, 990) in the context of selling tropical paradise. Scholars and social commentators alike debate the appropriate term to use for foreign women who vacation and—intentionally or unintentionally—make exchanges for sex. Several argue that "romance tourism" is a more appropriate term when dealing with female travelers because the exchange of sexual services is usually not strictly for cash and these travelers often reference romance and companionship when describing their relationships (Pruitt and LaFont 1995).

Yet the use of the word "romance" obscures the fact that these relationships are ultimately economic and business exchanges, despite the views of novelist Terri McMillan and other popular cultural observers to the contrary. As Polly Pattullo points out, exploitation is always present because the exchange relies on the dependency of the host. Beyond being just a "romance holiday," the exchange gives a woman "power over a man in a way that she does not have in New York or Manchester," even if she is oblivious to this global power position (Pattullo 2005, 98). Her ability to exchange what she has to offer—be it anything from money to "temporary [or even permanent] access to the First World"—hinges on her geopolitical and socioeconomic superiority over her Caribbean companion. The industry, which depends on the image of the island as desirable and consumable, necessarily creates a space of otherness that allows the female foreigner to feel sufficiently attracted to and safe from the island paradise so she can fully engage both her socioeconomic superiority and her sexual fantasy. And female sex tourism is significant business. According to one estimate, between 1980 and the early 2000s nearly 600,000 women worldwide traveled for the purposes of sex tourism (Belliveau 2006).

The local men and boys who traverse the beach areas and resort towns proffering services and/or companionship to foreign women are integral to the informal economy of tourism, yet their presence in the "sexscape" is rarely understood as a survival strategy. Instead, locals regularly mock them and visitors sometimes fear them. While observers have noted that the standard practice for male sex-tourism providers across the region is a performance of exaggerated and stereotypical masculinity that simultaneously evokes attraction and disdain, little work has challenged *why* and *how* this particular stereotype developed across disparate nation-states and as part of diverse institutional economic strategies.

Just as Hilary Beckles (2004) argues for an understanding of masculinity as a historically evolving script based in "violent subordination of black males by white men" under slavery (228), female sex tourism demands historical analysis to uncover the origins of an archetype among male sex workers that is overtly masculine yet servile, carefree yet threatening. This conflicted gender identity among male sex workers is grounded in the economic and historical development of the region's tourism industry and highlights the difficult and nuanced problems of selling travel—particularly for sex—as the solution to Caribbean underdevelopment.

Although sex tourism was first mentioned in a scholarly context in a 1978 study that addressed the young men or "hustlers" who combed the beaches of Barbados for female companions, the practice reaches back to the beginnings of female tourist travel (Matthews 1978, 67). While the report referred to the men broadly as "hustlers," it was clear that sex was more often than not a part of the equation. Since then, the practice by men has grown throughout the region alongside the growth of the tourist industry and the increase of global North women traveling independently.

Female sex tourism in Hispaniola began to grow significantly in the 1970s and 1980s as a result of resort development on both sides of the island and relied on the generalized male archetype emerging across the Caribbean. As Padilla notes of the Dominican Republic, "The sanky-panky identity—based on a linguistic Dominicanization of the English phrase "hanky panky"—emerged in response to the growing presence of young, well-built men who made a modest living by hustling foreign men and women in tourist-oriented beach areas" (Padilla 2009, 147). While male sex tourists tend to parse the various merits of "chicas" of different nationalities the discourse on beach boys focuses on a single, dependable archetype of the laid-back, often dreadlocked, extremely fit, and dark-skinned male beach dweller.[10] Ethnographers argue that these men originally catered to gay tourists on guided tours in the late 1970s but soon transitioned to servicing women, who provided them with more money and presented less risk of stigma (Herold, Garcia, and DeMoya 2001). Now such "beach boys," who often work jobs that bring them in contact with tourists, tend to project a friendly, flattering, and nonthreatening attitude toward visiting foreign women and position themselves as ideal vacation companions. As Kempadoo argues, this "construction of the hypersexual male" positions sankies and beach boys "as subjects that can provide sex on demand—as the quintessential black male stud" (1999, 25).

Yet two elements of this performance of masculinity contrast with normative understandings of men's role in the patriarchal power structure and have implications for the island's male sex workers. First, the denationalized nature of the play for the attention of visiting female tourists—an essential part of the "island paradise" fantasy—marginalizes male sex workers from narratives of national identity. Second, the ambivalent nature of the male service provider's role—performing as a laid-back yet knowledgeable guide while also explicitly accepting the socioeconomic nature of his inferior relation to the female guest—challenges existing normative expectations that the island's male citizenry be masculine, authoritative heads of household.

In a study in Puerto Plata in the late 1990s, investigators interviewed twenty-five male sex workers and fourteen female tourists (Herold, Garcia, and DeMoya 2001, 981). In addition to being in beach areas, the men were also often associated with all-inclusive resort areas and commonly held jobs in the industry that provided legitimate excuses for them to meet tourist women. Many admitted to using foreign women to supplement their meager incomes and were aware that they were capitalizing on the emotional vulnerability of female tourists. Almost all sankies, who were generally from vulnerable socioeconomic backgrounds, came to beach enclaves from various parts of the island in search of greater economic opportunities.[11]

While scholarly focus has mostly centered on the Dominican side of the island, sex work is embedded in the development of informal beach economies that have been growing on both sides since the middle of the twentieth century. Yet the practice remains relatively underinterrogated, particularly in relation to the construction of the island—literally and metaphorically—as a paradise fantasy for global North travelers. Philosopher Linden Lewis (2004) argues that "although not included in the tourism brochures, everyone knows that an important part of the tourism industry [in the Caribbean] is the availability of exoticized sex" and the black male bodies that are an integral part of the "libidinal economy" (246). As scholars, we need to begin to delve into the subtext of all the ways these islands are being sold to foreign visitors and interrogate the connection between promotions of paradise and a livelihood that operates to marginalize Dominican and Haitian men from accepted narratives of nation and masculinity. This is certainly not to say that such normative discourses of identity are desirable but rather to question the repercussions for men across Hispaniola who are constructing performances of self that at once undergird and also subvert standard, heteronormative understandings of nation and gender.

Conclusion

Historically, sankies and beach boys have not been policed in the same literal way as female sex workers. Many have flexible economic arrangements that allow them to slip in and out of this informal economy. They are also generally not subject to arrest or police harassment in the same way as female sex workers. However, they are not immune to social critiques and cultural policing of their survival strategies by both local and foreign observers. According to commentators on the social site dr1.com, sankies are characters to be wary of. To one blogger, they are "Dominican con-men who prey on unsuspecting female tourists."[12] According to another post, individuals can "catch [the sanky] in their lies" by following some precautionary steps. While more laudatory of the diverse social and sexual skills and abilities of the sanky ("*rasgos exóticos y habilidades amatorias*"), one Dominican commentator noted that it was this type of behavior that brought HIV to the island and would continue to bring drug addiction, moral degradation, and death to the Dominican people.[13] Like Legba, the typical beach boy is slick, suave, and uber-masculine yet also the portent of the damning elements of development.

What does it mean that Dominican and Haitian men who supplement their incomes through sexual exchanges with foreign women are viewed as morally corrupt con men and hustlers who have been othered by their own people as a direct result of a historically constituted foreign gaze? If we believe popular culture or even some feminist theory that posits female sex tourism as "romance holiday," the fault lies with the men themselves. Yet the men working in beach enclaves across the island can be seen merely to be grappling with a limited number of choices. They are often forced into survival strategies due to the particularities of the tourism economy and seek advancement by strategically deploying an exotified island manhood as an embodied commodity.

In the process of these sexual or romantic exchanges between foreign women and local men, various identity markers for male sex workers—such as race, nation, class, and sexuality—are subsumed while their masculinity serves in a performatively exaggerated yet practically limited way. As they are selling both their bodies and their gendered performance to foreign buyers, they embody a trans-Caribbean identity that remains divorced from more local ideas about manliness and masculinity. Engaging the transnational Hispaniola paradigm, this chapter begins the work of digging out this particular denationalized hypermasculinity from the intertwined histories of tourism and development on both sides of the island. It argues that sankies and beach boys across the island are not just a modern phenomenon of mass tourism but are also deeply embedded in centuries-old practices that have sought to sell the place—dating back to Columbus—as an imminently consumable paradise.

Imagining a Hispaniola community of male sex workers through this particular subsector of the tourism industry highlights how projects that sell the islands as tropical paradises both constructed an exoticized image of its male inhabitants and unintentionally created the spaces for many to work as providers. Paradoxically, sex tourism, one product of neoliberal economic development policies, promotes global interactions that perpetuate dangerous stereotypes among consumers and create conflicting understandings of identity for the providers. Given the impacts of tourism as a major development pillar both in the region and globally, interrogating the continuities of sex tourism across Hispaniola continues the project of thinking about and through constructs of nationalism on an island that has generally been analyzed by scholars through separate colonial lenses. Finally, working through these intersecting histories of sex tourism and tourism more generally reveals that the historical and discursive projections of the islands and their inhabitants as breathtakingly beautiful, undeniably relaxing, and constantly for sale are directly linked to contemporary and often contradictory understandings of Caribbean masculinity.

Notes

1. *Heading South*, dir. Laurent Cantet, 2006, Soda Pictures, DVD.

2. While de Albuquerque makes this reference in an anecdotal manner, other sources, such as women's travel writings and memoirs, provide additional evidence that women, while not necessarily traveling with the express purpose of sex, took advantage of opportunities to have relationships with local men (Colley 2008).

3. While Columbus wanted his writings to convince his readers of the land's openness to colonial exploitation, they serve as a powerful first impression of the land and its inhabitants. See "Letter from Christopher Columbus to Luis de Sant Angel Announcing His Discovery, 1493," in Eliot (1909).

4. Only later did most participants in the industry realize that significant capital was necessary to develop the kind of resort enclaves that would draw large numbers (Gmelch 2003, 7).

5. Before World War II, approximately 100,000 people traveled to the Caribbean each year. By 1985, that number was 10 million, and in 2000, it had reached 17 million (Gmelch 2003, 8).

6. All this purported progress came, of course, at a cost that went beyond just sovereignty. The presence of the United States and its marine forces aggressively promoted U.S. business interests, encouraged military-dictatorship-style rule, set limits on public dissent, and fostered the development of a national guard, a continued dependence on the exportation of primary goods, increased racial tensions, and the growth of anti-imperial nationalism and the space for predatory governments, like those of Trujillo and Duvalier (Winters and Derrell 2010, 603).

7. Unfortunately, it withered again as a result of political instability that began in 1986. It started to come back in the late 1990s. Following the earthquake, Haiti's Department of Tourism began a campaign to promote beach-based tourism, including the development of the small island of Ile-à-Vache, Jacmel, and possibly the historic island of Tortuga. For more on their recent efforts, see Haiti Support Group (2015, 1–2). For a critique of these plans see Adams (2014).

8. In 1970, 89,700 foreign tourists came to the Dominican Republic; by 1992, that number was 1.6 million (Pattullo 2005, 11).

9. More research needs to be conducted on the attitudes of female tourists about travel focused on sex and on the accompanying statistics (Sánchez Taylor 2001, 751). Moreover, there is no scholarly research on female-to-female sex tourism. While the industry is predominately heterosexual, there is no reason to believe that such exchanges do not occur.

10. Klaus de Albuquerque argues that beach boys are easy to spot because they usually sport "T-shirts, baggy swimming trunks, and Teva sandals, gold bracelets, and brand-name sunglasses," often wear their hair in dreadlocks, and are "without exception physically fit" (de Albuquerque 1998, 50–51). Nearly all participate either formally or informally in the tourist economy by renting beach chairs, working in local bars or tourist shops, or running tours, and virtually all navigate the coastal regions of the islands. They

are called many things: sanky-pankys, beach boys, rent-a-dreads, jineteros, the Foreign Service, and they have coined names for the women who become their clients.

11. Herold, Garcia, and de Moya argue that "all . . . are black," which is significant because it adds "an exotic nature" to the encounter (Herold, Garcia, and DeMoya 2001, 982). Their "covert strategies to procure financial gain" can be successful: many reported earning nearly $1,000 a month (compared to the Dominican average of $60) (Cabezas 2009, 999).

12. See "Sankie 101," DR1, http://dr1.com/forums/forumdisplay.php/39-Sankie-101, accessed October 11, 2007; and "Curso de Sankies for Dummies," Nistido.com, November 4, 2005, http://www.nistido.com/2005/11/curso-de-sankies-for-dummies-1-3/. Accessed September 11, 2015.

13. Presumably this stereotype pervades in Haiti, where a discourse developed in the 1980s that blamed the island nation for the AIDS crisis. See Haiti Support Group (2015, 50).

Works Cited

Adams, David. 2014. "Neglected Islanders Resist Plans for Haiti Tourist Revival." Reuters, April 7. http://www.reuters.com/article/2014/04/07/haiti-tourism-idUSL1N 0MX01F20140407. Accessed September 11, 2015.

Albuquerque, Klaus de. 1998. "In Search of the Big Bamboo." *Transition* 77: 48–57.

Beckles, Hilary. 2004. "Black Masculinity in Caribbean Slavery." In *Interrogating Caribbean Masculinities Theoretical and Empirical Analyses*, edited by Rhoda Reddock, 225–243. Kingston, Jamaica: University of the West Indies Press.

Belliveau, Jeannette. 2006. *Romance on the Road*. Baltimore, MD: Beau Monde Press.

Brennan, Denise. 2004. *What's Love Got to Do with It? Transnational Desires and Sex Tourism in the Dominican Republic*. Durham, NC: Duke University Press.

Cabezas, Amalia L. 2004. "Between Love and Money: Sex, Tourism, and Citizenship in Cuba and the Dominican Republic." *Signs* 29 (4): 987–1015.

———. 2009. *Economies of Desire: Sex and Tourism in Cuba and the Dominican Republic*. Philadelphia: Temple University Press.

Colley, Linda. 2008. *The Ordeal of Elizabeth Marsh: A Woman in World History*. Reprint edition. New York: Anchor.

Duval, David Timothy. 2004. *Tourism in the Caribbean: Trends, Development, Prospects*. London; New York: Routledge.

Eliot, Charles William, ed. 1909. *American Historical Documents, 1000–1904*. New York: Collier. http://www.bartleby.com/43/. Accessed September 4, 2015.

Gmelch, George. 2003. *Behind the Smile: The Working Lives of Caribbean Tourism*. Bloomington: Indiana University Press.

Goldberg, Alan. 1981. "Commercial Folklore and Voodoo in Haiti: International Tourism and the Sale of Culture." PhD diss., Indiana University.

Gregory, Steven. 2014. *The Devil behind the Mirror: Globalization and Politics in the Dominican Republic*. Berkeley: University of California Press.

Haiti Support Group. 2015. "Tourism in Haiti: New Pirates of the Caribbean." *Haiti Briefing* 79. June. http://haitisupportgroup.org/download/new-pirates-caribbean-hb79/. Accessed October 16, 2017.

Hernández, Tanya K. 2005. "Sex in the [Foreign] City: Commodification and the Female Sex Tourist." In *Rethinking Commodification: Cases and Readings in Law and Culture*, edited by Martha M. Ertman and Joan C. Williams, 222–242. New York: New York University Press.

Herold, Edward, Rafael Garcia, and Tony DeMoya. 2001. "Female Tourists and Beach Boys: Romance or Sex Tourism?" *Annals of Tourism Research* 28 (4): 978–997.

Kempadoo, Kamala. 1999. "Continuities and Change: Five Centuries of Prostitution in the Caribbean." In *Sun, Sex, and Gold: Tourism and Sex Work in the Caribbean*, edited by Kamala Kempadoo, 3–33. Lanham, MD: Rowman & Littlefield.

Laferrière, Dany. 2009. *Heading South*. Translated by Wayne Grady. Vancouver: Douglas & McIntyre.

Lewis, Linden. 2004. "Masculinity, the Political Economy of the Body, and Patriarchal Power in the Caribbean." In *Gender in the 21st Century: Caribbean Perspectives, Visions and Possibilities*, edited by Barbara Bailey, Elsa Leo-Rhynie, and Mona Academic Conference, 236–261. Kingston, Jamaica: Ian Randle.

Matthews, Harry G. 1978. *International Tourism: A Political and Social Analysis*. Cambridge, MA: Schenkman Pub. Co.

Meehan, Kevin. 2009. *People Get Ready: African American and Caribbean Cultural Exchange*. Jackson: University Press of Mississippi.

Meyer-Arendt, Klaus J., Richard A. Sambrook, and Brian M. Kermath. 1992. "Seaside Resorts in the Dominican Republic: A Typology." *Journal of Geography* 91 (5): 219–225.

Padilla, Mark B. 2008. "The Embodiment of Tourism among Bisexually-Behaving Dominican Male Sex Workers." *Archives of Sexual Behavior* 37 (5): 783–793.

———. 2009. "The Limits of 'Heterosexual AIDS': Ethnographic Research on Tourism and Male Sexual Labor in the Dominican Republic." In *Anthropology and Public Health: Bridging Differences in Culture and Society*, edited by Robert A. Hahn and Marcia C. Inhorn, 142–164. Oxford: Oxford University Press.

Pattullo, Polly. 2005. *Last Resorts: The Cost of Tourism in the Caribbean*. 2nd ed. New York: Monthly Review Press.

Plummer, Brenda Gayle. 1992. *Haiti and the United States: The Psychological Moment*. Athens: University of Georgia Press.

Pruitt, Deborah, and Suzanne LaFont. 1995. "For Love and Money: Romance Tourism in Jamaica." *Annals of Tourism Research* 22 (2): 422–440.

Renda, Mary A. 2001. *Taking Haiti: Military Occupation and the Culture of U.S. Imperialism, 1915–1940*. Chapel Hill: University of North Carolina Press.

Sánchez Taylor, Jacqueline. 2001. "Dollars Are a Girl's Best Friend? Female Tourists' Sexual Behaviour in the Caribbean." *Sociology* 35 (3): 749–764.

Sheller, Mimi. 2003. *Consuming the Caribbean: From Arawaks to Zombies*. London; New York: Routledge.

Thompson, Krista A. 2006. *An Eye for the Tropics: Tourism, Photography, and Framing the Caribbean Picturesque*. Durham, NC: Duke University Press.

Ward, Evan R. 2008. *Packaged Vacations: Tourism Development in the Spanish Caribbean*. Gainesville: University Press of Florida.

Williams, Erica Lorraine. 2013. *Sex Tourism in Bahia: Ambiguous Entanglements*. Urbana: University of Illinois Press.

Winters, Cecilia Anne, and Robert Derrell. 2010. "Divided Neighbors on an Indivisible Island: Economic Disparity and Cumulative Causation on Hispaniola." *Journal of Economic Issues* 44 (3): 597–613.

Wonders, Nancy, and Raymond Michalowski. 2001. "Bodies, Borders, and Sex Tourism in a Globalized World: A Tale of Two Cities—Amsterdam and Havana." *Social Problems* 48 (4): 545–571.

9

Global Capital Disguised as Sustainability in Post-Earthquake Haiti

KIRAN C. JAYARAM

What restorative action can be taken after a heavily populated area has experienced large-scale environmental destruction? This chapter takes as its case study the international response to the earthquake on Hispaniola on January 12, 2010. Although the phrase "build back better," taken from an article in the *UN Chronicle* by UN secretary general Ban Ki-moon (2010), gained currency, another way of framing the response came in the disguise of sustainable development. In recent years, particularly since the establishment of the UN's Millennium Development Goals in 2000 and the new Sustainable Development Goals of 2015, much political economic activity has occurred that has been disguised as sustainable development. Different versions of this disguise are created whenever and wherever various assemblages of funds, commodities, and personnel combine with an ideological framework in which sustainability is not only a given, but also a good.

In what follows, I argue that the elaboration and implementation of sustainable development in Haiti after the earthquake served empires of capital rather than the direct needs of the majority of the Haitian people in distress.[1] Furthermore, as I will show through historical precedents and events that unfolded in the time after the earthquake, the official plan for sustainable development continued a long tradition of matching international political economic interests with the needs of a national economic elite, at the expense of the general public.

Conceptual Framework

In addition to the transnational Hispaniola framework, this chapter draws on studies of sustainability, capitalism and development, and disaster.

At first glance, this chapter could seem to be a partial mismatch with the transnational Hispaniola framework. Initially, the *transnational* part of transnational Hispaniola makes sense, as it invokes "the ways in which imperialism, global capitalism, and inequalities in the international system continue to wreak havoc and devastation on the island" (Mayes et al. 2013, 28). A focus on Haiti, though, seems to present a disjuncture with the other chapters in this volume, which address the "cross border, cross linguistic, and cross ethnic interactions [that] have long characterized relations between Dominicans and Haitians" (Mayes et al. 2013, 27). Yet, much as Michel-Rolph Trouillot's experiences in Dominica enriched his analytic framework, my research in the Dominican Republic and experiences of mobility across Hispaniola have enabled me to see connections beyond those that are visible through the nationalist methodological lens.

Anthropologists who have written about disasters have primarily analyzed relationships between processes and groups of actors. Anthony Oliver-Smith (2010) writes that after the moment of altruism following the initial event, when "humanitarian assistance arrives, class and ethnic differences re-emerge, private property concerns reawaken, and old schisms reappear" (14). Building on this observation and integrating ideas from Naomi Klein, Mark Schuller and Julie Maldonado examine the concept of *disaster capitalism*, by which they mean the process of "national and transnational governmental institutions' instrumental use of catastrophe (both so-called 'natural' and human-mediated disasters, including post-conflict situations) to promote and empower a range of private, neoliberal capitalist interests" (2016, 62). To Schuller and Maldonado, disaster capitalism includes donors awarding no-bid contracts to private entities (instead of to the state) and the implementation of radical policy reforms that would have been difficult even to propose prior to the disaster. In this chapter, I examine the divisions that appeared in Haiti after the post-disaster euphoria ended to see whose interests were favored.

Paying attention to how development projects integrate industrialized market relations can produce insights into how these endeavors affect people at different moments and locations of commodity exchange. This approach builds on insights from Immanuel Wallerstein's (1974) world systems theory. Wallerstein argues that certain core states will benefit from the development of capitalism, to the detriment of peripheral areas. Julia Elyachar (2005) describes how the introduction of specific forms of market exchange alters social relationships and behaviors and dispossesses the poor. Thus, capitalist development involves unequal national and international power relationships generated by the expansion of market exchange.

It is important to define the concept of sustainability. Anthropologists, among others, have argued that sustainability relates to "the ability of a people to preserve and defend its way of life" (Fratkin and Means 2003, 113). However, other definitions exist. Jeffrey Sachs best summed up a frequently used meaning of sustainable development when he described it as continuous "economic development and environmental sustainability" (Sachs and Annan 2010). When Sachs talks of economic development, he means the ability to share "in the benefits of expanding world markets" (Sachs 2000, 580). Yet countries can only do that if they attract investment and expand the reach of monetized social relations. Today, attaching the word sustainable to project proposals makes them attractive to potential funders. As Sachs points out, "Developing countries that successfully attract foreign direct investment and thereby become part of those global production systems have benefited with faster economic development" (Sachs 1999, 99). This definition, which draws directly from the ideas of the Brundtland Commission, certainly differs from the notions of sustainability that emerged within the U.S. environmentalist movement of the 1960s[2]. Implicitly critiquing the ideas of Jeffrey Sachs, Wolfgang Sachs notes that "sustainable development has been explicitly conceived as a strategy for sustaining 'development,' not for supporting the flourishing and enduring of an infinitely diverse natural and social life" (Sachs 2010, 13). For present purposes, I will use the critical understanding that W. Sachs has of sustainable development while recognizing that policymakers may advocate something like what J. Sachs offers.

Methods

This chapter employs a mixed-methods approach that includes history, political economy, and ethnography. Material used to describe the period before the earthquake comes from government documents, organizational policies, professional reports, and some secondary historical sources. Information about actions after the earthquake comes from newswires, industry reports, and secondary sources. The material on the Haitian mango industry is based on research I conducted during the summer of 2016 on the question of what mangoes mean to Haitian agriculturalists. During that time, I conducted interviews with two dozen families involved in the mango industry, held an interview with the head of a mango export project, and did participant observation in a village in northern Haiti.

From Hispaniola to *Goudoumgoudoum*

Before delving into the details of the post-earthquake reconstruction efforts, it is useful to summarize the significant continuities in Haiti's economic history. The colonial history of Hispaniola began with the arrival of Christopher Columbus in December 1492, but the historical trajectory of the island split when it was divided in 1697 by the Treaty of Ryswick, in which Spain delivered the western part of the island to the French. Over the next ten decades, Saint Domingue became France's most valuable colony, producing sugar, coffee, indigo, and other commodities at levels that surpassed that of all of France's other colonies combined. In 1791 and the years following, massive numbers of Africans and their children and *milat*,[3] both rich and poor, took up arms against France and then against Spain and England. This indigenous army fought and won a bloody war against all the major world powers at the time and established the first modern black republic in the world, Haiti. Slave insurgents-turned-republicans declared their independence on January 1, 1804, because they wanted to end this history of foreign domination, of generation of wealth for foreign entities, of unfair access to land, and of inhumane living and working conditions.

For approximately the next 100 years, various factions within Haiti vied for control of the state apparatus. After the betrayal and murder of Jean-Jacques Dessalines, the country split into the Kingdom of Haiti in the north (under Emperor Henri Christophe) and the Republic of Haiti in the south (under Alexandre Pètion). It was not until the administration of President Jean-Pierre Boyer that Haiti and then the island became unified under a single government in 1818. In 1844, the Dominican Republic declared its independence from Haiti, initiating a period of internal divisions and political struggles for state power that continued for decades, during which time the inhabitants of Haiti carried out their quotidian tasks related to production and reproduction. The property regimes in postrevolutionary Haiti and the subsequent changes in legal structures contributed to the development of both statutory and customary practices of land tenure in Haiti, a social fact that complicated the development of a modernized land tenure system in contemporary Haiti (Jayaram 2010).

In 1915, the United States occupied Haiti and the next year it occupied the Dominican Republic. The U.S.-controlled government quickly set on a course to alter Haiti. In 1918, a new constitution allowed foreigners to own land for the first time in Haitian history.[4] Roads were built with the idea that they would facilitate the transport of crops from the interior to export markets, part of a plan of agricultural intensification. In 1925 and 1926, the military government began the process of a cadastre (property register) by using the new technology of the airplane to take aerial photographs of the countryside. This project came to a grinding halt when the building that stored the data burned down in a mysterious fire (Schmidt 1995). Given armed Haitian resistance to U.S. Marines from the start of the occupation (the Caco Wars of 1915 and 1918–1920 and Charlemagne Peralte's revolt of 1917–1919) and political resistance led by intellectuals (Jean Price-Mars and the other members of the *indigène* movement), it is likely that the fire was purposely set in an effort to end the occupation government's attempts to regulate land claims.

It is clear that control of land and tenure regulation played a large role in the push toward so-called modernization in Haiti. The underlying logic of this drive to regulate land for easier market exchange reveals who the primary beneficiaries were supposed to be. For example, after the end of the Duvalier dynasty, a group of foreigners published a report on land reform in Haiti (Bloch, Lambert, and Singer 1988).[5] After describing existing land-tenure relations, this extensive and informative document detailed a type of "agricultural development" that the Haitian government should pursue in order to achieve its economic goals. The projects described in the document endeavored to increase land values, which would have meant that more farmers would have had to go through formalized legal structures to protect their land (instead of relying on traditional systems of tenure based on kinship and social ties); promoted the "increased commercialization" of agriculture, which would have brought farmers into a more moneyed economy; and outlined more systemic changes in state legal structures (Bloch, Lambert, and Singer 1988, 71). The most salient contribution of this report was the fact that while its authors articulated a development logic that tied Haiti's well-being to the land question, its authors viewed the "land question" in limited ways—as a problem with tenure, lack of monetization, and absence from market exchange. The authors implicitly considered traditional systems based on reciprocity of labor and social ties to be barriers to modernization or development.

In 1990, in the first open and uncontested elections that allowed universal adult suffrage in Haitian history in 1990, Haitians elected Jean-Bertrand Aristide as their president. Aristide suffered his first coup d'état seven months later. President Bill Clinton eventually decided to use U.S. and UN forces to restore democracy, but at a price. In 1993, Aristide was forced to sign the Governor's Island Accord, whereby he agreed to "technical and financial assistance for development" (Article 5a) and to administrative, judicial, and security reforms (Articles 5b, 5c, and 7), which were to be verified by the UN and the Organization of American States (Article 10). This included $37.5 million to pay arrears so Haiti could borrow more from international institutions for "development" oriented projects (United States Department of State 1993). While the Governor's Island Accord provided little more than a skeleton plan for future political economic policy, President Aristide provided a more detailed plan in August 1994 (Gouvernement de la République d'Haïti 1994), just months before U.S. troops arrived to facilitate his return. This plan included ideas such as "eschewing foreign exchange controls, price controls, and other policy-induced distortions" and reliance on "a vibrant, private sector with an open foreign investment policy" in order to create "a rigorous macroeconomic framework anchored on programs supported by international financial institutions" (1, 5). The strategy prioritized the export sectors of agriculture and assembly manufacturing, requested favorable tariff treatment from the United States, suggested the liquidation of state goods and services that could be replaced by the work of private companies, and relied on "the private sector or qualified NGOs" for service delivery (5).

International donors' conferences that took place after Aristide's removal in 2004 have supported a similar concept of sustainable development. For example, in 2006, the Madrid Donors' Conference encouraged the Haitian government's stance. Premised on the idea of the state as "regulator and corrector of market imperfections and as promoter of private initiative" (International Monetary Fund 2006), it laid out a plan of sustainable development based on light assembly, agricultural intensification with and additional emphasis on exports, improvement of infrastructure, and tourism. Moreover, it included the desire to secure private property rights and land titles, all with the goal of courting private investment. A donors' conference in 2009 supported an almost identical platform that was put forth jointly by the Haitian government and the Inter-American Development Bank (2009).

Just in time for the 2009 meeting, the UN released the Collier Report (Collier 2009)[6]. In the name of promoting sustainable development and creating jobs, Collier advocated for the expansion of export zones for mango production and the apparel industry. Apparel manufacture in Haiti had already been given a boost by the Haitian Hemispheric Opportunity through Partnership Encouragement Acts (HOPE I in 2006 and HOPE II in 2008),[7] which the U.S. Congress passed to provide incentives for investors to participate in the development of the Haitian apparel industry (Hornbeck 2010). To accomplish these goals, the Collier Report prioritized the need to clarify property rights and the ability to "ensure that land is rapidly available for acquisition in Export Zones with titles that cannot subsequently be challenged" (Collier 2009, 12). To provide support for infrastructure in these zones, the report advocated a cluster model of investment on the grounds that "it is much easier and quicker to provide the infrastructure and services that the industry needs by creating a few islands of excellence rather than by trying to improve standards across the entire country" (Collier 2009, 11). In this report, sustainable development became the means by which the Haitian government and its financial backers would court the attention of international companies, venture capitalists, and angel investors.

In summary, there were multiple connections in a long history of modernization and, more recently, sustainable development in Haiti in the time leading up to the earthquake:

An interest in courting capital from foreigners or Haitian elites

An interest in having the majority of Haitians be laborers and secondary recipients of any investment

A push to orient national production, including agriculture, toward international consumption

A push to orient land tenure along the lines of a generalized politico-legal structure

A push toward a moneyed economy rather than one that supports reciprocal social relations

A push for national legislation to facilitate the aforementioned trends

The Earthquake and Subsequent Plans

Around 4:53 p.m. on January 12, 2010, there was an earthquake, or *goudoumgoudoum*, near Leyogàn that registered 7.0 on the Richter scale.[8] Approximately 300,000 people died. Estimates suggest that 600,000 people from Port-au-Prince traveled to the Haitian countryside, to the Dominican Republic, or beyond Hispaniola as a response to the humanitarian crisis the earthquake created. Over 1.5 million people were immediately affected. Roughly 300,000 houses were either damaged or destroyed (DesRoches et al. 2011). Some 1,300 schools (preschool through university level) were also destroyed. Only a few government buildings remained intact. The capital's port was also rendered completely ineffective.

In the weeks after the earthquake, Haitians across the globe began conceiving informal and formal plans for reconstruction. In the Dominican Republic, some people suggested making Haiti the fifty-first state in the United States of America. Others suggested turning Haiti into a U.S. protectorate, like Puerto Rico. Online discussion boards frequented by members of Haitian diasporas (mainly those living in the United States) included similar sentiments and a variety of ideas about how to react to the destruction in Haiti. Within Haiti itself, the Fondation Haïtienne pour le Développement Intégral Latino Américain et Caribéen (FONHDILAC) came up with a singular idea. The organization advocated that the country be decentralized, that the capital be relocated in the central plateau, and that a joint committee for reconstruction be formed that would include the Haitian state, the Haitian private sector, Haitian civil society, and the Haitian diaspora (FONHDILAC 2010). This idea, however, had no chance for consideration, as the "real development" plans were already being developed—and not in Haiti.

An initial summit about Haiti's reconstruction occurred at the end of January in Canada, followed by two more in March, the first in Santo Domingo, Dominican Republic, and the next in New York. A final conference in late May and early June was held in Punta Cana, Dominican

Republic. By the time the second meeting occurred, the Haitian government had already released the Plan d'Action pour le Relèvement et le Développement Nationale d'Haïti (PARDN). The PARDN was based on a "new idea of cooperation" and the concept of "sustainable development" (Gouvernement de la République d'Haïti 2010, 3, 45). Authors of the PARDN described four areas of reconstruction. For territorial development, the plan included road construction, a land survey, and changes in laws in order to facilitate large projects, among other activities. For economic development, there were provisions for clothing-assembly factories, for tourist zones, and for agricultural export. For social development, the PARDN proposed support for more schools and health centers. The authors also advocated changes in laws to facilitate the execution of the PARDN. This plan resembled much of what has historically been proposed, and it almost exclusively prioritized foreign capital investment interests over those of the Haitian masses.

The plan billed itself as "Haitian" because, according to its authors, "the principal sectors of Haitian society were consulted," including Haitians living in the country and Haitian expatriates (Gouvernement de la République d'Haïti 2010, 3, my translation). However, this claim to autochthony might have misrepresented the breadth of participation in the reconstruction plans. Several factors suggest that the PARDN and other reconstruction plans reflected the ideas of a powerful group of high-level government officials instead of being informed by ideas from a broad cross-section of Haitians. According to Guy Alexandre (1945–2014), former Haitian ambassador to the Dominican Republic, no significant consultation about reconstructions occurred with experts, government officials, or the population of Haiti (Guy Alexandre, personal communication, June 2010). After the plan was published, Haitians living in Haiti and members of the Haitian diaspora in the United States were invited to provide testimony at an international donor's conference in New York. They were given sixteen minutes total, or eight minutes for each group.[9] Two points of so-called common sense in Haiti should be remembered regarding the contribution of the Haitian diaspora to the official reconstruction plan (beyond the fact that these actors were not identified). First, *tout moun se moun, men tout moun pa menm* (everyone is a person, but not all people are the same).[10] It is almost certain that not all Haitians living in the United States share a single set of values, and it is even more unlikely that all Haitians who reside in France, the Dominican Republic, Brazil, and the United States think the same way. Second, in Kreyòl, *dyaspora* (diaspora) refers to Haitians who have limited to no understanding of contemporary issues within Haiti, and the word traditionally carries a negative connotation when applied to a person. Given the linguistic bias against the members of the *dyaspora* as an equal partner in Haiti's reconstruction, it is a stretch for the authors of the PARDN to claim that all were consulted and a consensus had been reached that could be identified as the "*dyaspora*'s plan" for Haiti's reconstruction. Instead, it makes sense to look at other contributors to assess which sectors within Haiti stood to benefit from these reconstruction efforts.

Portrait of the PARDN at an Early Stage: Seeds

Central to the PARDN's success are agricultural exports and textile manufacture. Starting in 2009, the Earth Institute at Columbia University began an investigation into future projects in Haiti, including what would become something akin to a Millennium Village, a model of sustainable development. It produced a report that voices support for a national cadastre and for some legal reform to address land tenure issues (Jayaram 2010).[11] In the spring of 2010, the institute developed a plan to provide seeds of preexisting crops and chemical fertilizer (reportedly from a Dominican company) to Haitian farmers. These were to be free for two years, then the Earth Institute would slowly remove subsidies over five years. The hybrid seeds, which the Haitian Ministry of Agriculture approved, came from the Monsanto Company.[12] As of summer 2010, however, that plan had been placed on hold to assess the possibility of reorienting Haiti toward mango production.

The Earth Institute was not the only group interested in boosting mango production for export. Internally, Haitians such as Jean Maurice Buteau have been pushing for the intensification of mango production for years. After the earthquake, his company received additional media attention.[13] On an international scale, the Coca-Cola Company teamed up with the U.S. Agency for International Development (USAID) for a $7.5 million project to increase mango production, which was then linked to the Odwalla Haiti Hope Mango Lime Aid drink.[14] The Clinton-Bush Fund provided additional money for farming collectives, nurseries, and collection centers (USAID 2010), all of which were oriented toward mango production with the goal of producing a single variety, *mango fransik*, for market. In 2016, as the five-year USAID-funded project ended, I conducted the first phase of fieldwork on parts of the initiative. To understand this project, some ethnographic detail is required.

Previously, private growers would pick their mangoes, store them, and sell them to an export-processing transporter through a growers' association. The association would set a price per dozen[15] that was higher than what independent speculators would pay. CorporaWise,[16] the nongovernmental organization hired to conduct a purportedly fair trade mango-export project, created its own organizations that competed with existing grower cooperatives. In addition to compensating the growers at a slightly higher rate, these new cooperatives received compensation in the form of small community projects at the end of the year. In other words, in exchange for *mango fransik*, the producers received a cash incentive and the community was given a small improvement. The more farmers who sold, the more money the community would collect. Unfortunately, the rate per dozen was negotiated in 2010. Since 2011, the average annual rate of inflation has been 7–8 percent and the value of the exchange has decreased significantly for the farmers.[17] Many agriculturalists complained to me about the need for higher compensation, and they were shocked to know that although they were paid about fifty cents for a dozen mangoes, each so-called fair trade mango sold in the United States for about three dollars. When I asked the head of CorporaWise in Haiti about this, he responded that the exporters have "no incentive to compensate growers in a manner that reflects inflation" (personal communication, August 6, 2017). With limited options for income, many rural Haitians felt compelled to produce *mango fransik*. In fact, one prominent community promoter admitted to openly pressuring people to cut down their other mango trees to produce the export variety.

Portrait of the PARDN at an Early Stage: Seams

In addition to agriculture, the textile industry loomed large in the post-earthquake development of Haiti. Continuing in the spirit of the HOPE agreements signed before the earthquake, the U.S. Congress passed and President Obama signed the Haitian Economic Lift Program (HELP) in May 2010, which extended until 2020 the mostly unaltered provisions of the prior agreements. The bill received praise from Presidents George W. Bush and Bill Clinton, who remarked in a joint statement that it provides "more tools to lift [Haitians] from poverty, while standing to benefit U.S. consumers" (quoted in Charles and Clark 2010).

As a result, several projects were initiated. First, the Korean-based Sae-A Trading Company signed an agreement to set up factories in the displaced persons camp known as Corail-Cesselesse. Former secretary of state Hillary Clinton billed the project as providing "good jobs with fair pay that adhere to international labor standards" (Clinton 2010). The company assembled products for Walmart, Target, Gap, Banana Republic, and Levi Strauss (Katz 2010). Another section of the "seams" economy involved the Haitian Apparel Center. This project was a joint endeavor of the Haitian government, USAID, and CHF International (now Global Communities). It included a 6,000-square-meter building where workers would enter a USAID training program and then assemble a variety of garments. These commodities figure largely in Gap clothing stores (Kaiser Family Foundation 2010).

Portrait of the PARDN at an Early Stage

Other sectors of the economy changed in accordance with the PARDN.[18] The sale of Teleco, the Haitian national telephone company, to the Vietnamese company Viettel, for instance, was finalized after the earthquake. Dozens of other projects related to economic development and education were launched under the PARDN framework, most of which provided few results. For example, building on an idea it first launched in Rwanda, the Macy's department store company launched a "Heart of Haiti" home-accents line whereby the company purchased Haitian quilts, paintings, jewelry, metalwork, and ceramics from artisans to sell in their stores (Dickenson 2010). The Clinton Global Initiative, in conjunction with the University of the People, agreed to give 250 students the opportunity to engage in online learning so they could earn an associate's degree in computer science or business administration because these fields would help students "contribute to sustainable economic development programs and infrastructure in their homeland" (Ford 2010).

Despite the bricolage of incentives, ideas, and initiatives, a discernible pattern emerged within sustainable development in Haiti. First, sustainable development according to the PARDN involved a plan to render land tenure more friendly to markets by making more Haitian land available to both foreign and domestic investment capital. Second, the model included large-scale intensified agricultural production for export, including exports under the fair trade label. Third, these projects focused on extending foreign capital into Haiti and increasing the volume of capital accumulation driven by the availability of Haitian labor. This is most evident in the support given to assembly factories. In other words, the "new" sustainable development looks very much like older proposals for capitalism. Sustainable development is little more than a marketing strategy to advance market-driven economic policies that have not worked for Haiti in the past.

Why Sustainable Development in Haiti Is Wrong

Sustainable development in post-earthquake Haiti is wrong because it is simply an updated form of a type of exchange that has, throughout history, mostly benefited national elites and international markets instead of those in need. First, as shown above, post-earthquake initiatives privilege capitalist exchange and relations.[19] Second, the plan for sustainable development directs funds toward Haiti's economic elite, including many who live in the diaspora, and expects that the benefits will trickle down. The economic elite in Haiti (such as the Apaid, Mevs, Brandt, Bigio, Madsen, and Accra families) have traditionally placed their financial and personal interests before Haiti's interests and needs. Plans for post-earthquake development in Haiti failed to transform this fundamental fact. It is also true, however, that denying the traditional elite any role in discussions of Haiti's future is unlikely to happen.

Conclusion

The above examination demonstrates that any sense of inclusiveness intended in post-earthquake Haiti under the banner of sustainable development should be seen as a disguise for renewed connection to a capitalist system. During the provision of humanitarian assistance and subsequent "building back better," preference was given to funding the capitalist classes on either a national or international scale. Although the aftershocks of the disaster included a policy shift and the specific actors and commodities may be markedly different from those of earlier generations, the dependent status of Haiti was maintained. Sustainability within the PARDN meant first and foremost a continuous connection to a capitalist system. Future research within the transnational Hispaniola framework will be able to show parallels between the case of Haiti after 2010 and the case of the privatization of large sections of the Dominican economy after 1997.

Update: 2017

Since I presented an earlier form of this research at the Transnational Hispaniola conference in Santo Domingo (Jayaram 2010), much has happened. Cholera brought to the island by Nepalese UN troops in late 2010 killed over 10,000 people and sickened hundreds of thousands across Hispaniola. In 2011, Jean-Claude Duvalier and Jean-Bertrand Aristide returned to Haiti. President Michel Martelly failed to establish a working government during his five years in office. The recent election to the presidency of Jovenel Moïse marks the possibility of resumed governance but also the possibility of renewed emphasis on export-driven agriculture mentioned in the PARDN.

Some of the ideas in PARDN were realized and continue today. Garment factories were created, but not until May 2015 did then-president Michel Martelly raise the minimum wage for workers to 240 goud ($5.11) per day, less than the wages of Haitians working in construction or at supermarkets. Macy's Heart of Haiti line of products continues to be sold online. The tourism industry has grown in Haiti, increasing from 250,000 tourists in 2010 to almost 500,000 in 2015 (IndexMundi 2016). A number of luxury hotels have cropped up around Pétion-Ville, including a replacement for the Hotel Montana, which collapsed during the earthquake. As a result, several professional organizations have held their annual conferences in Port-au-Prince, including the Caribbean Studies Association and the Association of Caribbean University, Research and Institutional Libraries. Other small companies that have been created through private investment have sprouted up in the past few years to market Haitian agricultural products, including coffee, moringa leaves, and boutique soaps, but these have limited distribution beyond the upscale grocery stores around Pétion-Ville.

To date, several of the projects mentioned above have fundamentally changed, are no longer active, or were never actualized. For example, no national cadastre has occurred in Haiti, though the OAS provided $500,000 to the Haitian government to complete one in 2012. No hydroelectric dam was built. Although *mango fransik* continues to be produced and exported, CorporaWise's project ended, and it remains to be seen how effective the project has been in transforming the lives of Haitian agriculturalists.

The march of corporate capitalism as a supposed civilizing agent of development goes on. Whether sustainability as capitalist development will continue to guide Haitian policy or whether it will be replaced with another proposal, it is imperative to look behind the disguise to determine whether what is being proposed will benefit those historically marginalized populations. Any interventions should be truer to the more anthropological definition of sustainability Elliot Fratkin and Robin Mearns gave us, one that includes an implicit notion of sovereignty. To do otherwise is to perpetuate inequality.

To close with the words of the great Haitian scholar and poet, Michel Rolph-Trouillot:

Toupatou, yo sèl wa. Se pa nou ki sou do bèf la. Se bèf la ki sou do nou. Men jou ti katkat gen pou l tounen gwo chat pou yon lòt 1804.

Everywhere, they are the kings. We are not riding high. We are being ridden. But one day, the little guy will become the big man, for another 1804.

Notes

1. While some scholars in American studies or the field of history use the term *imperialism* for what I describe, I choose the term *empire(s) of capital* to promote an understanding of this phenomenon as being primarily in the service of an economic goal rather than a political goal of expanding a geographic domain.

2. The Brundtland Commission, formally known as World Commission on Environment and Development, was a United Nations initiative from 1983 to 1987 that linked the concept of development with the environment, suggesting that improvements in technology could improve the use of the environment to meet the needs of poor populations. The commission endeavored to coordinate international efforts in support of this idea. It ran counter to the philosophy of the 1972 UN Conference on the Human Environment, which emphasized protecting the environment.

3. *Milat* is a colonial term that referred to a child with one white parent and one black parent.

4. Article 5 deals with foreign land ownership, article 109 prevents the state from

levying taxes, and article 128 states that all actions by the government of the United States are "ratified and valid."

5. The presidency of François Duvalier (1957–1961) was followed by that of his son (1961–1986).

6. In 2008, UN Secretary General Ban Ki-Moon asked British economist Paul Collier to travel to Haiti and produce an economic development strategy that would build upon benefits of the Mission des Nations Unies pour la stabilisation en Haïti (MINUSTAH) and the favorable trade conditions under the U.S. Haitian Hemispheric Opportunity through Partnership Encouragement Act, or HOPE II, of 2008. This resulted in the Collier Report (Collier 2009).

7. In 2010, the Haitian Economic Lift Program (HELP) modified and extended these provisions and those of the Caribbean Basin Trade Partnership Act until 2020.

8. This neologism came out of the earthquake experience. The expressions used prior to January 12 were *tranblemanntè*, which still applies in general; the Creolized French *tranblemandetè*; or the French *séisme*. In the weeks after the earthquake, people used both *goudoumgoudoum* and *goudougoudou*.

9. Final program for the International Donors' Conference Towards a New Future for Haiti, 2010, in author's possession.

10. "*Tout moun se moun*" is a common Haitian aphorism.

11. To that end, the Office for a National Cadastre (ONACA) with the plans of the Organization of American States to conduct a national cadastre within the next few years (Organization of American States 2010).

12. A wealth of long-term research is now available that shows how similar seed and agricultural projects can lead to malnutrition and disease and can introduce toxins into the ecosystem as in Zambia (Bond n.d.) and how such programs attack biodiversity and overtax the soil (see Shiva et al. 1999). In addition, soil erosion could lead to the fertilizer leaching into the water supply, creating a public health disaster.

13. The National Public Radio program *This American Life* dedicated part of episode #408 to Buteau's work. "Episode 408: Island Time," *This American Life*, aired May 21, 2010, transcript at https://www.thisamericanlife.org/radio-archives/episode/408/transcript, accessed October 16, 2017.

14. "The Coca-Cola Company's Haiti Hope Project Momentum Continues," *Dominican Today*, September 11, 2010. The juice was not a product of Haiti.

15. In market exchanges, purchasers may consider a dozen to number anywhere from nine to eighteen mangoes, depending on size and quality. The additional units are included so that if a factory rejects mangoes from a middleman, twelve mangoes can still be sold.

16. A pseudonym.

17. "Haiti—CPI Inflation" (1980–2016), n.d., https://knoema.com/atlas/Haiti/CPI-inflation, accessed December 19, 2016.

18. Not all endeavors were successful. A Martinican company hoped to purchase a large piece of agricultural land for banana production near Jakmèl but was thwarted by land tenure and security issues. There were also plans to flood huge tracts of land to

create a hydroelectric dam, which would most likely have led to the displacement and further marginalization that occurred with the creation of the Peligre Dam (see Farmer 2006).

19. For more information on recent writings about the inherent limitations of capitalism, see Harvey (2006, 2010).

Works Cited

Ban Ki-moon. 2010. "Toward a New Future for Haiti." *UN Chronicle* 47 (1). https://un chronicle.un.org/article/toward-new-future-haiti. Accessed December 19, 2016.

Bloch, Peter C., Virginia Lambert, and Norman Singer. 1988. *Land Tenure Issues in Rural Haiti: Review of the Evidence.* Madison, WI: Land Tenure Center.

Bond, George C. n.d. "The Social History of an Agrarian 'Community' in Northern Zambia: History, Policy, and Practice." Unpublished manuscript, Teachers College, Columbia University. In author's possession.

Charles, Jacqueline, and Lesley Clark. 2010. "U.S. House Passes Textile Trade Bill for Haiti." *Miami Herald*, May 5.

Clinton, Hillary Rodham. 2010. "Remarks at the Signing of Two Memoranda of Understanding Regarding Haiti Recovery Projects." Office of Website Management, Bureau of Public Affairs, U.S. Department of State. https://2009-2017.state.gov/secretary/20092013clinton/rm/2010/09/147451.htm. Accessed December 13, 2017.

Collier, Paul. 2009. *Haiti: From Natural Catastrophe to Economic Security.* Report for the Secretary-General of the United Nations. Unpublished document. http://www.focal.ca/pdf/haiticollier.pdf.

DesRoches, Reginald, Mary Comerio, Marc Eberhard, Walter Mooney, and Glenn J. Rix. 2011. "Overview of the 2010 Haiti Earthquake." *Earthquake Spectra* 27 (1): S1–21. https://escweb.wr.usgs.gov/share/mooney/142.pdf. Accessed October 16, 2017.

Dickenson, Susan. 2010. "Macy's to Launch 'Heart of Haiti' Home Accents Collection in October." Home Accents Today, September 21. http://www.homeaccentstoday.com/article/531820-Macy_s_to_launch_Heart_of_Haiti_home_accents_collection_in_October.php. Accessed September 22, 2010.

Elyachar, Julia. 2005. *Markets of Dispossession: NGOs, Economic Development, and the State in Cairo.* Durham, NC: Duke University Press.

Farmer, Paul. 2006. *AIDS and Accusation: Haiti and the Geography of Blame.* Berkeley: University of California Press.

Fondation Haïtienne pour le Développement Intégral Latino-Américain et Caribéen (FONHDILAC). 2010. "Plaidoyer pour la refondation de l'Etat d'Haïti selon une vision haïtienne." http://tanbou.com/2010/FONHDILACPlaidoyerVF.pdf. Accessed October 16, 2017.

Ford, Anissa. 2010. "Haiti Gets Tuition Free Online University." Huliq, September 21. http://www.huliq.com/10178/haiti-gets-tuition-free-online-university. Accessed September 22, 2010.

Fratkin, Elliot, and Robin Mearns. 2003. Sustainability and Pastoral Livelihoods: Lessons from East African Maasai and Mongolia. *Human Organization* 62 (2): 112–122.

Gouvernement de la République d'Haïti. 1994. Strategy of Aristide Government for Social and Economic Reconstruction. Occasional Papers 4. University of Kansas, Institute of Haitian Studies.

———. 2010. *Plan d'Action pour le Relèvement et le Développement d'Haïti.* Port-au-Prince, Haiti.

Harvey, David. 2006. *Limits to Capital.* 3rd ed. London and New York: Verso.

———. 2010. *The Enigma of Capital and the Crises of Capitalism.* London: Profile Books Ltd.

Hornbeck, J. F. 2010. "The Haitian Economy and the HOPE Act." Congressional Research Service. http://amchamhaiti.com/home/HOPE_Act_revised_June_2010.pdf. Accessed December 13, 2017.

IndexMundi. 2016. Haiti—International Tourism. http://www.indexmundi.com/facts/haiti/international-tourism. Accessed December 20, 2016.

Inter-American Development Bank (IADB). 2009. "Third Conference on Haiti's Economic and Social Development." Press release, April 14. https://www.iadb.org/en/news/news-releases/2009-04-14/third-conference-on-haitis-economic-and-social-development%2C5349.html. Accessed November 18, 2010.

International Monetary Fund (IMF). 2006. *Haiti: Interim Poverty Reduction Strategy Paper.* IMF Country Report No. 06/411. http://www.imf.org/external/pubs/ft/scr/2006/cr06411.pdf. Accessed December 18, 2010.

Jayaram, Kiran. 2010. "Report on Land Tenure in Post-Earthquake Haiti." Earth Institute, New York.

Kaiser Family Foundation. 2010. "U.S.-Funded Center to Improve Haitian Garment Manufacturing Opens in Haiti." August 12. https://www.kff.org/news-summary/u-s-funded-center-to-improve-haitian-garment-manufacturing-opens-in-haiti/. Accessed August 12, 2010.

Katz, Jonathan. 2010. "US, Haiti Accord Paves Way for Korean Factories," September 20. http://www.businessweek.com/ap/financialnews/D9IC015G0.htm. Accessed October 10, 2010.

Mayes, April, Yolanda C. Martín, Carlos Ulises Decena, Kiran Jayaram, and Yveline Alexis. 2013. "Transnational Hispaniola: Toward New Paradigms in Haitian and Dominican Studies," *Radical History Review* 115: 26–32.

Oliver-Smith, Anthony. 2010. "Voices in the Storm: Social Relations of Relief and Reconstruction." *Anthropology News* 51 (7): 14–15.

Organization of American States. 2010. *Modernization of Cadastre and Land Rights Infrastructure in Haiti.* Project proposal Executive Summary. http://siteresources.worldbank.org/EXTARD/Resources/336681-1236436879081/5893311-1271205116054/RobergePaperCAP5.pdf. Accessed October 16, 2017

Sachs, Jeffrey. 1999. "Twentieth-Century Political Economy: A Brief History of Global Capitalism." *Oxford Review of Economic Policy* 15 (4): 90–101.

———. 2000. "Globalization and Patterns of Economic Development." *Weltwirtschaftliches Archiv* 136 (4): 579–600.

Sachs, Jeffrey, and Kofi Annan. 2010. "Prospects for 21st Century African Agriculture" Video sponsored by The Earth Institute and Columbia University. October 21. http://www.earth.columbia.edu/videos/watch/265. Accessed October 17, 2017.

Sachs, Wolfgang. 2010. *The Development Dictionary*. New York: Zed Books.

Schmidt, Hans. 1995. *The United States Occupation of Haiti, 1915–1934*. 2nd ed. New Brunswick, NJ: Rutgers University Press.

Schuller, Mark, and Julie Maldonado. 2016. "Disaster Capitalism." *Annals of Anthropological Practice* 40 (1): 61–72.

Shiva, Vandana, Ashok Emani, and Afsar H. Jafri. 1999. "Globalisation and the Threat to Seed Security: Case of Transgenic Cotton Trials in India." *Economic and Political Weekly*, March 6–13.

United States Department of State. 1993. "The Governor's Island Accord: A Victory for Diplomacy and Democracy in Haiti." Transcript of speech by Secretary of State Warren Christopher. http://dosfan.lib.uic.edu/ERC/briefing/dispatch/1993/html/Dispatchv4no30.html. Accessed June 1, 2010.

USAID. 2010. "The Coca-Cola Company's Haiti Hope Project Momentum Continues." Press release. August 18. https://reliefweb.int/report/haiti/coca-cola-companys-haiti-hope-project-momentum-continues-investment-united-states. Accessed May 1, 2018.

Wallerstein, Immanuel. 1974. *The Modern World-System*. New York: Academic Press.

10

Ties That Bind

La Sentencia and Citizenship in Contemporary Hispaniola

APRIL J. MAYES

In September of 2013, the Constitutional Tribunal of the Dominican Republic rendered its decision, Sentence 168-13 (La Sentencia), which stripped over 44,000 Dominicans of Haitian descent of Dominican nationality and threatened hundreds of thousands more with deportation. Some human rights advocates in the international media viewed La Sentencia and subsequent threats to deport undocumented Haitians as the natural outcome of a society steeped in denial of blackness and anti-Haitianism, a society that was poised, at any moment, to unleash genocidal violence against Haitian migrants and Dominicans of Haitian descent, as had occurred during General Rafael Trujillo's 1937 massacre (Grandin 2015a, 2015b, 2015c; Katz 2015).

Social justice advocates in the Dominican Republic viewed La Sentencia differently: as a coordinated backlash by the government against increasing support for Haitian (im)migrants and their children on the part of Dominicans; as the strategic outcome of a collaboration between economic elites connected to powerful political cadres; and as the culmination of a political strategy by which right-wing parties allied with the reigning Partido de la Liberación Dominicana (Dominican Liberation Party, PLD) gained control over the migration regime through exclusionary legislation, policies, and racist practices that have undermined the rights of Dominicans of Haitian ancestry since the early 2000s (Dominican@s X Derecho 2013).

In this chapter, I use a transnational Hispaniola framework to understand La Sentencia as a product of political developments in the Dominican Republic. La Sentencia evidences the successful uses of anti-Haitianism to guarantee Dominican political stability and the PLD's longevity as the dominant political party (Corten et al. 1995). Yet looking across the island as a whole, I also argue that La Sentencia's origins lie in the connected economic trajectories of Haiti and the Dominican Republic. Since the 1980s, both countries have embarked on a development model oriented around export-oriented production and the complete restructuring of both countries' economies. Key elements of these changes include the growth of apparel manufacture, tourism, banking, and construction as leading economic sectors (Betances and Spalding 1995, 15; Werner 2016).

While La Sentencia clearly draws on a long history of anti-Haitian xenophobia and arcane, static notions of Dominican national identity, it also demonstrates the continued manipulation of antagonisms and racist ideologies by powerful sectors in Dominican society (Hintzen 2014). Moreover, the implementation of the decision, including the inadequate and confusing "fixes" proposed in its wake, illuminates how "discrimination has been recast in forms that are more bureaucratically efficient and more in keeping with democratic procedural rules" (Martínez 2013). Yet procedural democracy is not the same as a substantive democracy concerned with protecting and nurturing its citizens. This chapter will show that in addition to escalating the vulnerability of Haitian migrants and their children in the Dominican Republic, La Sentencia undermines citizenship as a rights-bearing concept for Dominicans and Haitians across the island.

Uneven Development in Hispaniola

The story of La Sentencia as an institutionalized and "racialized project of exclusion" (Persaud 2004, 63) begins when the economies of Haiti and the Dominican Republic diverged significantly in the 1970s and 1980s. Prior to those decades, the gross domestic product was nearly even and Haiti's per capita income outpaced the Dominican Republic's. One explanation for the significant economic differences between the two countries that began to emerge in the 1950s was the important change in governing regimes. François "Papa Doc" Duvalier began his dictatorship in 1957 and General Rafael Trujillo's authoritarian rule ended with his assassination in 1961 (Khan 2010, 117). In each regime, the rulers enriched themselves and their families, but in the Dominican Republic, Trujillo incorporated the Dominican peasantry into his national development plan and financed infrastructure building (Khan 2010, 122–123). As Frank Moya Pons (1990) argues, Trujillo "protected and promoted the formation of a native industrial sector which, although subservient to the dictatorship, was rather independent financially from the dictator" (576). The Duvaliers did not take a similar course in Haiti. Instead, the more politically competitive environment in Haiti, which created a great deal more instability for the Duvaliers than Trujillo had experienced, prompted the Duvaliers to maximize short-term gains over long-term revenue generation (Khan 2010, 117). The economic policies of these dictatorships left each country in vastly different circumstances.

In the 1980s, however, the economic and political paths of Haiti and the Dominican Republic began to converge. Both countries faced the enormity of the crisis later known as Latin America's "Lost Decade," characterized by the end of state-driven economic nationalism, increased indebtedness to lending agencies such as the World Bank and the International Monetary Fund (IMF) as a result of high interest rates and currency devaluation, uncontrollable inflation and recession, and intensified internal stresses caused by the growth of social movements in the pursuit of democratization (Espinal 1995; Weisbrot 1997).

The United States, either directly or through its influence in the World Bank and the IMF, exerted pressure on both governments to implement the structural adjustment of their economies, privatization, and cuts in social expenditures and subsidies in order to pursue new development strategies that would encourage free trade, foreign investment, and the end of state-led economic modernization. Scholars and activists often refer to this package of solutions as the Washington Consensus, structural adjustment, or neoliberalism. Forced to align their economic strategies with those coming from the World Bank and International Monetary Fund, the Haitian and the Dominican governments accepted export-led manufacturing, "the development of a low-wage, export assembly industry of light manufactured goods" (Weisbrot 1997). This led to the growth of manufacturing zones known as free trade zones (FTZs) in the 1980s and 1990s. At their height in the 1990s, FTZs employed 200,000 workers in the Dominican Republic and, in 2008, about 60,000 Haitians (Werner 2011, 1578; Weisbrot 1997).

Alex Dupuy (2010) writes that throughout the 1990s and even after the earthquake in 2010, U.S.-derived development plans turned "Haiti into a supplier of the cheapest labor in this hemisphere for foreign and domestic investors in the export assembly industry and one of the largest importers of U.S. food" (196). Throughout the 1980s and 1990s, the United States and the United Nations also undermined the transition to democracy in Haiti by stifling the popular movements that brought Jean-Bertrand Aristide to power in 1990. A military coup led by Raoul Cédras ousted Aristide in 1991, but popular protests, a trade embargo, and the suspension of World Bank assistance weakened Cédras's administration. When Aristide returned to power in 1993, he promised to end the political violence, but his tenure as president was secured only after he agreed to commit to structural adjustment. In July 1994, U.S. troops landed in Haiti; by October of that year, Aristide had signed the Emergency Economic Recovery Program that the World Bank, the United Nations Development Program, the Inter-American Development Bank, and other international entities had developed (Schuller 2007, 150).

Since the 1980s, both the Dominican and the Haitian government have deregulated their economies, diminished social spending, and sold state-owned industries to private companies (Fatton 2014, 3). In the Dominican Republic, two successive PRD (Partido Revolucionario Dominicano, Dominican Revolutionary Party) administrations introduced structural and market reforms, with devastating results. In 1984, the Dominican gross domestic product grew at a rate of less than 1 percent while inflation increased by 44 percent. President Joaquín Balaguer refused to continue the economic program of his predecessors until his uncontrolled spending in public projects and an increase in oil prices forced him to raise gas prices 100 percent in 1989 (Espinal 1995, 63, 66, 67–68). The complete shift toward a neoliberal regime developed during Leonel Fernández's presidency in 1996. In the late 1990s, Fernández's government sold the majority share of ten state-owned sugar mills. This move destroyed the sugar industry and forced many Dominicans and Haitians into the informal economy (Gregory 2006, 29).

Haiti and the Dominican Republic are fully integrated into the global assembly line. As is the case in their counterparts across Asia, export-driven industry has exacerbated and deepened income inequalities in both countries. While the Dominican economy has grown 4 percent every year since 2000, the Haitian economy has shrunk significantly, especially since the 2010 earthquake. In 2012, the wealthiest 20 percent of Haiti's population consumed 46.9 percent of its national wealth and the poorest 20 percent had access to only 5.6 percent of the national income. Despite steady economic growth in the Dominican Republic, the numbers in 2012 were similar to those in Haiti: the top 20 percent of the economic quintile owned 51.5 percent of the national wealth, while the poorest 20 percent had access to only 5.0 percent (World Bank 2017a, 2017b). The lack of well-paying jobs in either country has reinforced international migration as a survival strategy. In 2012, remittances injected $4.262 billion into the Dominican economy and over $1.612 billion into Haiti's economy (World Bank 2017c).

While U.S. development plans for Hispaniola make economic dependence between Haiti and the Dominican Republic more visible, they also create competition between the two countries. As a result of the trade and financial embargoes the United States and the United Nations imposed on Haiti in the 1990s, the Dominican Republic assumed a more pronounced role in Haiti's economic affairs. Dominican business and political elites, for instance, received important concessions from U.S.-led trade agreements that provided tax-free duties for goods partially manufactured in Haiti but sold by Dominican corporations to the United States and, increasingly to Haiti (Fatton 2014, 69–70; Reyes-Santos 2015, 120). While such concessions and growing trade with Haiti resulted in gains for Dominican businesses, these advantages remained minimal until the 2010 earthquake. For example, in 2000, only 3 percent of Dominican exports went to Haiti; according to a 2012 World Bank report, 15 percent of Dominican exports went to Haiti. Between 2009 and 2011, Haitian imports from the Dominican Republic grew from $647 million to just over $1 billion. Indeed, it is estimated that fully 2 percent of the Dominican economy's 7 percent growth in 2010 resulted from the aftermath of the Haitian earthquake (Milfort 2013, 1; Fatton 2014, 68).

The Dominican economy's consistent 4 percent annual growth rate throughout the 2000s has led many economists to praise the Dominican Republic as a shining star in the Caribbean despite persistent underemployment and high rates of poverty. Some analysts have termed this the "Dominican paradox": "high growth, declining wages, stubborn poverty," and the expansion of the informal economy (International Labour Organization 2013, 1, 19–25). In other words, the Dominican economy is generating wealth, but that wealth has not created higher-wage jobs and it has not been invested in secondary and postsecondary education in order to produce a more educated and competitive workforce. However, the "Dominican paradox" is not an anomaly or an accident. Rather, this situation is the direct outcome of a development model that was shaped in Washington and adopted by Dominican administrations since the 1980s. This model relies on artificially maintained low wages, underemployment, and outright exclusion from the workforce. As Melissa Bretón writes, "The implementation of neoliberalism as a project for economic growth has been partly dependent on the state's ability to draw on historical constructions of the Haitian Other in order to maximize capital's need for cheap labor" (Bretón 2016, 4).

Indeed, neoliberalism in Hispaniola has created an informal labor market across the island that is characterized by low wages and persistent vulnerability. As Robert Fatton (2014) notes, post-earthquake interventions did little more than move Haiti further into the "outer periphery," which he defines as "the very bottom of the production process of the world system" (9). Haiti's comparably disadvantaged position vis-à-vis the Dominican Republic has created opportunities for Dominican businesses, an advantage the United States has cultivated in pre- and post-earthquake trade agreements. For example, the Interim Haiti Recovery Committee (IHRC), which was created by the Action Plan for the Reconstruction and National Development of Haiti and was co-chaired by former U.S. president Bill Clinton in March 2010, advocated strengthening Haiti's apparel industry and welcomed the U.S. Congress's passage of the Haiti Economic Lift Program (HELP). HELP extended the country's favored status under the Caribbean Basin Recovery Act to 2020. HELP also declared that apparel produced in Haiti and shipped through the Dominican Republic would be free from all taxation.[1]

The second iteration of the Haitian Hemisphere Opportunity through Partnership Encouragement (HOPE II) permitted the co-production of garments in the Dominican Republic and Haiti and provided that apparel could be exported from the Dominican Republic duty free. Indeed, Dominican business elites have long understood the expansion of free trade zones along the Haitian-Dominican border and in Haiti as important to alleviating the pressure to migrate for many Haitians (Dupuy 2015, 111). While these new agreements position Haiti in the "outer periphery," Dominican economist Wilfredo Lozano concludes that Washington's plan is "to make the Dominican Republic, as the neighboring country to Haiti, a partner dependent on the international community and, specifically, on the United States" (Lozano 2011, 566, 581–582).

The devastating effects of the 2010 earthquake on the Haitian economy

(Robert Fatton estimates that Haiti lost 120 percent of its gross domestic product) made Haiti even more dependent on international donors and non-governmental organizations. The earthquake may have also led to changes in Haitian migration patterns to the Dominican Republic. Survey data reveal that by 2012, 75 percent of Haitian migrants to the Dominican Republic intended to stay there permanently. In keeping with trends regarding the feminization of poverty throughout the Americas, Haitian migration to the Dominican Republic is also decidedly more female than in the past. In 2004, 22 percent of Haitian immigrants were women; by 2012, they accounted for nearly 35 percent of the immigrant population (Observatorio Político Dominicano 2013). Given these changes, some observers note that "remittances from Haitian migrants in the DR may be going to the lowest quintile of the Haitian population" (Kristensen and Wooding 2013, 5). Finally, Haitian migrant labor has moved beyond the agricultural sector, where the overwhelming majority of Haitians labor, to include construction, commerce, and the service industry. In 2012, the number of Haitians in agriculture had decreased to 35.7 percent. Twenty-six percent of Haitian migrants in the Dominican Republic labored in construction, another 16.5 percent worked in commerce, while another 10 percent were employed in the service sector (Observatorio Político Dominicano 2013).

In other words, as the Dominican economy shifted toward service and tourism, Haitian labor in the Dominican Republic moved beyond agricultural *bateyes* (rural compounds). The Dominican state has responded to this by manipulating differences in status, nationality, race, and gender to limit Haitians' mobility within this transnational and informal labor market. Stephen Gregory (2006) noted this phenomenon years ago in his study of the Dominican beach town Boca Chica: "It was through the policing of citizenship—its enabling discourses, practices, and logics of verification—that differences tied to race, class, gender, and national origin were embodied and articulated as a system of exclusions that was the foundation of the social division of labor" (37, 39).

More recently, Kare Kristensen and Bridget Wooding (2013) have argued that "anti-Haitian exclusionism [in the Dominican Republic] may also be understood as part of a post-nationalist demographic economy" that is driven by low wages (4). The Dominican state uses bureaucratic procedures to control access to the labor market and its artificially maintained low-wage structure by policing the legal status of (im)migrant workers and of the underemployed. In the Dominican Republic, as elsewhere, rules governing nationality and legality establish, as Myriam Chancy (2014) argues, "whether or not [an] individual is seen as a *desirable* citizen of the State." Mechanisms such as aggressive policing to determine who has the right to work and decisions such as La Sentencia further entrench the exclusion of the laboring poor because they are the most unlikely to have access to the documents they now need to prove their right to employment and their claims to any rights as citizens or residents.

Two Birds or One? Manipulating Anti-Haitianism for Political Gain

For the Partido de la Liberación Dominicana (PLD), the most dominant political party in the Dominican Republic, exploiting anti-Haitianism to protect both its political power and its economic agenda is nothing new. When analyzed alongside the consolidation of the PLD in the late 1990s, La Sentencia can be viewed as the result of a series of procedural changes enacted by the PLD's right-wing, xenophobic allies that has institutionalized Haitian exclusion and racism into the mechanisms of Dominican state governance (Marsteintredet 2014). Similar to its uses during General Rafael Trujillo's dictatorship (1930–1961), modern Dominican political parties, most notably the PLD but also the PRD and the PRSC (Partido Reformista Social Cristiano, Reformist Social Christian Party), use anti-Haitianism as a scapegoat for the nation's ills. The political uses of anti-Haitianism and the constant manipulation of legal status to define who can make demands on the state, in the end, produces a policing mechanism that also manages who has the right to access the state's diminishing resources, including state pensions, as in the case of sugar workers (Centro Bonó 2016).[2]

For example, during the Dominican debt crisis of the 1980s, President Antonio Guzmán Fernández (PRD) ordered that Haitian workers be deported from sugar estates at the end of the sugar season. President Guzmán's order coincided with the explosion of protests involving labor unions, community associations, and peasant organizations against increased taxes and lowered state subsidies on basic food items, gas, and cooking oil. After riots gripped the country in 1984 and 1985, President Joaquín Balaguer (PRSC) also capitalized on anti-Haitianism in an effort to divert attention away from the implementation of policies that devastated the Dominican poor. Then, in 1991, President Balaguer deported approximately 14,000 Haitians; another 40,000 people left to avoid violence (Wucker 2000, 132–137).

During the election year of 1996, when the PLD forged an alliance with Balaguer's party to guarantee a victory in the presidential elections, Leonel Fernández and the PLD leadership exploited anti-Haitian racism as a campaign strategy against its main political rival, the PRD. In that vitriolic campaign, the PRD's candidate, Francisco Peña Gómez, became the brunt of vicious jokes and racist assaults that questioned his right to run for president on the basis of his Haitian ancestry. PLD activists also claimed that Peña Gómez and the Haitian government encouraged voter fraud by allowing undocumented Haitians residing in the Dominican Republic to vote for the PRD. Leonel Fernández and the PLD won that election. With the exception of one term, 2000–2004, the PLD has since held the reins of political power in the DR (Sagás 2000, 105–113, 138–140).

The PLD's anti-Haitianism exploits long-held stereotypes about Haitians, but within a democracy, the government's stated loyalties to the rule of law, freedom, multiculturalism, and human rights force explicit racist ideologies to assume new forms. In the 1940s, official nationalist narratives cast Haitians as biological threats to a Hispanic-cultured nation on the brink of progress and modernity. From the 1990s to the present, governing institutions, such as local civil registries, and civil authorities such as doctors, nurses, and bureaucrats who check documentation, position both Haitian migrants and their Dominican-born children outside the imagined community by questioning Haitians' legal status and by emphasizing their cultural and presumed racial differences (see Clarke and Thomas 2006). As Haitian migration to the Dominican Republic has increased and transformed (Moya Pons 2010), Dominicanness has increasingly been defined by legality—legal versus illegal residence; documented versus undocumented persons.

Since the 2000s, the PLD has taken steps to narrow access to Dominican nationality. Immediately upon taking office in 2004, for example, President Leonel Fernández authorized a General Law on Migration that defined temporary contracted laborers or casual border crossers as non-resident persons "in transit." The 2004 law appears to have been an attempt to meet the demands of Dominican business elites aligned with the PLD who were interested in guaranteeing their continued access to vulnerable workers. Yet the law went further. Article 28 stipulated that nonresident foreign women who gave birth in the Dominican Republic had to register their children with the consulate of their citizenship unless the father was Dominican. Hospitals were ordered to offer these mothers pink birth certificates and to register their children in a log for foreigners.

A report published by OBMICA, a Dominican-based think tank, and the international political rights organization Open Society pointed out that the rule tied children's nationality exclusively to that of their mothers (in violation of international law) and that since many women lacked documents that proved their own residence in the Dominican Republic, children could lose their nationality based on assumptions about their mothers' residency status. Most important, doctors and nurses often determined the mothers' residency on the basis of their names or physical appearance. Those deemed "Haitian" were inscribed as such (OBMICA and Open Society 2013).

Three years later, the Junta Central Electoral authorized Resolution 12 and Circular 017, which allowed state officials to deny residents their birth certificates, passports, or *cédulas* (national identification cards) if there were indications of irregularities. Circular 017 defined inscriptions made by foreign-born parents who were unable to prove their legal status at the moment of their children's birth as "irregular." Then, the 2010 constitutional reform, shepherded by President Fernández, declared children born of "in-transit" parents to be noncitizens, affirming constitutionally what had been institutionalized in practice. In 2013 the Supreme Court of Justice, later called the Constitutional Tribunal, upheld the constitutionality of denying citizenship to those considered to be in "irregular migration situations" and to their Dominican-born children. Even more tragically, the tribunal applied the law retroactively, thus also ratifying the practice of denying nationality rights to Dominicans of Haitian ancestry on the merits of their parents' or even grandparents' legal status.

These exclusionary mechanisms and bureaucratic intransigencies produced a number of significant effects. Together, they nurtured and strengthened the idea that "Haitianness" radically differed from Dominicanness, but instead of relying on the racist tropes of the past, the government used legal status to re-create Haitian subordination to Dominican superiority. In the contemporary Dominican Republic, race-based exclusion assists the modernization of government and its institutions through the enforcement of the law and legal status, demonstrating "the modernity of prejudice rather than its primitivism" (Martínez 2013).

At the same time, the controversy over Dominican nationality provides important cover for Dominican president Danilo Medina to further his own political goals and shore up the power of his wing of the PLD. In September 2014, one year after La Sentencia went into effect, the widely read Dominican newspaper *Hoy* reported that Leonardo Grisanty, who was employed in the president's communications office, had created the hashtag #DM4 to solicit responses to the following tweet: "Danilo Medina should continue and deepen the transformations that he has realized since his presidency."[3] Then, in April 2015, Dominican newspapers published articles advocating for President Medina's reelection. Arismendy, reporting for the online newspaper *Espacio de Prensa*, quoted Nicolás Mateo, a member of the PLD's central committee, as stating that President Medina's reelection would "unify society" and guarantee "a tranquil campaign without surprises" (Arismendy 2015). On June 17, the deportation deadline, the Dominican Congress granted President Danilo Medina the constitutional reform he needed to run for reelection.

Conclusion

Soon after La Sentencia was published, the Dominican state implemented piecemeal "fixes" that have divided the community of those the policy affects. In the wake of social protest against the decision, President Danilo Medina signed Executive Order 169-14, the Naturalization Law (Ley de Régimen Especial y Naturalización) and the Regularization Plan for Migrants with Irregular Status (Plan Nacional de Regularización de Extranjeros, PNRE). The Naturalization Law separates those most directly affected by La Sentencia into two groups: the 24,000 who have valid Dominican identity papers, such as birth certificates and *cédulas*, can apply for citizenship immediately, while the 21,000 people who could prove their birth in the Dominican Republic between 2007 and 2010 but do not have valid documents can apply for naturalized citizenship after a two-year waiting period. For the nearly 500,000 people who live in the Dominican Republic without documents, the Regularization Plan was meant to provide them with a path to legality. Newspapers report that as of the June 17, 2015, deadline, 98 percent of the 288,466 foreign residents who had already submitted documents for residency or naturalization were Haitian. Another 150,000 persons boycotted the endeavor completely (Wooding 2014, 107; Rodríguez 2015).

Possible solutions to La Sentencia and its ongoing effects will continue to occupy discussions and activism within the Dominican Republic, Haiti, and abroad. Clearly, the Dominican Constitution needs to be changed and a general amnesty needs to be legislated, but at the moment the Dominican political consensus regarding immigration, as in the United States, weighs heavily toward policing and deportation, not inclusion and equity. While legal remedies are important because of the ways they might protect immigrants' human rights, they do not change the structural mechanisms and ideological arguments that have made undervalued Haitian labor both necessary and available to Dominican industry since the late nineteenth century. For example, for the thousands of undocumented cane workers who still do not have their pensions decades after losing their jobs when the Dominican sugar industry privatized in the 1990s, legalizing their status is important in the larger process of documenting their claims to benefits. Yet legal status alone will not guarantee that they will receive their hard-earned pensions. This raises (perhaps controversial) questions. What comes after legality? If citizens can no longer receive state benefits, is citizenship even worthy of the fight?

I have used an island-wide perspective to analyze La Sentencia and to attempt a response to these questions. In this chapter, I have shown that La Sentencia is an effect of the development policies and priorities imposed by international lending agencies on both countries (albeit under quite different circumstances). If one takes seriously the idea that export-oriented industrialization has created an island-wide work force that has been made flexible and expendable through low wages and exclusionary practices and that the United States and international funding agencies manipulate competition between Haitian and Dominican political and economic elites, La Sentencia can be understood as deeply rooted in historical anti-Haitianism *and* as a product of these contemporary structural conditions (Perez Hazel 2016). La Sentencia is the latest example of a longer process of "dehumanization entailed by the exclusionary transformations of citizens and political subjects into subjects of management and control" (Fischer 2007, 4).

The transnational Hispaniola framework used in this analysis can also help politically engaged scholars resist the "epistemological violence" occasioned by an anti-historical, identity politics–framed moralism that obscures the interactions between culture, power, the state, and economic development. Samuel Martínez (2014), who has long studied human rights discourses, finds that they tend to adopt a "naming and shaming" approach that lacks what he calls "global historical reflexivity." For Martínez, global historicity would include human rights organizations in the global North holding their own countries accountable for the failures of development aid and development policies. Such a human rights movement would broaden the circle of who bears responsibility for the situation of Haitian migrants and their children. In addition to advocating for immigrants' human rights, this human rights regime would "look into what is owed, by whom, to Haitian migrant and Haitian-descendant workers, to compensate for years of under-remunerated labor, unfairly extracted from them on the basis of restricted geographical and social mobility" (174–175).

Martínez's demand for historicity is a call for a different way to account for the failures of development in Hispaniola—a new narrative, as it were. In her study about political and social violence in Jamaica, *Exceptional Violence. Embodied Citizenship in Transnational Jamaica*, Deborah Thomas (2011) advocates that we move against culturalist arguments that "'naturalize a people and their social circumstances as the product of a moral deficit, deviance, or degeneracy'" and "obscure our understanding of the ways imperial and nationalist projects have been developed transnationally" (66, 68–69). Culturalist arguments make ahistorical claims that transform Dominican anti-Haitianism into a naturally occurring phenomenon.

This story, however, fails to capture the ways that La Sentencia emerges from an environment where there is little tolerance for rights-bearing citizenship. Indeed, the state's attacks on citizens' rights is precisely what the Dominican-based organization Reconoci.do emphasizes in its *vidas suspendidas* (suspended lives) campaign, which underscores the fact that the lack of a Dominican *cédula* obstructs people's access to education, marriage, and financial freedom. This environment and its by-products are historically produced, and U.S. and European capital play important roles in this unfolding drama. I am not arguing that the United States or Europe is responsible for La Sentencia. Nevertheless, U.S.- and European-backed development protocols for the island set the Dominican Republic and Haiti as competitors. The Dominican Republic, with its stronger economy and better structural position in key trade agreements, can use this leverage to enhance its elevated position over Haiti, maintain its role as an arbiter between the United States and Haiti, and police labor across the island.

Therefore, as a political crisis affecting all of Hispaniola, the problems of exclusion and dehumanization and their by-products—fear, xenophobia, interpersonal violence, and racism—may best be addressed by creating a transnational politics that also addresses the political economy at the center of this controversy. As activist scholars who advocate for the right of people to move elsewhere and to be treated equally in their new countries of residence, the current social movement for belonging in the Dominican Republic is about the right to stay put and live with dignity. This is clearly the common ground that unites movements across the island. While the plight of Haitian immigrants and their children in the Dominican Republic has captured the moral imagination of the movement, it is also true that even if the Dominican state resolves the issue of citizenship, Hispaniola's labor force will remain as vulnerable as ever, especially its poorest residents, and laboring communities will continue to migrate across the island or across the water in search of economic security and opportunity.

A new kind of politics that emerges from transnational analysis should reflect a commitment to changing a system that profits from labor exploitation and express moral indignation for the many human rights abuses that occur in the name of development. By looking across the entire island, activists and scholars can craft the necessary strategies to undertake the transformational work required to counteract the serious injustices that La Sentencia has produced and that the decree makes evident in the everyday lives of Hispaniola's residents.

Notes

1. Haiti Economic Lift Program Act of 2010, Public Law 111-171, https://www.congress.gov/111/plaws/publ171/PLAW-111publ171.pdf, accessed October 16, 2017.

2. "Compromiso social y político por un nuevo modelo de gestiones de las migraciones," which was signed by a number of foundations, nonprofits, trade unions, federations, and organizations in the Dominican Republic, many of which had worked on behalf of migrants and their families for years, called for a regularization plan months before La Sentencia.

3. *"Danilo Medina Sánchez debe continuar y profundizar las transformaciones que ha encarnado desde la Presidencia."* "Piden reelección del Presidente Danilo Medina en red

social," *Hoy Digital*, September 8, 2014, http://hoy.com.do/piden-reeleccion-del-presi
dente-danilo-medina-en-red-social/, accessed September 26, 2015.

Works Cited

Arismendy. 2015. "Asegura reelección es la garantía de la unidad del PLD." *Espacio de Prensa*, April 14. https://www.espaciodeprensa.com/2015/04/14/asegura-reeleccion-es-la-garantia-de-launidad-del-pld/ Accessed May 1, 2018.

Betances, Emelio, and Harold Spalding Jr. 1995. "Introduction." *Latin American Perspectives. The Dominican Republic: Social Change and Political Stagnation* 22 (3): 3–19.

Bretón, Melissa. 2016. "Neoliberalism, Citizenship and the Law: Migration and Labor in the Dominican Republic." Unpublished manuscript in author's possession.

Centro Bonó. 2016. "Compromiso social y político por un nuevo modelo de gestiones de las migraciones." Unpublished document. http://bono.org.do/wp-content/up loads/2013/05/Compromiso-Social-y-Politico-por-un-Nuevo-Modelo-de-Gestio nes-de-las-Migraciones.pdf. Accessed February 1, 2016.

Chancy, Myriam. 2014. "New Year's Resolution: Love Thy Neighbour." Myriam J. A. Chancy (blog), January 24. http://www.myriamchancy.com/new-years-resolution-love-thy-neighbor/.

Clarke, Maxine, and Deborah A. Thomas. 2006. "Introduction." In *Globalization and Race. Transformations in the Cultural Production of Blackness*, edited by Kamari Maxine Clarke and Deborah A. Thomas, 1–36. Durham, NC: Duke University Press.

Corten, Andre, Isis Duarte, Consuelo M. Soto, and Viviana Fridman. 1995. "Five Hundred Thousand Haitians in the Dominican Republic." *Latin American Perspectives* 22 (3): 94–110

Dominican@s X Derecho. 2013. "Análisis de la Sentencia No. 168-13 del Tribunal Constitucional de la República Dominicana." Unpublished document. https://domini-canosxderecho.files.wordpress.com/2013/10/puntos-de-anc3a1lisis-de-la-sentencia-no-168-13-definitivo.pdf. Accessed October 16, 2017.

Dupuy, Alex. 2010. "Beyond the Earthquake. A Wake-Up Call for Haiti." *Latin American Perspectives* 37 (3): 195–204.

———. 2015. "The World Bank and Haiti: Abetting Dictatorship, Undermining Democracy." In *Haiti: From Revolutionary Slaves to Powerless Citizens*, edited by Alex Dupuy, 93–114. New Brunswick, NJ: Rutgers University Press.

Espinal, Rosario. 1995. "Economic Restructuring, Social Protest, and Democratization in the Dominican Republic." *Latin American Perspectives* 22 (3): 63–79.

Fatton, Robert. 2014. *Haiti: Trapped in the Outer Periphery*. Boulder, CO: Lynne Rienner.

Fischer, Sibylle. 2007. "*Haiti*: Fantasies of Bare Life." *Small Axe* 11 (2): 1–15.

Grandin, Greg. 2015a. "There's a Vicious, Slow-Motion Pogrom Happening a Few Hundred Miles from the U.S." *The Nation*. June 5. https://www.thenation.com/article/theres-vicious-anti-black-pogrom-happening-few-hundred-miles-us/. Accessed October 16, 2017.

———. 2015b. "We Regret to Inform You That in 14 Days You and Your Family Will

Be Deported to Haiti." *The Nation*. June 15. https://www.thenation.com/article/we-re gret-to-inform-you-that-in-4-days-you-and-your-family-will-be-deported-to-haiti/ Accessed October 16, 2017.

———. 2015c. "Concentration Camps in the Dominican Republic?" *The Nation*. June 18. https://www.thenation.com/article/concentration-camps-in-the-dominican-repub-lic/. Accessed October 16, 2017.

Gregory, Stephen. 2006. *The Devil behind the Mirror: Globalization and Politics in the Dominican Republic*. Berkeley: University of California Press.

Hintzen, Amelia. 2014. "Historical Forgetting and the Dominican Constitutional Tribu-nal." *Journal of Haitian Studies* 20 (1): 108–116.

International Labour Organization. 2013. "Growth, Employment and Social Cohe-sion in the Dominican Republic." ILO Background Paper. http://www.ilo.org/wc msp5/groups/public/---dgreports/---integration/documents/meetingdocument/ wcms_204604.pdf. Accessed October 16, 2017.

Katz, Jonathan. 2015. "The Dominican Time Bomb." *New York Times*. July 2.

Khan, Wasiq N. 2010. "Economic Growth and Decline in Comparative Perspective: Haiti and the Dominican Republic, 1930–1986." *Journal of Haitian Studies* 16 (1): 112–125.

Kristensen, Kare, and Bridget Wooding. 2013. "Haiti/Dominican Republic: Upholding the Rights of Immigrants and Their Descendants." Executive Summary. https://www. files.ethz.ch/isn/172091/273b4770daf48a18c60d724a641f0470.pdf. Accessed October 16, 2017.

Lozano, Wilfredo. 2011. "Geopolítica de la reconstrucción de Haití y la cooperación in-sular en la Hispaniola." *Ciencia y Sociedad* 36 (4): 561–589.

Marsteintredet, Leiv. 2014. "Mobilisation against International Human Rights: Re-Do-mesticating the Dominican Citizenship Regime." *Iberoamericana. Nordic Journal of Latin American and Caribbean Studies* 44 (1–2): 73–98.

Martínez, Samuel. 2013. "The Political Economy of Dominican Anti-Haitian Exclusion-ism: A Post-National Nationalism?" Paper presented at the International Congress, Latin American Studies Association, May 31. Chicago, Illinois.

———. 2014. "A Postcolonial Indemnity? New Premises for International Solidarity with Haitian-Dominican Rights." *Iberoamericana. Nordic Journal of Latin American and Caribbean Studies* 45 (1–2): 173–193.

Milfort, Milo. 2013. "Haiti-Dominican Republic Trade: Exports or Exploits?" Haiti Sup-port Group, December 21. http://haitisupportgroup.org/haiti-dominican-republic-trade-exports-or-exploits/. Accessed October 16, 2017.

Moya Pons, Frank. 2010. "La Matriz transnacional haitiana." Paper presented at Transna-tional Hispaniola I, Santo Domingo, Dominican Republic, June 4.

OBMICA and Open Society. 2013. "Presentación al Comité para la Eliminación de la Discriminación contra la Mujer: Revisión de la República Dominicana." http:// www.obmica.org/images/Publicaciones/Informes/Informe%20alternativo%20 CEDAW%202013%20Discriminacion%20de%20genero%20en%20acceso%20a%20 la%20nacionalidad%20RD.pdf. Accessed October 16, 2017.

Observatorio Político Dominicano, Unidad de Políticas Públicas. 2013. "La presencia de inmigrantes haitianos en República Dominicana." September 11. http://www.opd.

org.do/index.php/analisis-politicas-publicas/936-la-presencia-de-inmigrantes-hai-
tianos-en-republica-dominicana. Accessed October 16, 2017.

Perez Hazel, Yadira. 2016. "¿Ajeno Siempre Será (Foreigners Forever)? The Spectacle of
(Un)Making Dominican/Haitian Identity." *Memorias. Revista Digital de Historia y
Arqueología desde el Caribe Colombiano* 12 (28): 136–166.

Persaud, Randolph B. 2004. "Situating Race in International Relations. The Dialectics of
Civilizational Security in American Immigration." In *Power and Postcolonialism and
International Relations. Reading Race, Gender, and Class*, edited by Geeta Chowdhry
and Sheila Nair, 56–81. London: Routledge.

Reyes-Santos, Alaí. 2015. *Our Caribbean Kin: Race and Nation in the Neoliberal Antilles*.
New Brunswick, NJ: Rutgers University Press.

Rodríguez, Ramón 2015. "Interior y Policía tiene listos 130 mil carnés del Plan Nacional
de Regularización." *Diario Libre*, September 9. http://www.diariolibre.com/noticias/
interior-y-policia-tiene-listos-130-mil-carnes-del-plan-nacional-de-regularizacion-
IH1191381. Accessed September 25, 2015.

Sagás, Ernesto. 2000. *Race and Politics in the Dominican Republic*. Gainesville: University
Press of Florida.

Schuller, Mark. 2007. "Haiti's 200 Year Ménage-à-Trois: Globalization, the State, and
Civil Society." *Caribbean Studies* 35 (1): 141–179.

Thomas, Deborah. 2011. *Exceptional Violence. Embodied Citizenship in Transnational
Jamaica*. Durham, NC: Duke University Press.

Weisbrot, Mark. 1997. "Structural Adjustment in Haiti." *Monthly Review* 48 (8): 25–39.

Werner, Marion. 2011. "Coloniality and the Contours of Global Production in the Dominican Republic and Haiti." *Antipode* 43 (5): 1573–1597.

———. 2016. *Global Displacements. The Making of Uneven Development in the Caribbean*.
Oxford: Wiley Blackwell.

Wooding, Bridget. 2014. "Upholding Birthright Citizenship in the Dominican Republic."
Iberoamericana. Nordic Journal of Latin American and Caribbean Studies 44 (1–2):
99–119.

World Bank. 2017a. "Income Share Held by the Highest 20%." https://data.worldbank.
org/indicator/SI.DST.05TH.20?locations=HT. Accessed October 16, 2017.

———. 2017b. "Income Share Held by the Lowest 20%." https://data.worldbank.org/in
dicator/SI.DST.FRST.20. Accessed October 16, 2017.

———. 2017c. "Personal Remittances, Received (Current US$)." https://data.worldbank.
org/indicator/BX.TRF.PWKR.CD.DT. Accessed October 16, 2017.

Wucker, Michelle. 2000. *Why the Cocks Fight: Dominicans, Haitians, and the Struggle for
Hispaniola*. New York: Hill and Wang.

4

Transnational Cultural Production

11

Interview with Paul Austerlitz

Engaged Scholarship and Engaged Creativity in the Dominican Republic and Haiti

PAUL AUSTERLITZ AND APRIL J. MAYES

Paul Austerlitz is an ethnomusicologist and musician who has spent decades studying and playing Dominican and Haitian music. Paul's first book, *Merengue: Dominican Music and Dominican Identity* (1996), was the first work published in English that offered a comprehensive history of the genre. In that book, Paul traces the early development of *merengue* and its transformation into the Dominican Republic's national music. His second book, *Jazz Consciousness: Music, Race, and Humanity* (2006), uses W. E. B. Du Bois's concept of double consciousness as a springboard for thinking about music and race and looks at jazz in a variety of settings ranging from New York City to the Dominican Republic and Finland, the country of Paul's birth. Paul is also an accomplished musician; his musical creativity is documented on several CD recordings.

Given Paul's extensive experience playing and researching Dominican and Haitian musical genres and their historical development both across the island and from the island to New York City, the editors of this volume invited Paul to give an interview, conducted by April Mayes, in the fall of 2016. What follows is an edited and revised transcription of the interview, organized to highlight three intellectual and personal threads that emerged during their conversation: Paul's arguments regarding the similarities and differences between Dominican and Haitian musical genres, his comprehensive overview of the Dominican roots music movement, and his engagement with Caribbean musics as a scholar, teacher, musician, activist, and spiritual practitioner.

APRIL: Hello, Paul! As we start this interview, would you please share with me your background?

PAUL: So, I'm Paul Austerlitz. Whew, I don't know how far back you want to go! Well, I was born in Finland, my mother is Finnish, and I was one year old when I came to the United States. My father was from Romania and he was Jewish, but he was not a practicing Jew and I wasn't raised Jewish. He moved to the U.S. when he was fifteen and became a linguist. He was doing research in Finland when he met and married my mother. But I grew up in the U.S., so my identity is very North American. Still, I think the fact that I'm an immigrant really shaped me. I speak Finnish fluently and I maintain strong relationships with my relatives.

APRIL: How did you discover Caribbean music, especially Dominican music, and start playing it?

PAUL: I grew up in New York City and I lived there after college, in the early 1980s. I had always loved various forms of African-based music, as many white people do. If you think about it, it's interesting that the most popular forms of music all around the world, among people of all races and ethnicities, are African-influenced. From the U.S. to Europe and Asia, people are listening to hip-hop, jazz, rock, reggae, and salsa. Anyway, I always loved all forms of African-influenced music and especially liked anything with lots of drumming, like salsa and Latin jazz. After college, I started playing in New York's Latin bands. I learned that the saxophone played a position of importance in *merengue*, contributing to the music's rhythmic texture by interacting structurally with percussion instruments. Previously, I had considered becoming a conga player because I loved percussion, but when I discovered *merengue* I thought: "Well, no, I can play just as rhythmically on the sax in *merengue* bands." And I loved it! I adored the music and I also loved the culture, responding to the warmth I discovered in the Dominican community. I moved to Washington Heights and began learning Spanish.

I played with many lesser-known bands but also had opportunities to play with stellar figures like Joseíto Mateo, who had been the "King of *Merengue*" in the 1950s. Mateo had played a pivotal role in the historical development of the music during the period of Rafael

Trujillo's dictatorship (1930–1961). So when I went to graduate school for ethnomusicology at Wesleyan University, I opted to do my dissertation on *merengue*, partly because people like Joseíto agreed to help me. I interviewed Joseíto and many other *merengueros*, doing oral historical work, piecing together the history of the music, which wasn't well documented at the time. People knew anecdotally about Trujillo's role in promoting *merengue* as a national music, but it wasn't really written down anywhere. So I kind of came upon the topic at the right time. The fact that I met these *merengue* musicians on the bandstand gave me entrée into their worlds. Joseíto invited me to his house; I interviewed Johnny Ventura; I jammed with Tavito Vásquez and Félix del Rosario. I played, as a guest artist, with *típico* musicians like El Ciego de Nagua and Rafaelito Román.[1]

APRIL: When did you start playing sax?

PAUL: I started playing in college. As a young kid, I played different instruments—violin, piano, and guitar—and then in high school, clarinet.

APRIL: What else did you learn in college that has helped you understand Dominican and Haitian musics?

PAUL: I studied at Bennington College with Bill Dixon and Milford Graves, who were important people in what they called the "New Black Music," or freely improvised avant-garde jazz. Bill Dixon founded a separate Black Music Division (or department) at Bennington College. Dixon argued that because the existing Music Division taught European repertoires, it was actually a "white music" department. He convinced the college administration that if the school had a White Music Division, it should also have a Black Music Division. That was how a lot of the Black Studies programs were founded—they were demanded. I focused much of my work with Bennington professor Milford Graves, a drummer who focused on African-influenced musics as well as healing traditions and spirituality from around the world. He introduced me to ethnomusicology. Graves's perspective is African-centered but also universalistic: he looks at African-based traditions as manifestations of something that is fundamentally human, something that *all* people share. Graves set the agenda for the rest of my career. My *Jazz Consciousness* book, for example, looks at music in a way very influenced by Graves and even ends with a chapter co-written by him. My parents were liberals who taught me about Martin Luther King, but in college, I read Malcolm X's autobiography, which inspired to examine my *own* positionality, to think deeply about my lived racial consciousness. It was through music cultures that I made connections. I grew immeasurably by working in African American, Dominican . . . and, later, . . . Haitian music scenes. Music can't make everything a level playing field because class, race, and gender are inextricable from our everyday lived experience. At the same time, influenced by Paul Gilroy's arguments about "strategic universalism" and "planetary humanism,"[2] I have noticed that music can indeed build bridges, that *musical consciousness raising* can actually occur. People utilize music and other means to make *strategic gestures of universalism*, not to minimize points of privilege, but as a necessary response to injustice.

As mentioned, after graduating from Bennington, I got my PhD in ethnomusicology at Wesleyan University, whose rich program stressed performance as well as scholarship. Later, I taught ethnomusicology at Brown University, where I affiliated with Africana studies in addition to the Music Department. Lewis Gordon[3] was there at the time, and he encouraged me to work with a rich theater program housed in Brown's Africana Studies program. At Gettysburg, where I now teach, I have a joint appointment in music and Africana Studies. Much of this grew directly out of my Bennington experience, and even today, Milford Graves and I meet regularly; we're in touch all the time.

APRIL: Well, let's talk about music. When I think about Dominican and Haitian music traditions fitting into a broader narrative, I think about this on two levels. The first is how Dominican and Haitian musics relate to each other, how they speak to each other. The second is how they connect to the larger, umbrella term "Afro-diasporic music." Would you explain how you view these relationships?

PAUL: They relate to each other very closely because not only are they both Afro-diasporic, but also because they emerged on the same island, so the relationships are fundamental. I will add, though, that the two countries' musical cultures are also quite different. Actually, they are astoundingly different, considering how small the island is.

And each country also has a stunning amount of diversity, especially among the more rural "folkloric" noncommodified genres.

APRIL: And are you saying that this diversity is a product of the different ethnic groupings across the island?

PAUL: Yes, yes—that's a big part of it, but there are also other factors. The ethnic traces are interesting and influential. For example, Dominicans are very Congolese. Haiti has a lot of Congolese but also a lot of Dahomey (Fon), Yorùbá, and other ethnic groups. Hispaniola didn't see the extent of pan-African homogenization that happened in the U.S., for example. In North America, we can't easily identify separate strains of Yorùbá or Congolese culture, but in Haiti (and places like Cuba and Brazil), we can. The extent to which these ethnic influences have been maintained within Vodou practice, for instance, is remarkable. The D.R. is a more of a mixed-race society, so the African influences in Dominican popular religion are more syncretic.

At the same time, Dominican musical aesthetics are extraordinarily African. And as I said, the African influences on Dominican music are primarily Congolese rather than West African. *Palos* drumming, for example, is primarily Congo. *Palos* was maintained through the *cofradías*, which were fraternal aid societies founded by the Catholic Church.[4] In fact, the first black *cofradías* were actually founded in Spain under the auspices of the Church by Africans living there. The D.R. had a lot of maroon societies, too, which had an enormous impact on the development of Afro-Dominican traditions of resistance.[5] But Afro-Dominican ritual musics such as *palos* and *salve* (religious songs) are completely different than Haitian ritual music.

APRIL: I appreciate your response to that question. My colleague at Scripps College, Martha González, a recording artist with the group Quetzal, and a feminist *artivista*, discusses a number of genres in her scholarship and blends them in her musical performances. Many of these rhythms are African-derived, such as *son jarocho*, the musical genre connected to *fandango*, the ritual-based celebrations. While she and her band have been central to the popularization of these forms in Chicano music in the United States, González maintains their distinctiveness even as she connects, integrates, and fuses them with other genres.[6] What I'm basically saying is this: your insights confirm how diaspora can be a productive framework to think about diversity and difference, not just sameness.[7] Are you essentially saying that the diversity you note in Haitian and Dominican music has less to do with ethnic differences and more to do with their uses in ritual practices and with each country's historical developments?

PAUL: Yes, but there are also lots of connections.

APRIL: I think that within African diaspora studies Haiti can sometimes be viewed as the seed culture, right? And then you have the movement of people from Saint Domingue to Cuba, to Puerto Rico . . .

PAUL: And Santo Domingo.

APRIL: And Santo Domingo, Trinidad, and they are sort of seeding these islands and their cultures from the Haitian cultural tableau.

PAUL: I agree and I think it's very relevant. Dominican *merengue* is part of a larger complex of styles including Haitian *méringue*, Venezuelan *merengue*, the Puerto Rican *danza*, and the Cuban *danzón*. These are all syncretic dance forms influenced by the French *contredanse* and the Spanish *contradanza*. The early history of *merengue* is undocumented, so we don't know where it started. But we do know that like the other genres I mentioned, it ultimately developed as an Afro-Caribbean transformation of the contredanse. Black cultures in the Caribbean transformed the European dance musics into uniquely Afro-Caribbean styles. Alejo Carpentier, the Cuban writer, argued that the *cinquillo*, a signature rhythm of Cuban music, came from Haiti. So I agree that Haitian influence is fundamental throughout the Caribbean, including the D.R.[8] But the influences go both ways. For example, there is a kind of folk wisdom that the Petwo division of Haitian Vodou was founded during the colonial era by a Spanish speaker from the eastern side of the island called Don Pedro. Petwo is the most revolutionary, militant side of Haitian Vodou. Much later, during the Trujillo era, Dominican music was very popular in Haiti and exerted a very strong influence on the advent of the preeminent form of Haitian popular music, *konpa*, which grew with a very strong influence of Dominican *merengue*. François "Papa Doc" Duvalier utilized *konpa*, just as Trujillo used *merengue*, although to a lesser degree.[9] And significantly, former Haitian president Michel Martelly, who was a *konpa* star prior to entering politics, is also a Duvalista. Gage Averill says that *merengue* is the "leitmotif" of Hispaniola dictatorships.[10] That's something else the two countries have in common musically.

APRIL: Stepping back and summarizing: Hispaniola is a great example of how the search for origins is perhaps not as productive as thinking about how musical and performance genres cross ethnic, colonial, and then, later, national boundaries. This reminds me of the idea of sociosonic circuitry that some scholars have used to explain the development of contemporary genres such as *dembow* and *reggaetón*.[11] Dominican and Haitian musics have their own historical developments, yet they are also products of cultural movements across the Caribbean. Can you give me a chronology of the Afro-Dominican roots music movement? Did it emerge from this interaction between musicians who were based in the U.S. or in the Dominican Republic or was that mostly from D.R?

PAUL: Afro-Dominican roots music had its origin during the Doce Años (The Twelve Years, 1966–1978) of President Joaquín Balaguer's regime and began as the Dominican expression of Nueva Canción and Nueva Trova, folkloric music movements that were popular throughout Latin America at the time.[12] The first important Dominican Nueva Trova group was called Convite, derived from the Haitian Kreyòl word *konbit*, which is also used in the D.R. when people do communal labor accompanied by work music. Convite wasn't just a musical ensemble, though—it was also an educational group. Some members, such as Dagoberto Tejeda, were not musicians. Still today, Tejeda stands at the forefront of engaged scholarship on Afro-Dominican culture.[13] The late, great Dominican musician Luís Dias also started out as a member of Convite. Like other Nueva Canción and Nueva Trova groups, Convite worked from a Marxist perspective, placing class, rather than race, at the center of their celebration of Dominican roots. In the 1970s, it wasn't necessarily an Afro-Dominican music movement; it was a Dominican Nueva Trova movement that included Afro-Dominican elements. During the Balaguer period, the Dominican revolutionary spirit came alive and the first expressions of *négritude* in the D.R. emerged.[14] In countries such as the U.S.,

Cuba, and Brazil, the elevation of black culture occurred earlier, but Trujillo made it impossible for this to happen in the D.R. during his rule. It's interesting that in Haiti, the *noiriste* movement, which celebrated blackness, emerged as a reaction to U.S. military occupation (1915–1934) as the mulatto elites reacted to the racism of the occupying Yankees. In the D.R., *négritude* developed belatedly and perhaps, rather weakly, during and after Balaguer's Doce Años. With time, people started talking about an Afro-Dominican music movement. I would argue that, today, Toné Vicioso, José Duluc, and Xiomara Fortuna are the foremost figures in this area.

I'd like to back up a bit and talk about (Haitian) *rara* in the Dominican Republic, where it's called *gagá*. Originally developing in Haiti, *rara* is a form of processional, sacred/secular music performed during Lent, leading up to Easter. In the D.R., it's performed during Holy Week, the last week of Lent, mainly on *bateyes*.[15] June Rosenberg, who, like myself and Martha Ellen Davis, was a white, North American scholar, lived in the D.R. and wrote about *gagá* during Balaguer's presidency, celebrating it as a manifestation of *Dominican* culture even though it was mainly confined to the Haitian-Dominican community.[16] This was very courageous of her at that time, because Balaguer's repressive regime had articulated a virulently anti-Haitian and racist ideology; I think Rosenberg was somewhat shielded by the fact that she was a U.S. citizen. During the same period, the Dominican folklorist Fradique Lizardo also emerged with adamant assertions about the African basis of Dominican traditional culture. He insisted that *merengue* was of African origin.[17] He also argued that as the most widely diffused genre of Dominican traditional music, *palos* ritual drumming should be embraced as the national music of the D.R. With the growth of the Afro-Dominican music movement,[18] *gagá* became one of the most prominent roots genres. José Duluc, for example, made a point of living on a *batey* to learn *gagá* drumming, song, and dance, and also imbibe the ritual traditions that surround the music. Duluc developed into a master *gagá* musician and dancer who blends traditional wisdom with his own street-smart songs. He is also extremely well versed in *palos, salve*, and all the other forms of Afro-Dominican music. Toné plays a lot of *gagá*, as does Xiomara. And new forms of *merengue* such as those performed by artists such as Amarfis and Tulile also incorporate lots of *gagá* influences. So, it's really interesting that *gagá*, which came to the D.R. from Haiti, has become fully Dominican, as June Rosenberg demonstrated in her book so long ago.

Roldan Marmól has produced several recordings featuring music by the major Dominican roots musicians as well as his own *gagá* fusions. In 2011, he instigated a "Cultural Caravan" to foment solidarity between the D.R. and Haiti following the devastating earthquake of 2010. Dozens of Dominican artists traveled together on a bus to perform in and demonstrate solidarity with Haiti. I had the privilege of participating in this.[19] The accomplishments of Convite, Duluc, and their colleagues amount to a significant social movement. I remember talking to you about this a while back, and you said, "Yeah, but it's always the same people who show up at those events." But the question remains: is this a social movement? And my response is that certainly it's a movement, even if it's a small movement . . .

APRIL: In a very conservative, authoritarian country where people like me wonder: where are the victories? We often forget how authoritarian everything is: Dominican politics, Dominican society. Those authoritarian legacies go on. It just keeps going . . .

PAUL: My response is that *the victory is the survival*. The fact that during any given weekend rural areas of the D.R. boast multiple Afro-Dominican rituals and that in Santo Domingo a small but dedicated group of cultural workers continue to use music as a means to affirm Afro-Dominicanness is significant. It's a triumph unto itself.

APRIL: What have you seen more recently among your friends and your colleagues in the music world and how all that is changing Dominican and Haitian musics in the United States?

PAUL: Well, I was thinking of a particular, very important musician, Toné Vicioso. Toné was born in the Dominican Republic and lived in Venezuela as a child. With Duluc, he co-led an important roots band called Los Guerreros del Fuego in the D.R. during the 1980s, maybe already in the 1970s. Moving to New York in the early 1990s, he started another group, called Asa-Difé, of which I was a member when it was founded. This was a great honor for me. Toné taught me a lot about traditional Dominican music, and actually he taught a lot of people. Even Xiomara Fortuna, a major figure in this movement in her own right, told me that Toné was her teacher. When I met Toné, he felt that what he was doing was not gaining acceptance in the Dominican Republic. He thought that he might have more success in New York, so he started promoting his Afro-Dominican fusion music there in the Dominican community and in the wider community in the hopes that any acceptance he would get in New York would be a form of capital to bring back to the Dominican Republic, that once Dominicans on the island saw that this music can thrive in the U.S., they'd be more prone to embrace it. Much later, he did, in fact, move back to the D.R. And to a certain degree, his plan might have worked, but not to a very great extent. Still, this interplay between the Dominican diaspora and the D.R. is beneficial for both groups. Toné, Duluc, Xiomara, and the other innovators of Dominican roots music have certainly had an important impact. Many young Dominicans have been influenced by them, starting their own bands which celebrate Afro-Dominican culture. Of course, the situation in the country is not particularly progressive in terms of race, so this impact has major limitations.

APRIL: I wanted to go back to a couple of things, such as what victory may look like. I think for many of us in the diaspora, victory may include ending anti-blackness in the D.R.; another kind of victory might be of a sort of reevaluation or acknowledgment of anti-Haitianism within certain discourses of Dominicanness and its role in Dominican society. One critique of what you've just described might be, "Well, there might be an Afro-Dominican music movement, but it's not changing how people think about blackness." Have you heard that critique?

PAUL: Well, what we are doing with Transnational Hispaniola could be criticized for the same reasons. How much of an impact has engaged scholarship had on Dominicans living on the island? Certainly not as much as we would like. But we keep going.

APRIL: I guess I'm saying, for someone who's raised in diaspora, especially in the United States, you take on a certain racial identity and that racial identity is going to be about elevating a certain critique of racial power in U.S. society that one might think operates exactly the same in D.R. And so I might be looking for a movement that's going to speak against anti-blackness very explicitly and we're also going to have this particular critique of white supremacist capitalist patriarchy. Does the music movement push some of those questions around what blackness is, what anti-blackness has been—you know in ways that the diaspora-minded folks want?

PAUL: I think the answer is "Yes!" I mean it's exactly what people are doing. I don't think there's much difference between the perspectives presented at the Transnational Hispaniola meetings and the perspectives promoted by Duluc, Toné, and Dagoberto Tejeda. In fact, Toné, along with a great New York–based Dominican roots drummer, Ernesto Rodríguez, performed at the second TH conference. Haitian roots musicians Sanba Zao and Jacobo were also there. We all played together and it was great! I would change the question: Why is the progressive Dominican movement in the U.S. so separate from the Afro-Dominican movement in the D.R? This is unfortunate. I thought you were asking about how successful we have been.

APRIL: Well, has it been successful? I'm actually saying that everyone you've mentioned has been doing it right for a long time. I agree with you, but I think there's impatience within the diaspora . . .

PAUL: Oh! I'm so impatient—to be honest, sometimes I just feel like giving up. I have witnessed anti-Haitianism in the D.R. that just turns my stomach. And the worst part is that in some cases, anti-Haitianism is spewed by people—friends of mine—who purport to be progressive, or "revolutionary," as they say. Duluc and I have often discussed this. We're really close. More than once, I've asked him, "Man, how do you, how can you take it? How can you stand living in the D.R., with all this negativity about Haiti, all this rejection of blackness?" And he says, he always says, "Well, the progress is slow, but it's getting a little better all the time." And I say, "Duluc, that's what you said twenty years ago!" On the last occasion we talked about this, Duluc said to me, quietly this time, "You know, Paul, this is my home. I have to stay positive." Even for me, Dominican culture has also become part of who I am, so I also can't give up. And those of us in the U.S. can play a role in supporting people who have been fighting the good fight in the D.R. all these years; we can help.

APRIL: I would like to return to what grounds you as a musician, as a scholar, as a human being. You spoke before about the profound impact of Milford Graves on your formal education and racial consciousness while at Bennington. You brought this back to New York as you pursued a living playing in various bands. What about this part of your journey informs your work as a teacher?

PAUL: So I teach at Gettysburg College, where every year for the last four years, we do a trip to the Dominican Republic. We stay in housing provided by Xiomara Fortuna's Rancho El Campeche, in the San Cristóbal area, and visit the local community where Xiomara does a lot of meaningful social work. We also work with MUDHA (Movimiento de Mujeres Dominico-Haitianas, Inc.), an activist group fighting for Dominican-Haitian rights. They bring us to *bateyes*, educating us about labor conditions and human rights. We do workshops with members of MOSCTHA (Socio-Cultural Movement of Haitian Workers), whose lawyers teach us about the legal battles they fight, not only in the D.R. but also at the International Court of Justice.[20] Duluc is involved: he teaches Afro-Dominican drumming and dance classes. Also, I have good contacts with *servidores de misterios* (Vodou practitioners), especially in the Haina area, who invite us to ceremonies. You can be sure that my collaborators in the D.R. consider their work—and our visit—as part of a larger social movement. Music gives the students an entrée into that world. Their drumming classes with Duluc introduce them to *palos* drumming, so when they meet ritual drummers, they can have a more informed kind of conversation. Duluc always tells my students that he's doing the same thing that enslaved people and maroons did: they're using music as a way to create a liberatory space.

APRIL: That sounds really powerful. So when you're teaching, what are some of the main objectives that you want to get across to students?

PAUL: One thing that I have noticed is that students respond to my work on *merengue*: it's a really good way to think and talk about race. The contradictions are surprising and troubling. My students are always surprised to learn that a Dominican president, Trujillo, who was of Haitian descent, massacred Haitian-Dominicans. It's also surprising that, while Trujillo made Vodou illegal according to the Dominican Constitution, evidence shows that he himself believed in the efficacy of African-based mystical practice. And while Trujillo-era folklorists insisted that Dominican music was derived primarily from Europe,[21] it was precisely its Afro-Caribbean aesthetic that made *merengue* such an effective form of propaganda for the dictatorship. As a white, middle-class, North American male, it's of course awkward for me to raise these issues. To help my students—and myself—through the confusion and contradiction, I draw on my personal history.

I mentioned earlier that my father was Jewish, but I wasn't raised Jewish. My father never talked to me about the Holocaust, he never even talked to me about being Jewish! It was my mother who told me, when I was about ten years old, that my father was Jewish. After my father died, I found out that I had two relatives in the Czech Republic whom I didn't know about. They were Holocaust survivors who had been in Auschwitz, and I had the privilege of visiting them several years ago. I was going through a spiritual period of my life where I was visiting the graves of all my ancestors. That meant I had to go to Auschwitz, so I made the pilgrimage, and made offerings to my ancestors there. I used to be mad at my father, thinking, "Why didn't you teach me about this part of my heritage?" But, then I realize that I hadn't gone through what he lived. He was doing the best he could. *He* was the one whose cousins were in Auschwitz, not me. I don't know what I would have done in his position. Maybe the Dominican situation is kind of similar. For example, the abolition of slavery is not officially celebrated in the D.R. From a spiritual standpoint, and from a psychological standpoint, it can't be healthy to disregard one's own ancestors, one's own bloodline, in this way. But when I thought about my father, it gave me perspective. Slavery, colonialism, and genocide create trauma which causes people to do things that we might wonder about, but it's all part of the struggle to survive. That's one thing I've talked to my students about.

APRIL: Thank you for sharing that. I really have appreciated this discussion about your spiritual foundations. Where do you now find yourself?

PAUL: Afro-Caribbean spiritual traditions are a big part of my life. I look at those traditions as conduits of African philosophies. If you

study the different *lwa*, for example, or *orishas*,[22] you are studying fundamental concepts like change, technology, health and
disease, sexuality, fertility. It's a mode of learning that I have found
very helpful in my own life, even though I come from a completely
different culture. My own spiritual practice grew out of my musical work because it was through music that I met people that were
involved in those traditions and had the social networks necessary
to pursue them. Joseph Campbell, the great religious studies scholar,
wrote the preface to Maya Deren's seminal book on Vodou,[23] not-
ing that Deren's status as a creative artist (filmmaker) rather than
as an anthropologist informed her sensitivity to Haitian religion.
Maybe my work within Caribbean culture and my participation in
its religious traditions are informed by my musicality. I used to think
that my *merengue* book was separate from my musicianship because
it doesn't directly address my experiences as a performer, but looking
back, I think I could never have written that book if I hadn't become
involved with the music as a player. This raises methodological and
even epistemological questions.

Academia is removed from the cultures that have nurtured wisdom traditions in the African diaspora. Academia is Eurocentric, it's
disembodied, it's verbal-centric. Even as a child, I was aware of the
limitations of linear thinking. And now that I'm no longer a spring
chicken (as a colleague once said), if I can influence anyone, I'd like
to influence people to pursue multi-modes of discourse. Of course,
rigorous academic work is valuable and I'm dedicated to being as
good a scholar as I possibly can. But my exposure to Afro-Caribbean
spirituality has given me additional tools, ones that transcend verbal
and linear discourse. I've entered the world of Afro-Caribbean
spirituality through my musicality, with my body, with my intuition,
and I try to convey some of this to my students. Scholarship about
Vodou can teach you a lot, but to really understand these traditions,
there is no substitute for traditional courses of study, which consist
of various forms of initiation, dreamwork, ritual, and oral traditions.
Since I was young, I was drawn to Afro-Caribbean religion, not as a
research topic, but as a deeply felt spiritual yearning. I was baptized in
the 21 División (or Dominican Vodou) by Señora Jenny Cabrera and
received the *kanzo* level of initiation in Haitian Vodou from the late

Max Beauvoir and Manman Nicole Miller. And I've grown *a lot* from the process!

As a white, middle-class U.S. male spending time in the Dominican Republic, I sometimes feel awkward because when I'm there, I'm often promoting my concerts on the radio or on Dominican TV. And interviewers ask my opinions about what's going on in music or in culture. As a white male, I used to operate under the erroneous assumption that I had the privilege of saying whatever I wanted whenever I wanted. I'm ashamed to admit this mistake, but I'm grateful to have grown. I used to publicly speak out, in the D.R., against the government's anti-Haitian policies, but later realized that I'm not the right person to talk about these issues. A white North American lacks the moral authority to preach to Dominicans about these issues. I came to the conclusion that it was better to use music as a vehicle for making my statements.

I've had a band in the Dominican Republic for about eight years, and for a while I was going three or four times a year to perform with them. Now we usually just perform once a year. All the members of the group are Dominicans. Duluc is in the band, and we focus on my compositions and arrangements, which fuse *merengue, palos,* and other Afro-Dominican musics with jazz. We also play some Haitian songs. Now this is just a coincidence, but the only vocal music that we do is in Haitian Creole. We perform mainly for upper-middle-class people because that's the audience for jazz in the D.R. Many of my audience members embrace jazz as a North American thing and might be attracted to the idea of a gringo playing jazz fused with *merengue.* But they also see us playing *palos* and even singing Haitian Vodou songs. And it's interesting—sometimes middle-class Dominican jazz fans even sing along, in Creole, in those venues—they seem to know some of the words or they'll sort of mouth along! Toné once told me, "Paul, that's what you should do. You don't need to go on TV and talk about your opinions, you're making a statement through your music." I just consider it a privilege to be part of that and continue to grow and learn from people like Toné, Duluc, and Xiomara by being welcomed as part of that social movement. I have also had the privilege of playing with Haitian roots bands, like Foula, and I'm currently recording a CD with a Haitian drumming group called Asakivle, along with bassist Chico Boyer and guitarist Monvelyno, who are major innovators in Haitian roots music.

I started out as a white guy who just wanted to play Caribbean music. Then I became a scholar of *merengue* and of Caribbean culture. But later, I became a participant in Dominican musical and social movements. And that's how I see myself now.

Notes

1. Tavito Vásquez, an alto saxophonist who rose to prominence in the 1950s and was active until his death in 1995, was a brilliant figure in Dominican jazz. Del Rosario was an innovative *merengue* bandleader, and El Ciego de Nagua and Rafaelito Román are major figures in accordion-based *merengue*. Paul Austerlitz, *Merengue: Dominican Music and Dominican Identity* (Philadelphia: Temple University Press, 1996), 58, 59, 87–88, 94, 122, 144; Paul Austerlitz, *Jazz Consciousness: Music, Race, and Humanity* (Middletown, CT: Wesleyan University Press, 2006), 106–117.

2. Paul Gilroy, *Against Race: Imagining Political Culture beyond the Color Line* (Cambridge, MA: Harvard University Press, 2000).

3. Lewis Gordon and Jana Anna Gordon, eds., *A Companion to Africana Studies* (Malden, MA: Blackwell Publishing, 2008).

4. The earliest documents referring to black *cofradías* in Santo Domingo, which were also associated with particular African ethnic groups ("tribes" or "*naciones*"), date to the sixteenth century. Martha Ellen Davis, "Afro-Dominican Religious Brotherhoods: Structure, Ritual, Music" (PhD diss., University of Illinois, 1976).

5. Maroon communities refer to settlements of runaway enslaved people who lived free from nearby plantations, having freed themselves in the process of escaping from slavery. Carolyn Fick ascribes much of the success of the slave insurgency against the French in colonial Saint Domingue to the support rebels received from runaways (maroons) and from the broader practice of *marronage*, which included individuals who left plantations without necessary permission and more collective actions that could involve groups of enslaved people who sought escape and defended the autonomy and liberty of their communities. Carolyn Fick, *The Making of Haiti: The Saint Domingue Revolution from Below* (Knoxville: University of Tennessee Press, 1990).

6. Martha González, "Creating a Mexican-Afro-Cuban-American Beat. The Rhythms I Play and Dance Collided on the American Continent—Then I Made Them My Own," Zócalo, December 5, 2004, http://www.zocalopublicsquare.org/2014/12/05/creating-a-mexican-afro-cuban-american-beat/chronicles/who-we-were/.

7. Brent Hayes Edwards, "The Uses of Diaspora," *Social Text*, 19, no. 1 (2001): 45–73; Tiffany Ruby Patterson and Robin D. G. Kelley, "Unfinished Migrations: Reflections on the African Diaspora and the Making of the Modern World," *African Studies Review* 43, no. 1 (2000): 11–45.

8. Alejo Carpentier, *Music in Cuba*, edited by Timothy Brennan, translated by Alan West-Durán (1944; repr., Minneapolis: University of Minnesota Press, 2001).

9. Gage Averill, "Haitian Dance Bands, 1915–1970: Class, Race, and Authenticity," *Latin American Music Review* 10, no. 2 (1989): 221; Gage Averill, *A Day for the Hunter, a Day for the Prey: Popular Music and Power in Haiti* (Chicago: University of Chicago Press, 1997, 71–77).

10. Averill, "Haitian Dance Bands," 234.

11. Wayne Marshall, Raquel Z. Rivera, and Deborah Pacini Hernandez, "Introduction: Reggaeton's Socio-Sonic Circuitry," in *Reggaeton*, edited by Raquel Z. Rivera, Wayne Marshall, and Deborah Pacini Hernández (Durham, NC: Duke University Press, 2009), 11.

12. Deborah Pacini Hernandez, "La lucha sonora: Dominican Popular Music in the Post-Trujillo Era," *Latin American Music Review* 12, no. 3 (1991): 105–123.

13. Dagoberto Tejeda Ortíz is an anthropologist and a founder of Afro-Dominican ethnology in the Dominican Republic. See Dagoberto Tejeda Ortíz, *Mana: monografía de un movimiento mesiánico abortado* (Santo Domingo: Alfa y Omega, 1978).

14. Leopold Senghor defined *négritude* as "the whole complex of civilised values—cultural, economic, social, and political—which characterise the black peoples or, more precisely, the Negro-African world." Leopold Senghor, "Negritude and African Socialism" (1961), in *The African Philosophy Reader*, edited by P. H. Coetzee and A. P. J. Roux (London: Routledge, 1998), 440. The significance and expressions of négritude change according to the context in which they emerge. In the Dominican Republic, it might be said that négritude consisted of the effort to recognize the African origins of Dominican cultural elements and was an attempt to systematize intellectual and artistic production that elevated those cultural elements as part of the national narrative.

15. Barracks and small villages on sugar estates that house mostly Haitian migrant workers. They are usually poorly resourced—often lacking electricity and running water—and are usually located in the cane fields, far from government services.

16. June Rosenberg, *El gagá: Religión y sociedad de un culto dominicano* (Santo Domingo: Universidad Autónoma de Santo Domingo, 1979); Fradique Lizardo, *La cultura africana en Santo Domingo* (Santo Domingo: Sociedad Industrial Dominicana, 1979).

17. Hugo Antonio Ysálguez, "El merengue tiene su origen en Africa," *Ahora* 8, no. 630 (1975): 50–51.

18. Angelina Tallaj-García, "Performing Blackness in a Mulatto Society: Negotiating Racial Identity through Music in the Dominican Republic" (PhD diss., City University of New York, 2015).

19. Joselin Rodríguez, "RD y Haití unidos por la cultura," *Hoy*, July 17, 2011, http://hoy.com.do/rd-y-haiti-unidos-por-la-cultura/, accessed January 22, 2017; "La Caravana Cultural será en Haití," *Hoy*, July 12, 2011, http://hoy.com.do/la-%c2%93caravana-cultural-de-la-isla%c2%94-sera-en-haiti/, accessed January 22, 2017.

20. For more information and to support their causes, visit their websites. MUDHA: mudhaong.org/en/; MOSCTHA: www.mosctha.org.

21. Flérida de Nolasco, *La Música en Santo Domingo y otros ensayos* (Ciudad Trujillo: Editora Montalvo, 1939), 71.

22. *Lwa* are the spiritual entities invoked in Vodou. *Orishas* are the spirits invoked in Yorùbá religion as practiced in Nigeria, Cuba, Brazil, Trinidad, and elsewhere.

23. Joseph Campbell, "Foreword," in Maya Deren, *Divine Horsemen: The Living Gods of Haiti* (New Paltz: McPherson, 1970), xiv–xv.

12

Translating Hispaniola to the Digital Realm

On Teaching Alternative Histories of the Americas

KAIAMA L. GLOVER AND MAJA HORN

Almost nowhere are issues of linguistic borders and their challenges to mutual legibility more striking than in the case of Haiti and the Dominican Republic—two nations that share the same 30,000-square-mile island of Hispaniola and over five centuries of interconnected history but are deeply divided in ways that reflect broader geopolitical phenomena grounded in a dialectic of commonality and conflict.

The geopolitical border that separates Haiti from the Dominican Republic is a divide that echoes long-held perspectives on race and culture that circulate far beyond the island of Hispaniola. That divide posits blackness as contaminant or contagion and is often deployed to justify Haiti-related policies and practices in both the United States and the Dominican Republic. The border between Haiti and the Dominican Republic is in many ways marked by the peculiarity of borders in general—what postcolonial scholar Chris Bongie (1998) describes in *Islands and Exiles* as those disconcerting "interstitial zones that paradoxically divide and unite" (210).

Borders are essential to maintaining the integrity of what they contain, but they are necessarily situated at the extremities of the spaces they circumscribe. Because of this, borders are constantly threatened. Permeable and pregnable (and in using the term "pregnable" we mean to evoke a mixing of blood via procreation—the Haitian-Dominican romantic couplings and the politically liminal, stateless children these couplings produce), borders trouble the comfort—and the comfort zones—of nation-state identity. They function to demarcate and to limit, but they are constantly disputed, which is of course a mark of their arbitrariness.

Ultimately, the border dividing Hispaniola is a testament to the elusiveness of true transnational hybridity. Although the border region has long been a place of cultural intermingling, various regimes in the history of Hispaniola have put policies in place that made crossing the border prohibitively difficult. A dividing line in the non-space between two countries, the border region is a particularly absurd iteration of the arbitrary divisions that have been established and are maintained throughout the Americas, one of many legacies of a colonial past that persists into contemporary reality. The spatial logic of contiguous geography, the temporal logic of common colonial origins, and the social logic of shared cultural practices are often overridden by grudges passed down from Europe and maintained by self-interested elite power brokers in Hispaniola and, perhaps less obviously, in the United States.

Over the last years, the two of us—researchers and teachers of the literature and culture of Haiti and the Dominican Republic, respectively— have come to realize that our positioning in the academy is in fact part of this story. Colleagues at Barnard College in the French (Glover) and Spanish and Latin American Cultures (Horn) departments, both passionately interested in and professionally focused on the same Caribbean island, we were confronted with the shocking realization that we had never been in sustained scholarly or pedagogical dialogue with one another. It became starkly apparent to us that the same fracturing that has long marked the geopolitical realities of the Caribbean has been mapped onto scholarship of the region. Thus, we began to think pointedly about the disciplinary balkanization of the Americas—the fact that the Anglophone, Hispanophone, Francophone, and Dutch-speaking Caribbean have been fixed within the boundaries of university departments in accordance with national European languages, a phenomenon that in many ways un-self-reflectively reproduces a European imperial model of world history. Although times are changing and Caribbeanists increasingly have been pushing against this model through working groups and centers (such as the Advanced Institute for Critical Caribbean Studies at Rutgers University), with few exceptions, the academy has been remarkably slow to change.

With these realities in mind, we began thinking in earnest about what it means—or, rather, what it should mean—to be a scholar of the

Caribbean in the context of a region that is still fundamentally bounded by the legacies of North Atlantic imperialism. It became clear to us that Hispaniola offers a singularly generative space from which to think of Caribbean Studies and in which to examine how legacies of the colonial past in the Atlantic region and beyond determine global hierarchies and contemporary neoliberal structures of inequality. Phenomena like multilinguality, transnationalism, creolization, and globalization—all those trendy buzzword concepts that have become so prominent in the academy in recent years—are in the very DNA of both Haiti and the Dominican Republic, both independently and in relation to one another. These reflections seemed to be the stuff of pedagogical possibility. In other words, in addition to and beyond the opportunity for mutual enrichment of our respective scholarly perspectives, we were able to imagine boundary-transgressing approaches to engaging our students.

We are fortunate to hold faculty positions in a college/university situated in New York City, perhaps the most significant nodal point of both the Haitian and Dominican diasporas. As such, we set about devising a course that would tap into the many and diverse academic and cultural resources at our disposal. Over a period of six months, we developed the first iteration of a seminar course on Hispaniola that would put Haiti and the Dominican Republic in substantive dialogue with one another from a long-historical perspective, while pointedly addressing the metacritical obstacles or challenges to such a conversation. Thus was born our team-taught undergraduate seminar "Translating Hispaniola." The class was launched as part of a Barnard College Critical Consortium for Interdisciplinary Studies (CCIS) initiative as one of its first CCIS lab courses. The CCIS mandate—"fostering innovative faculty research on the transnational and intersectional contexts of social difference"—was to be supported in part by these CCIS lab courses, each of which would represent original interdisciplinary and collaborative pedagogical projects developed by two faculty members. "Translating Hispaniola" was clearly aligned with these objectives and found an ideal home in CCIS.

We had initially experimented with an iteration of the course designed for first-year students as a pair of linked seminars that met independently for the most part but came together regularly to discuss particular events in Hispaniola's history. Our tandem development of "Translating Hispaniola: Haiti" and "Translating Hispaniola: The Dominican Republic" was immensely valuable because it enabled us to identify and elucidate points of intersection, collaboration, and conflict that marked the evolution of Hispaniola from the fifteenth century to the present. It soon became apparent to us that, although this format brought into close and constant contact the distinct but interrelated histories and contemporary realities of the two nations concerned, it did so inadequately. By proposing course materials to students from two separate academic departments and classroom spaces who came together only intermittently, we were unwittingly facilitating the retrenchment of some of the biases and presuppositions we were committed to upending.

This inadequacy inspired us to overhaul the course content and structure within the frame of CCIS and, just as important, with a significant digital component that we believed would make most plain the imbricated and multiple histories that link Haiti and the Dominican Republic. We realized that in order to meet our objectives we would need to think not only across borders but also across disciplines. We were interested in content-based inquiries regarding the two countries and, perhaps more crucially, in methodologies and tools for resisting existing historical narratives. We recognized from our initial experience in presenting the materials to students that we needed to actively and aggressively undermine a number of conventional narratives about the relationship between Haiti and the Dominican Republic. Specifically, we wanted to avoid—or at the very least complicate—the prevailing narrative of impoverished, victimized Haitians and racist, predatory Dominicans that we felt underpinned the early iteration of the course. We knew there would be no avoiding certain very dramatic facts of history—the massacre of 1937, the human rights abuses of Haitian migrant laborers working on the sugar plantations of the Dominican Republic in the present day, the notorious 2013 Dominican supreme court ruling and its denationalization of Dominicans of Haitian descent, and so forth. We knew that these facts could not be elided or underplayed. Yet we were also committed to vigilance concerning narratives of the Dominican Republic's intractable antagonism that are easy to (re)produce inadvertently.

To that end, we dedicated the course to realizing three principal objectives: 1) facilitating a rigorous examination of social and political actors who, both historically and in the present day, have determined the sociopolitical frontiers of life on Hispaniola; 2) tracing alternative comparative histories of the two nations; and 3) intervening critically in existing narratives of Hispaniola. As part of our effort to broaden the narratives about

Hispaniola, including our own, we organized a lecture series that would parallel the course. We invited five accomplished scholars to speak about their own work and critical interventions. We were fortunate to have Sibylle Fischer (New York University), Raphael Dalleo (Bucknell University), Ginetta Candelario (Smith College), Gina Athena Ulysse (Wesleyan University), and Carlos U. Decena (Rutgers University) come to campus to present their work to our students.

The point of departure for our course was necessarily the past and present issue of human rights abuses against economically and politically disenfranchised Haitians in the Dominican Republic. We felt that we needed, above all, to thoroughly consider the facts that "cross-border, cross-linguistic, and cross-ethnic interactions have long characterized relations between Dominicans and Haitians" and "governing elites and their supporters have purposefully denied their peoples this history" (Mayes et al. 2013, 27). Relying on the elegant concept of "state against nation" that Michel-Rolph Trouillot (2000) has introduced, we sought to develop a course that would pay close attention to class by differentiating elite and state agendas from the lived realities of the majority population of the two countries. A substantial aspect of this endeavor involved triangulating the relationship between Haiti, the Dominican Republic, and the United States. We wanted to shed a light on the ways the United States, with its racist and racialized cultural underpinnings, has affected—if not infected—interactions between the two countries. We were convinced that understanding U.S. involvement in Hispaniola would give our students context for discourses within the international media and elsewhere that have long posited Haiti's dysfunctionality as entirely self-generated and the Dominican Republic as a relatively "successful" nation that plays well with free-market others—context for the notion of a deep-seated feud between *all* Dominicans and *all* Haitians.

Accomplishing this end meant moving away from grand historical narratives and conventional forms of evidence and moving toward alternative archives. It meant encouraging our students to recognize the constructed nature of history, particularly when it comes to places—like the Caribbean—that have been subject to the stereotyping impulses of the world outside their borders.

We believed that digital technologies might offer a useful point of departure for such an intervention into history-telling. Specifically, we were interested in how digital tools could: 1) enable us to place side by side what are too often the separately told histories of the two nations; and 2) empower our presumably technologically savvy students to inquire on their own how these histories might relate and intersect in ways we had not anticipated. Part of our preparation was the realization that we each needed to understand the limitations of our discipline—the fact of our respective lacunae with regard to the "other side" of that frontier of nation and language—as a reality embedded in the wider scholarly community. With this in mind, it became important to us to imagine how students might become cross-border "translators" of sorts who could make an intervention into the field of Caribbean Studies that would be direct, relatively quick, and impactful for a broader audience.

After toying with a variety of platforms and possibilities, we determined that digital timelines would be the most effective tool for our pedagogical objectives. We placed our students in teams of four and asked each group to investigate a topic that would lend itself to a comparative historical analysis of a particular Haitian and Dominican social, cultural, or political phenomenon. Each group was expected to present its research findings as an interactive digital timeline. We were very fortunate to have the assistance of Alex Gil, the digital scholarship coordinator for Columbia University, who is a Caribbeanist by training. We prepared a sample comprehensive multimedia timeline that featured historical and political data points that figure in "traditional" histories of the two countries.[1] We introduced our students to the timeline platform and held an in-class training session, in which we outlined the data-entry process and the bells and whistles of the finished product. We also encouraged students to rely on the support of Barnard librarians Miriam Neptune and Vani Natarajan for help with navigating technology challenges and for guidance in the research process. The librarians generously prepared a rich online resource guide for our course, which they presented to the class early in the semester. This guide included texts, online databases, and archives that greatly expanded students' awareness of the vast range of potential sources and means of accessing materials beyond scholarly monographs and academic journals.

Getting students to fully understand and accept the assignment was no easy task. We had expected—presumptuously, as it turned out—that our students would be apostles of all things digital, so were surprised to encounter what ranged from wariness to outright resistance. The students were decidedly daunted, both by what they imagined would be the assignment's technological demands and by the unfamiliar concept of a final project that did not include a research paper. Allaying fears about the former turned out to be the easier task. The timeline-making tool we chose—the TimelineJS Embed Generator—required no advanced programming knowledge or particular technological skills. In addition to its simple, clear design and intuitive data-entry process, which was perfectly manageable for anyone with a basic command of Excel or similar spreadsheet programs, the advantage of this platform was its ability to accommodate multiple thematic strands. This feature allowed for the simultaneous presentation of several chronologies in a single visual presentation, thus providing immediate opportunities for comparison.

We limited our students to four thematic strands for each of their topics and instructed them to establish distinct responsibilities for putting the timeline together. Each student was required to do the research for one of the four strands of the timeline. This enabled the group members to work collaboratively yet independently and allowed for maximum accountability regarding individual contributions to the project. In addition, each student was to assume a specific logistical/managerial role: project management (scheduling, task checklists); coding and development of the timeline; data entry; and liaising with librarians. More challenging, ultimately, was helping students understand the very nature of the assignment—the kind of data the timelines should contain and the overall methodology needed in order to conduct their research efforts to gather that data. We insisted that the project be envisioned as a carefully curated digital exhibit of information on a particular topic rather than as an answer to a specific research question. We wanted students to understand that they would be generating a resource that would identify and showcase relevant sources, events, and individuals from which other users, scholars and students alike, could draw informed conclusions.

In conclusion, translating Hispaniola to the digital realm offered both new pedagogical opportunities and some unexpected challenges, including the fact that the digital medium necessarily meant adjusting foundational pedagogical expectations to which students had become accustomed. This first experience with including a significant digitally based final assignment also taught us that students must work throughout the semester with digital tools rather than working in a digital format only at the moment of completing the final assignment. This all being said, the digital component succeeded in facilitating our primary objective in several key ways. It enabled us to offer what amounted to a fourteen-week crash course on 500 years of Hispaniola's history to a group aged 18 to 22, most of whom had limited knowledge of the island and the region, and to have them come away with 1) minds opened—through praxis—to the constructed nature of history; 2) new perspectives on alternative ways of representing knowledge and creating space for questioning established and simplistic narratives of the two sides of Hispaniola; 3) appreciation for the benefits and challenges of collaborative scholarship; and 4) increased proficiency in a digital context.

We anticipate offering this course every two years. In the next iteration, we will introduce incremental digital assignments alongside the more conventional project proposal and annotated bibliography that precede the final digital project. We also want to introduce a digital mapping tool. Our objective would be to allow students to trace and highlight diachronic relations between the two countries instead of focusing primarily on teleological historical narratives. We expect that this will open additional paths for identifying and examining the networks of relations that crisscross the border of Hispaniola and that link the island to broader geopolitical realities. This will, we believe, be the next pedagogical step toward foregrounding the interwoven histories and manifold connections that international mainstream media discourses and official accounts of the two nations' pasts and possible futures all too often pervert or ignore.

Note

1. We are grateful for the historical timeline that Anne Eller generously shared with us that served as our point of departure.

Works Cited

Bongie, Chris. 1998. *Islands and Exiles: The Creole Identities of Post/colonial Literature*. Stanford, CA: Stanford University Press.

Mayes, April, Yolanda C. Martín, Carlos Ulises Decena, Kiran Jayaram, and Yveline Alexis. 2013. "Transnational Hispaniola: Toward New Paradigms in Haitian and Dominican Studies." *Radical History Review* 115 (Winter): 26–32.

Trouillot, Michel Rolph. 2000. *Haiti: State Against Nation*. New York: Monthly Review Press.

Epilogue

APRIL J. MAYES AND KIRAN C. JAYARAM

Two republics on a bit of an isle caught between history and geography, between a past of conflicts and a geographical present of local and immediate
exigencies. Two republics stuck between time and space.

Michel-Rolph Trouillot (1949–2011)

We begin our final reflections with another exchange of letters, another
gesture of invitation to a conversation. The year was 1934. The *antillanista*
project had failed to become reality and U.S. intervention and occupation
had become the new norm (Haiti, 1915–1934; Dominican Republic, 1916–
1924). So, too, would dictatorship, facilitated by U.S. complicity and, later,
buttressed by Cold War policy that positioned Hispaniola's authoritarian
regimes as bulwarks against Communist Cuba. General Rafael Trujillo's
dictatorship in the Dominican Republic would last from 1930 until his
assassination in 1961. In Haiti, François "Papa Doc" Duvalier assumed
control in 1957, and then his son, Jean-Claude "Baby Doc" Duvalier, kept
the regime going until it finally collapsed under popular pressure and
international scorn in 1986.

In 1934, Hispaniola's activist women reached across national boundaries. The interaction we wish to highlight began when women's educa-
tor and founder of Dominican Feminist Action (Acción Feminista Dominicana, AFD) Abigaíl Mejía de Fernández (1895–1941) sent a letter to
Madeleine G. Sylvain Bouchereau (1905–1970), the first Haitian woman
to earn a law degree and a practicing attorney in Port-au-Prince. Mejía
de Fernández and Sylvain Bouchereau had been in touch before, apparently so often that Mejía expressed sentimental attachment to Sylvain:
"As I have already had the opportunity, on other occasions, to write to
you and to receive news about you, I [have] come to believe myself your

long-distance friend, or, better yet, your sister."[1] In that sisterly vein, Mejía asked, "Could you try to establish in Port-au-Prince a Feminist Association like ours? It could be our sister [organization]: 'Haitian Feminist Action'"[2] (in Candelario, Ginetta, Mayes, and Manley 2016, 539).

Sylvain responded with cautious enthusiasm. Although she believed that the acceptance speech she had given at Haiti's Palace of Justice upon her swearing in as an attorney had "prepared the groundwork" for feminist activism, Sylvain wrote, "in general, feminism is not very well known or understood here."[3] To address this problem, Sylvain made a few suggestions, asking Mejía to "send [her] . . . magazines, books, feminist newspaper articles."[4] Sylvain then made an extraordinary request regarding the AFD's radio program: "Your Friday radio chats would interest me, too. . . . Would you find a date to send a message in French for Haitian women?"[5] Regarding Mejía's idea of visiting Haiti, Sylvain replied, "I think the idea of coming to give conferences here . . . is excellent, but . . . June or July might be too late."[6] Finally, she promised to "bring together some feminine personalities and [try to] discuss what opportunity, if any, there is for establishing a League here right now"[7] (in Candelario, Ginetta, Mayes, and Manley 2016, 540).

Drawing on the activist networks built throughout the 1920s, when Haitian women protested U.S. military occupation, Alice Garoute, a leading anti-occupation activist, and Sylvain Bouchereau had founded La Ligue Féminine d'Action Sociale (The Women's League for Social Action, LFAS) in 1934. Similar to the platform of Dominican Feminist Action, which had been written in 1931, the Ligue Féminine sought to address "the physical, intellectual, and moral improvement of Haitian women's condition"; "the protection of children, women, and the elderly"; and "the fight for civil and political equality" (Saunders 2013, 103).

According to Grace Saunders (2013), while there is no firm evidence that the LFAS founders drew their platform from the AFD's manifesto,

> oral [histories] among Haitian feminists and their families consistently maintain that when Alice Garoute and Madeleine Sylvain sat down to draft their plans for the first Haitian women's political organization, an unnamed woman from the Dominican Republic's feminist movement was present. (104)

In March, perhaps as a substitute for traveling to Haiti but certainly mindful of assisting the process of founding Haitian Feminist Action,

Mejía dedicated the AFD's airtime to encouraging Haitian women to organize: "[it will not be by] revolution, but rather humanity's evolution,
that we will win our rights, the forgotten Women's Rights; but we have to
fight to get them"[8] (in Candelario, Ginetta, Mayes, and Manley 2016, 617).

Then, as now, the lives of Haitian and Dominican women were connected by political and economic policies forged in Washington, such as
the U.S. intervention and occupation, export-driven industrialization,
and international loans. They had in common the ways that color, class,
education, and mobility divided them (Mayes 2008; McPherson 2010).
They were bonded by the legacies of colonialism, slavery, dictatorships,
sexual violence (Wright 2016) and left- and right-wing political movements that did not always address gender equality. And they were linked
by the commitments to democracy and to gender equity (Charles 1995).
As we mentioned in the introduction to this volume, Haitian and Dominican women's contemporary political activism provided a ready vehicle
for thinking about the politics of gender and sexuality transnationally.
Yet thinking about what those movements had in common and where
their interests diverged, and why, pushed our analysis beyond the way we
originally formulated "transnational." For example, the aforementioned
letter exchange invites the possibility of writing a history of Hispaniola
feminism that transcends national boundaries, but the evidentiary trail
equivocates about Dominican women's direct interactions with first-
wave Haitian feminism. At the same time, the broader historical context
in which Dominican and Haitian feminism emerged—U.S. intervention
and occupation—returns us to the necessity of thinking about these two
events together.

Challenges from the Volume

Our main goal with this book was to provide a space for critiquing some
received wisdom and unquestioned assumptions about Haitians, Dominicans, and Hispaniola through research and persuasive arguments.
Our goal is to counteract the retrograde nationalisms, xenophobia, ex-
ceptionalisms, and racist idealizations of Dominicans and Haitians that
promote conflict and exclusion and silence moments of commonalities
and solidarity. In this effort, we see our work as building on important
shifts in Dominican scholarship. In his characteristically prescient manner, the late Haitian anthropologist Michel-Rolph Trouillot noticed a key

development in Dominican historical research of the 1980s and 1990s: "Behind their historical writings or their critical analysis of the Haitian situation in the Dominican Republic[,] the idea is sneaking in that neither [Haitians nor Dominicans] will make it for good without at least taking into consideration the presence of the other." This change, Trouillot concluded, was "an invitation to rethink the time and space of Hispaniola" (1999, 7). Rethinking time and space necessarily begins with rewriting history.

The eloquently argued chapters that constitute the first section of the book reveal that the alternative stories needed today were always present in the archives. The stories these chapters tell about the individuals, families, and communities who moved back and forth across imperial allegiances and political loyalties reveal that the Dominican archive, in particular, has long been weaponized by the powerful to defend anti-Haitian nationalism. Fidel Tavárez's finding that "the *antihaitianismo* that runs through Dominican nationalistic political discourse was not present among most of the political leaders of Dominican independence" is a damning and carefully argued and evidenced critique of a type of nationalism that continues to hold sway among some Dominican intellectuals and is taught in Dominican schools. Nathalie Bragadir's and Anne Eller's chapters also make equally strong assertions that trouble any notion of a fixed Dominicanness or Haitianness that can be traced from the past into the present.

In other important ways, too, the chapters in this section address Trouillot's (1997) insights about silences in the archive that hinder whose stories get told and how the very organization of the archives creates those silences in the first place. Trouillot's goal was not to lock historians into an intellectual and ethical impasse or to make history writing impossible. Rather, he wanted to nudge historians away from a comfort with empiricism that also made them complicit with power; to embrace critical introspection about their historical narratives; and, to grapple with the power relations embedded in the production of historical narratives derived from purposefully incomplete documentation. The chapters here demonstrate that the archive remains a productive site from which to tell the stories that counter nationalist pretensions and to reveal the relations and structures of power behind those stories (Lora H. 2012; González Canalda 2013).

This collection offers new narratives of Hispaniola beyond the conflict model while acknowledging historical and contemporary traumas the Dominican government perpetuates. The chapters in part 2 deal more directly with the often conflicted, uneasy relations between Dominicans and Haitians. The chapters here do not make an argument for perfection in those relationships; they advocate for continued engagement. For example, it might be easy to express disappointment in Aída Cartagena Portalatín, who for many is a revered leftist feminist icon but whose silences and problematic engagement with Haiti in her work, according to Elizabeth Russ, appear to evidence a Dominican reluctance to accept Haitians as equals and blackness as part of *dominicanidad*. Russ's critical treatment of Cartagena refuses any temptation toward singularity and treats Cartagena in her full complexity. Russ shows that intellectual and personal engagement across the island does not require perfect human subjects, untainted by historical baggage, internal contradictions, or ethical shortcomings. Régine Jean-Charles places those contradictions, human failures, violence, and traumas front and center in her analysis of Haitian women's literary tussles with the Haitian-Dominican border and its long, bloody history. Jean-Charles asks, how can one community's "geography of grief" become "a crossroads where the physical and spiritual meet"? Russ and Jean-Charles beautifully show that engagement across the island requires the willingness to go through fear and confront the past.

Another goal of the book is to expose the nationalist presumptions of historical and social science research and to critically evaluate "Hispaniola" as a geopolitical and geohistorical unit of analysis. We wondered what would happen if a perspective that considered the island in its totality is used to study recent developments in Haiti and the Dominican Republic. The chapters published in part 3 attempt this island-wide framing through analyses of political economy. As the chapters by Kiran Jayaram and April Mayes argue, export-driven economic development and the turn to sustainable development have not fundamentally changed Hispaniola's subordinate position in the global economy. They were never meant to do so. However, contemporary economic policies have profoundly transformed social and political relationships and have generated new ways of thinking about citizenship, the state, and power.

Elena Valdez's and Elizabeth Manley's chapters are powerful reminders that the relationship between capital and labor or about state and nation in the context of regional integration, globalized economies, and export-driven industrialization also involves the intimate realm—the arena of love, sex, romance, and transnational relationships between Haitians and Dominicans and between Haitians, Dominicans, and foreign tourists. Valdez argues that contemporary portraits of sex workers in Haitian and Dominican novels and novellas show how sex tourism has turned Hispaniola into a "sexscape." As a result, Dominican and Haitian writers are grappling with the implications of sex work on gender relations, economic mobility, and national identity. Manley's chapter makes an important contribution to the scholarship about sex work across the island by bringing attention to male sex workers and their expectations and experiences within this economy. What spaces of resistance do intimacy and sex occasion in this landscape? Can these kinds of engagements provide templates for a new politics that reaches across borders? What kinds of power relationships does sex reveal and what forms of change, if any, does sexual agency facilitate?

Contributors to this book view Haiti and the Dominican Republic as productive spaces from which to analyze the pathologies produced by development agendas. The chapter by Kaiama Glover and Maja Horn, for example, discusses the lessons that can be drawn from the challenges and the joys of teaching alternative histories of Hispaniola and, by extension, the Americas. Their pedagogy declares that Hispaniola is "a singularly generative space from which to think about Caribbean Studies and in which to examine how legacies of the colonial past in the Atlantic region and beyond determine global hierarchies and contemporary neoliberal structures of inequality." This is a powerful claim because it asks what would happen to narratives about Hispaniola if the island were allowed to occupy a central place in the conceptualization of the key questions and guiding concepts that continue to shape Caribbean studies.

Raj Chetty makes an equally important argument in his chapter about black affirmation in Dominican literary texts produced in the late 1960s and early 1970s. Chetty shows that in that period there was

> a struggle over national identity. . . . This struggle did not stem from confusion over blackness as a component of Dominican identity. Instead, it stemmed from a conflict between those who espoused a logic of white supremacy and those who argued for a racial identity founded on a mulatto mixture that included African ancestry and an affirmative connection to enslaved forbearers.

For Chetty, Hispaniola is a reminder that "what blackness looks like" is a matter of perspective, nurtured by historical and political developments, among other forces. Both the chapter by Chetty and the one by Glover and Horn make a provocative demand that is well aligned with the collective goals of all the contributors to this volume: to understand and treat Hispaniola's conflicts, shortcomings, and contradictions as productive and generative, not just as evidence of pathology.

Paul Austerlitz's story about his life work as a musician and instructor is also a helpful and hopeful corrective to the destructive narratives about Haitians and Dominicans. As Austerlitz's scholarship shows, research that spans Hispaniola benefits tremendously from historical specificity and, most important, the archive in which we can do the arduous work of historical investigation is not limited to documents. The depository for the kinds of historical memories that help us create new narratives resides in music, in dance, and in ritual.

Transnational Hispaniola's Challenge to Area Studies

The contributors to this volume want new narratives that question how Hispaniola is imagined, to hold scholars and activists accountable for the stories they tell about Hispaniola, and to elevate Hispaniola's importance in the broader story of freedom through new representations. The international responses to the 2010 earthquake brought into sharp relief a point Michel-Rolph Trouillot (1990) noted years ago about Haiti's representation in popular media and even in academic scholarship. Haiti, he noted, was often represented as "weird." Trouillot pointedly responded, "The more Haiti appears weird, the easier it is to forget that it represents the longest neocolonial experience in the history of the West" (6–7)—and the longest experiment in Black republican freedom (Eller 2016). That neocolonial experience also includes the Dominican Republic, which shares the island's ecology with Haiti and where hundreds of thousands of Haitians and Dominicans of Haitian ancestry live and work. For this reason, Michel-Rolph Trouillot's invitation "to rethink the time and space of Hispaniola" cannot work unidirectionally; it must include all of those who study Haiti and the Dominican Republic, but perhaps not in the same ways.

The transnational Hispaniola framework joins with the effort of Haitianist scholars to radically rewrite Haiti through new narratives. We argue that a Dominicanist rapprochement with Haiti (and vice versa) is part of this effort. The scholarly request for new narratives for Haiti might benefit from looking across to the Dominican Republic. It is through challenging narratives that Haitianists and Dominicanists can find the common ground that might provide the foundation for greater future engagement. For this reason, we embrace a critical ecological approach for transnational Hispaniola. It is critical because it recognizes and seeks to demonstrate the full range of inequalities that people across the island experience. It is ecological in its recognition of humans as biocultural organisms dependent on a context that includes personal, local, national, regional, and global factors that affect the people of Hispaniola. Integrating ecology forces scholars to reach beyond disciplinary boundaries.

We also argue that a common ground may also be found in the important political work that creating new narratives about Haiti and the Dominican Republic accomplishes. The problem with standard narratives of Haitian and Dominican alterity resides in how these differences justify, implicitly or explicitly, Hispaniola's neocolonial subordination to the West. The call to dialogue presented in this collection is anchored in a critique and a rejection of exceptionalist narratives that reinforce a geopolitics of knowledge that continues to locate deviancy in Haiti (Polyné 2013, xx; Clitandre 2011). As has been argued here and elsewhere, narratives about Haiti and Hispaniola have done the political work of buttressing anti-blackness, elevating white supremacy, and denying Haiti's important role in the modern world. In future interactions and iterations of our work, the Transnational Hispaniola collective will embrace the challenge forwarded by Kaiama Glover and Alessandra Benedicty-Kokken, who ask: How are those of us who write about Haiti implicated in the construction of these narratives about Haiti? What political work do *we* do with our engagement with the island (Glover and Benedicty-Kokken 2016, 2, 6)?

This book proposes that the entanglement of the Dominican Republic and Haiti can produce a rich opportunity to rescript Hispaniola and do different kinds of political work in key areas of scholarship such as gender and sexuality, ecology, methodology, and, rural studies. New narratives that "think with Haiti" can help "cultivate the sense that the alternatives crafted in the country need not be exceptional" and that Haitians and Dominicans have the capacity to resolve their collective problems (Dubois 2016, 89). The vigorous defense of Hispaniola through new narratives, thus, does the dual work of exposing the power relations that naturalize the West's destructive engagements with Hispaniola and redefines the West's failures in its interactions with Hispaniola as Haitian and Dominican pathologies.

Along with the achievements of this book, though, there is also a glaring fault: a lack of balanced engagement with Haitian scholars and with Haitian social science research. Although Haitianists have certainly been a part of the Transnational Hispaniola collective, organizing conferences and contributing to its intellectual and creative formations, it is necessary to ask the question: does the imbalance in this collection in favor of Dominicanists suggest that the transnational Hispaniola framework may be an invalid one, at least where Haitianists are concerned?

To shed light on this question, we recall a dialogue between the former Dominican ambassador to Haiti, Rubén Silié, and the former Haitian ambassador to the Dominican Republic, Guy Alexandre (1945–2014). This conversation between long-time friends and intellectual *cómplices* (accomplices) was the featured event at the opening reception of Transnational Hispaniola I in Santo Domingo. Both men, speaking Spanish and some French, reminisced about their work as academics and how they viewed their professional lives in politics as extensions of their scholarship. They critiqued the rightward shift of the political parties that had once proclaimed themselves representatives of the masses and they urged solidarity in the rebuilding of Haiti after the earthquake.

When Ambassador Silié was asked about the necessity or appropriateness of including an island-wide perspective on Dominican and Haitian research, he replied enthusiastically that this was necessary, while Ambassador Alexandre responded more critically. We are paraphrasing his response: "For Dominicans, Haiti and Haitians occupy a great deal of mental energy. The opposite is not true for us. We just don't think about you very much. There is no need to exorcise the Dominican from our minds as it is for Dominicans to grapple with the Haitian in theirs."

If Ambassador Alexandre was correct that imagining Haiti in new ways is more of a question for Dominicans and Dominicanists to address, then Transnational Hispaniola may always and necessarily involve more Dominicanists because Dominicans and those in Dominican studies bear a particular historical burden that Haitians and Haitianists do not. However, as we argued above, we feel that transnational Hispaniola provides a way forward for Haitian and Haitianist engagement, albeit necessarily different from the way Dominicanists do. Ambassador Alexandre's insight troubles any notion that an invitation to dialogue is a neutral gesture. As scholars of Dominican ancestry or as Dominicanists, we need to attend to completing some ideological, intellectual, ethical, and moral groundwork so that the invitation to Haitianists does not appear to deny or diminish historical or contemporary injustices that incur violence and trauma against Haitians. These questions bring us to consider what is truly at stake in new research about Haiti and the Dominican Republic: the meanings of Hispaniola sovereignty and Black freedom more broadly in the twenty-first century. Deborah Thomas (2016) argues that "thinking about what sovereignty feels like . . . can also compel us to cultivate a sense of mutual recognition that not only exposes complicity but also demands collective accountability" (152). We argue that defending Haitian sovereignty and autonomy requires an island-wide perspective because to insist on Haiti's freedom is to necessarily insist on the freedom of Hispaniola, the Caribbean, and, indeed, all African descendants in the Americas. Transnational Hispaniola is one part of that effort.

Notes

1. "*Como ya he tenido en otras ocasiones la oportunidad de escribirle y de recibir noticias suyas, me creo su lejana amiga, o más bien su hermana.*"

2. "*No podría Ud. tratar de establecer en Puerto Príncipe una Asociación del Feminismo como la nuestra? Podría ser nuestra hermana: 'L'Action Feministe Haitienne, siempre en relación con nosotras.*"

3. "*Yo había comenzado ya a preparar el terreno con mi discurso en el Palacio de Justicia*"; "*En general el ideal feminista no es muy bien conocido ni comprendido aquí.*"

4. "*Por eso estaría contenta yo de que Ud. me enviara . . . revistas, libros, artículos de periódicos feministas.*"

5. "*Vuestras charlas por radio los viernes me interesarían también. . . . ¿No podría Ud. a una fecha fijada entre nosotras enviarnos un mensaje en francés para las mujeres haitianas?*"

6. "*La idea de venir aquí a dar algunas conferencias acerca de vuestros trabajos es excelente; pero yo creo . . . junio o julio sería demasiado tardía.*" Sylvain had proposed to Mejía that she visit Haiti in April or May.

7. "*Voy a tratar de reunir a algunas personalidades femeninas y trataremos de discutir la oportunidad que hubiere para fundar en este momento una Liga aquí.*"

8. "*No es por una revolución ahora, sino por la evolución de la humanidad, como conseguiremos nuestros derechos, los olvidados Derechos de la Mujer, pero hay que luchar por conseguirlos.*"

Works Cited

Candelario, Ginetta, April J. Mayes, and Elizabeth Manley, eds. 2016. *Cien años de feminismos dominicanos*. Tomo II, *1931–1965*. Santo Domingo: Archivo General de la Nación.

Charles, Carolle. 1995. "Gender and Politics in Contemporary Haiti: The Duvalierist State, Transnationalism, and the Emergence of a New Feminism (1980–1990)." *Feminist Studies* 21 (1): 135–164.

Clitandre, Nadège. 2011. "Haitian Exceptionalism in the Caribbean and the Project of Rebuilding Haiti." *Journal of Haitian Studies* 17 (2): 146–153.

Dubois, Laurent. 2016. "Haiti, Gender and Anthrohistory: A Mintzian Journey." In *The Haiti Exception: Anthropology and the Predicament of Narrative*, edited by Alessandra Benedicty-Kokken, Kaiama L. Glover, Mark Schuller, and Jhon Picard Byron, 74–92. Liverpool: Liverpool University Press.

Eller, Anne. 2016. *We Dream Together: Dominican Independence, Haiti, and the Fight for Caribbean Freedom*. Durham, NC: Duke University Press.

Glover, Kaiama L., and Alessandra Benedicty-Kokken. 2016. "Editors' Introduction." In *The Haiti Exception: Anthropology and the Predicament of Narrative*, edited by Alessandra Benedicty-Kokken, Kaiama L. Glover, Mark Schuller, and Jhon Picard Byron, 1–14. Liverpool: Liverpool University Press.

González Canalda, María Filomena. 2013. *Libertad Igualdad: Protocolos notariales de José Troncoso y Antonio Abad Solano, 1822–1840*. Santo Domingo: Archivo General de la Nación.

Lora H., Quisqueya. 2012. *Transición de la esclavitud al trabajo libre en Santo Domingo: El Caso de Higüey (1822–1827)*. Santo Domingo: Academia Dominicana de Historia.

Mayes, April J. 2008. "Why Dominican Feminism Moved to the Right: Class, Colour and Women's Activism in the Dominican Republic, 1880s–1940s." *Gender & History* 20 (2): 349–371.

McPherson, Alan. 2010. "Personal Occupations: Women's Responses to U.S. Military Occupations in Latin America." *The Historian* 72 (3): 568–598.

Polyné, Millery. 2013. "Introduction." In *The Idea of Haiti: Rethinking Crisis and Development*, edited by Millery Polyné. Minneapolis: University of Minnesota Press.

Saunders, Grace L. 2013. "La Voix des Femmes: Haitian Women's Rights, National Politics and Black Activism in Port-au-Prince and Montreal, 1934–1986." PhD diss., University of Michigan.

Thomas, Deborah A. 2016. "Haiti, Politics and Sovereign (Mis)recognitions." In *The Haiti Exception: Anthropology and the Predicament of Narrative*, edited by Alessandra Benedicty-Kokken, Kaiama L. Glover, Mark Schuller, and Jhon Picard Byron. Liverpool: Liverpool University Press.

Trouillot, Michel-Rolph. 1990. "The Odd and the Ordinary." *Cimarron: New Perspectives on the Caribbean* 2 (3): 3–12.

———. 1997. *Silencing the Past: Power and the Production of History*. New York. Beacon Press.

———. 1999. "Peoples of the Jumbled Lands: The Republic of Hispaniola." *Creole Connection* 5 (3): 1–9.

Wright, Micah. 2016. "'Protection against the Lust of Men': Progressivism, Prostitution, and Rape in the Dominican Republic under US Occupation, 1916–1924." *Gender & History* 28 (3): 623–640.

APPENDIX

Course Syllabi

Transnational Hispaniola: Histories of Haiti and the Dominican Republic

PROFESSOR ANNE ELLER

Course Description

Since the 1500s, the histories of the Dominican Republic and Haiti have informed the histories of the broader Caribbean and the Atlantic world. The early decline of plantation slavery in the Spanish colony enabled free peasants to create a remarkable rural society in the east of the island. In the French-dominated western territory, revolution was born amid brutal plantation slavery. The Haitian Revolution (1791–1804), the most spectacularly successful anti-slavery fight in modern history, engulfed the region in revolutionary ferment. Independence from formal colonialism led to complicated political contests in an extremely hostile climate, however. The struggles of Haiti and Santo Domingo/the Dominican Republic during the 1800s raised questions of state formation, autonomy, and citizenship that were being asked throughout the hemisphere as slavery ended and new nations formed.

We will review how the island became a focal point of U.S. military, political, and economic imperialism by the earliest decades of the twentieth century. Rural and urban residents across the island forged common narratives and practices of resistance during this period. Subsequently, the class will consider the rise and fall of dictatorial political regimes. Finally, we will discuss the impact of neoliberal economics and the tremendous political, economic, and cultural importance of the island's diaspora.

Throughout this lecture course, we will be considering the history of the two island communities together. Conflict has sometimes preoccupied official nationalist narratives, particularly in the Dominican Republic. These attitudes have supported virulent *antihaitianismo* that has led to episodes of considerable violence. We will interrogate elite and popular narratives about identity and belonging across the island with a critical eye with the goal of crafting a far more comprehensive understanding of the interconnected history of Hispaniola.

Required Books

Danticat, Edwidge. 1999. *The Farming of Bones.*
Dubois, Laurent. 2005. *Avengers of the New World: The Story of the Haitian Revolution.*
Johnson, Sara E. 2012. *The Fear of French Negroes: Transcolonial Collaboration in the Revolutionary Americas.*
Nicholls, David. 1996. *From Dessalines to Duvalier: Race, Colour and National Independence in Haiti.*
Trouillot, Michel-Rolph. 1990. *State Against Nation: The Origins and Legacy of Duvalierism.*
Turits, Richard. 2003. *Foundations of Despotism: Peasants, the Trujillo Regime, and Modernity in Dominican History.*

Weekly Topics

Week 1: Introduction and the Indigenous Caribbean
Week 2: Slavery and Development
Week 3: Diaspora Politics, Cultures, and Resistance
Week 4: The Haitian Revolution
Week 5: Revolution in the Atlantic World
Week 6: Peasants and the State
Week 7: The War of Restoration
Weeks 8–9: Liberals, Modernity, and the State
Week 10: The Occupations
Week 11: Trujillo
Week 12: The Duvaliers
Week 13: Democracy and Development
Week 14: Transnational Hispaniola

Transnational Hispaniola: A Social Science Approach

PROF. KIRAN C. JAYARAM

Course Description

This class will present and foster analysis of Hispaniola, the collective of islands where the countries of Haiti and the Dominican Republic are located, from a social science perspective. Content will derive from anthropology, biogeography, cultural geography, history, and political economy. This course should help students formulate an answer to the question of how social science can contribute to an understanding of issues affecting the people of Haiti and the Dominican Republic.

Required Books

Roorda, Eric, Lauren Derby, and Raymundo González. *The Dominican Republic Reader.*
Schuller, Mark, and Pablo Morales. *Tectonic Shifts: Haiti Since the Earthquake.*

Weekly Topics

Week 01: Introduction, Overview, and Course Justification
Week 02: Geography of the Islands
Week 03: Biogeographies
Week 04: Peopling of Hispaniola
Week 05–07: History of Scholarship, Scholarship of History
Week 08–09: Political Economy
Week 10: Languages and Education
Week 11: Gender, Sexuality, and Health
Week 12: Migration, Mobilities, Diasporas
Week 13: Environmental Issues
Week 14: Disasters
Week 15: The 2013 *Sentencia* in the Dominican Republic and Its Aftermath

Ispanyola Transnasyonal

PROF. APRIL J. MAYES

Course Description

The main objective of this course is to provide an overview of the historical, linguistic, economic, and cultural interactions between Haiti and the Dominican Republic. This one-week course at the Institute for Social Work and Social Science in Haiti will be taught in Kreyòl. Due to the intensive nature of the course, the class will emphasize in-class activities and provide opportunities for discussion of outside readings.

Daily Schedule

Day One: Overview of the Course

- Guest Lecturer: Ephesian Bury (Haitian History)
- Class Activities
  - Map Exercises
    - Political map of Haiti
    - Geographic map of Haiti

Day Two: Dominican History

- Lecturer: April Mayes
- Translator: Jean-Jeef Nelson
- Class Activities
  - Map Exercises
    - Political Map of the Dominican Republic
    - Geographical Map of the Dominican Republic

Day Three: Haitians in the Dominican Republic: Historical Migrations and Contemporary Cultural Change

- Guest Lecturer: Dr. Renauld Govain (Kreyòl in the Haitian-Dominican border town)

Day Four: Neoliberalism in Contemporary Hispaniola

- Field trip to the residence of the Dominican Ambassador to Haiti, Rubén Silié, for discussion about contemporary Haitian-Dominican relations

Day Five: Our Traditions, Our Knowledge Are in the Music: Haiti's Influences throughout the Caribbean

Translating Hispaniola: Undergraduate Seminar

PROF. KAIAMA GLOVER AND PROF. MAJA HORN

Weekly Topics

Week 01: Course Introductions
Week 02: Haitian-Dominican Border Crises of 1937 and 2013
Week 03: Colonial Hispaniola and Digital Timeline Workshop
Week 04: Haitian Revolution and the "Reunification" of Hispaniola
Week 05: Nationalisms and Other Founding Fictions
Week 06: U.S. Imperial Interventions and Their Gendered Implications
Week 07: Dictatorships: Race-Based State Formations
Week 08: Literary Engagements with Dictatorship
Week 09: Dictatorships: State Feminisms?
Week 10: Women's Voices
Week 11: Haitians Writing in The Diaspora
Week 12: Dominicans Writing in The Diaspora
Week 13: Queer Voices

Haiti and the Dominican Republic: History and Culture

PROF. ROBIN (LAUREN) DERBY

Course Description

This course is intended to provide an introduction to the island of Hispaniola, thus the history and culture of Haiti and the Dominican Republic. It surveys the key historiographic issues surrounding these two nations, which formed along very different paths. In the eighteenth century, Saint Domingue (Haiti) became the jewel in the crown of the French empire: in 1770, it produced more wealth than all other French colonies combined through an intensive sugar plantation economy. By contrast, the Dominican Republic was a colonial backwater that became a key site for contraband and the central source of meat production and cattle for the booming economy of the eastern portion of the island. The course will survey the contrastive, symbiotic, and at times hostile relationship between the two nations and seek to explain the emergence and impact of episodes of state-sponsored violence. The class will also consider the relationship between popular Catholicism and Vodou beliefs and practices that both divides and unites the island and the emergence of a racialized national identity under the dictatorships of François Duvalier and Rafael Trujillo. The course is intended as an introduction for those who wish to engage in service learning on the island, particularly with Yspaniola, a non-governmental organization which supports the educational needs of Haitians in the Dominican sugar sector.

Required Books

Roorda, Eric, Lauren Derby, and Raymundo González, eds. 2014. *The Dominican Republic Reader: History, Culture, Politics.*
All other readings have been scanned onto the course website.

Weekly Topics

Week 1: Introduction
Week 2: The Haitian Revolution: Sugar versus Cattle
Week 3: Haitians in the Dominican Republic Sugar Sector

Week 4: Race and National Identity
Week 5: Catholicism and Vodou
Week 6: The Protestant Invasion
Week 7: Poverty and the Informal Sector
Week 8: Food and Popular Culture
Week 9: Development Paradoxes under Neoliberalism

Transnational Hispaniola: Haiti and the Dominican Republic

PROFESSORS: AMELIA HINTZEN AND RYAN MANN-HAMILTON

Course Description

This course will examine the historical, political, and cultural development of the island of Hispaniola, which is currently divided into the countries of Haiti and the Dominican Republic. In this course, we will call into question popular narratives that portray Haiti and the Dominican Republic as locked in an ahistorical, continuous conflict. We will study the island's long history of Haitian-Dominican collaborations and networks. Residents on both sides of the island have worked together to fight against enslavement, colonization, state-led repression, and discrimination. At the same time, as an island that is split between two nations, Hispaniola presents as an interesting case study for understanding borders and their impact on national identity.

Required Books

James, C.L.R. 1989. *The Black Jacobins: Toussaint L'ouverture and the San Domingo Revolution.*
Franco, Franklyn. 2015. *Blacks, Mulattos, and the Dominican Nation.* Translated by Patricia Mason.
Danticat, Edwidge. 1998. *The Farming of Bones.*

Weekly Topics

Week 01: Introduction
Week 02: Conceptualizing Hispaniola

Week 03: Economic Growth and Imperial Conflict
Week 04: Haitian Revolution
Week 05: The Haitian Revolution Part Deux: The View from Santo Domingo
Week 06: Beyond the Revolution
Week 07: Nineteenth Century Nation Building
Week 08: Twentieth Century Occupations
Week 09: Dictatorships—Trujillo, Duvalier, and Anti-Haitianism
Week 10: Massacre and Memory
Week 11: Migration and Sugar
Week 12: Citizenship, Statelessness, and Race
Week 13: Afro-Caribbean Popular Culture
Week 14: The Diaspora Strikes Back

CONTRIBUTORS

Paul Austerlitz is professor of music and Africana Studies at the Sunderman Conservatory of Music, Gettysburg College, Gettysburg, Pennsylvania. He specializes in Afro-Caribbean music. Austerlitz is the author of *Merengue: Dominican Music and Dominican Identity* and *Jazz Consciousness: Music, Race, and Humanity*. As a jazz composer, bass clarinetist, and saxophonist, he has collaborated with Haitian and Dominican musicians. He has held several artistic residencies, received multiple grants for composition, and developed multicultural music with grassroots community organizations in the United States and the Dominican Republic on projects to foster social change.

Nathalie Bragadir is a faculty member in the Department of Spanish and Portuguese at the University of Southern California in Los Angeles. Her teaching and research interests include Latin American and Caribbean studies and (post)colonial, border, and transatlantic studies. She completed her PhD in Spanish at New York University. Her dissertation, "Contested Topographies: Border Passing in Colonial Hispaniola," examines borderland encounters in the late eighteenth century through archival research conducted in the Dominican Republic, France, and Spain.

Raj Chetty, assistant professor of English at St. John's University, Queens, New York, specializes in Caribbean literature in English, Spanish, and French with a focus on Black and African diasporas. His current project studies the articulations between Dominican literary and expressive arts in the post-Trujillo period and conceptualizations of the Black and African diasporas. He is coeditor of a recent special issue of *The Black Scholar* on Dominican Black studies. His work has appeared in *Callaloo*,

Anthurium, Palimpsest: A Journal on Women, Gender, and the Black International, and *Afro-Hispanic Review.*

Anne Eller is associate professor of history and affiliate professor of Spanish and Portuguese at Yale University. Her research focuses on popular politics in the emancipation-era Caribbean in and beyond traditional archives. She has published in *Small Axe, The American Historical Review,* and other journals. Her first book is *We Dream Together: Dominican Independence, Haiti, and the Fight for Caribbean Freedom.*

Kaiama L. Glover is associate professor of French and Africana Studies at Barnard College, Columbia University. She is the author of *Haiti Unbound: A Spiralist Challenge to the Postcolonial Canon* and coeditor of a number of essay collections, including the forthcoming *Haiti Reader.* Glover has published English translations of several works of Haitian literature and has won multiple awards for her scholarship. She is a founding coeditor of *SX Archipelagos* and the director of a digital humanities project on Afro-Atlantic intellectual history. She is currently completing a monograph about individualism, self-regard, and representations of womanhood in Caribbean fiction.

Maja Horn is associate professor of Spanish and Latin American Cultures at Barnard College. She specializes in contemporary Hispanophone Caribbean literature, visual and performance art, gender and sexuality, and political culture. She is the author of *Masculinity after Trujillo: The Politics of Gender in Dominican Literature* and is currently completing a second monograph on queer Dominican literature and visual and performance art.

Régine Michelle Jean-Charles is associate professor of romance languages and literatures and African and African Diaspora Studies at Boston College. She is the author of *Conflict Bodies: The Politics of Rape Representation in the Francophone Imaginary* and is currently completing a second book on contemporary Haitian literature. Her work has appeared in *American Quarterly, Callaloo, French Forum, Journal of Haitian Studies, Journal of Romance Studies, Research in African Literatures,* and *Small Axe.*

Kiran C. Jayaram is assistant professor of anthropology at the University of South Florida and cofounder of the Transnational Hispaniola project. He specializes in an anthropology of political economy, mobility, and education and has taught university-level courses in the United States, Haiti, and the Dominican Republic. His research has included fieldwork in the Dominican Republic, Haiti, Cuba, and the United States. He has held leadership positions in the Haiti–Dominican Republic Section of the Latin American Studies Association and the Society for Latin American and Caribbean Anthropology. He has published several articles and book chapters and is coeditor of *Keywords of Mobility*.

Elizabeth S. Manley is associate professor of history at Xavier University of Louisiana. She received her PhD in 2008 from Tulane University and is the author of *The Paradox of Paternalism: Women and the Politics of Authoritarianism in the Dominican Republic, 1928–1978*. She has also recently begun a research project on the history and development of female sex tourism in Haiti, the Dominican Republic, and Jamaica.

April J. Mayes is associate professor of history at Pomona College in Claremont, California, and an affiliated faculty member of the Instituto Superior Pedro Francisco Bonó in Santo Domingo, Dominican Republic. Dr. Mayes is the author of *The Mulatto Republic: Class, Race, and Dominican National Identity* and has published articles in women's and gender history. She teaches classes in Caribbean and Latin American history, gender and women's studies, and Africana studies.

Elizabeth C. Russ is associate professor of Spanish at Southern Methodist University, Dallas, Texas. She is the author of *The Plantation in the Postslavery Imagination* and numerous scholarly articles and chapters, including studies of Dominican writers Aída Cartagena Portalatín, Rita Indiana, and Junot Díaz. She is currently writing a book on representations of Haiti, race, and Hispaniola identity in post-1937 Dominican and Dominican-American literature.

Fidel J. Tavárez is a Provost's Postdoctoral Scholar at the University of Chicago. His work focuses on the administrative, intellectual, and economic history of the Spanish Empire during the eighteenth century. At present, Fidel is completing his first book manuscript, *The Imperial Machine:*

Assembling the Spanish Commercial Empire in the Age of Enlightenment. Fidel's future research plans include a book project that is tentatively titled *Empirical Statecraft: The Emergence of an Information Empire in the Eighteenth-Century Spanish Atlantic.*

Elena Valdez holds a PhD in Spanish from Rutgers, the State University of New Jersey. Her research interests include U.S. Latino/a literature, Hispanic Caribbean literature, the Latin American novel in the twentieth and twenty-first centuries, gender studies, and queer theory. She has published articles on urban space and queer sexuality in various scholarly journals and is currently working on a book manuscript on the politics of gender, sexuality, and urban space in the Hispanic Caribbean. She is currently a lecturer at Christopher Newport University in Newport News, Virginia.

INDEX

www.ingramcontent.com/pod-product-compliance
Lightning Source LLC
Chambersburg PA
CBHW020844270326
41928CB00006B/534